One Simple Change
Makes Life Easy

The Balanced View Team

The Library of Wisdom Classics

Fourth Edition 2012
Balanced View Media: Mill Valley, California USA 2012

One Simple Change Makes Life Easy by Balanced View Team is licensed under a Creative Commons Attribution-Noncommercial-No Derivative Works 3.0 United States License.

Based on a work at www.balancedview.org
ISBN 978-0-9886659-1-0

Dedication

Open Intelligence, Wisdom and Compassion for All

One Simple Change Makes Life Easy

Table of Contents

Note to the Fourth Edition	vii
Editor's Introduction	ix
Author's Introduction	xi
1. One Simple Change Makes Life Easy	1
2. Be Gentle with Yourself	11
3. Obedience to the Unenforceable	21
4. Love and Relationships	33
5. Sex and Desire	45
6. A Balanced View	56
7. Skillful Means	66
8. A New Way of Being	75
9. Afflictive States	86
10. A Beautiful Death	99
11. Practices	109
12. Meditation	120
13. Total Well-being	133
14. The Personal Identity	145
15. The Mind is Gifted	158
16. Exhausting Faults and Perfecting Qualities	170
17. The Natural Wisdom of Open Intelligence	180
18. No Effort, No Special Circumstances	193
19. Direct Teachings	203
20. Maintaining Open Intelligence in Sleep and Dreams	215
21. Complete Perceptual Openness	222
22. Decisions Without Decision-Making	233
23. The Qualities of Open Intelligence	241
24. Beyond Cause and Effect	251
25. Compassionate Benefit	263
26. It's Up to You, and It's Up to Me!	272
Balanced View Resources	286

Note to the Fourth Edition

We have been very encouraged by feedback from readers who have enjoyed and benefitted from the first and second editions of *One Simple Change Makes Life Easy*, and it is with great pleasure that we are now able to bring out a revised and updated edition of the book.

As part of the ongoing effort in Balanced View to find the best possible language that speaks skillfully to the most participants, a shift in the use of language came about in 2011 that found great resonance. Whereas previously the terms "clarity" and "points of view" had been used in the texts, the new terms "open intelligence" and "data" spontaneously came into use and were received with great enthusiasm, as these new terms seem to speak to readers in an even more direct way.

As a result, all of the Balanced View books are being updated to include this new and very powerful language. The content of this book is essentially the same as the first and second editions with only a few minor edits, and in addition that has been this shift to using "open intelligence" instead of "clarity" or "awareness" and "data" instead of "points of view."

The phrase "to rest" from the original language of the first and second editions is retained in this edition. This phrase means essentially the same as to rely on open intelligence, and also has the further implication of remaining at ease and letting things be as they are in the encounter with all data streams. "To empower" is also used in the same manner within the context of the empowering nature of open intelligence.

The change in language should make the message of the book even more powerful and clear.

Editor's Introduction

The material for this book comes from public talks given by Candice O'Denver, the founder of Balanced View, in India, the United States and Sweden. The tone and style of the various chapters reflect the atmosphere present in those talks—warm, friendly, intimate and conversational. As a result, the language one finds here is generally informal and relaxed and is meant to make it as simple as possible for the reader to benefit from what is spoken.

However, it is not the words or ideas themselves that are the most important aspect of the communication, but rather the ease of being inherent in these words and ideas. The reader is encouraged to allow her or himself the opportunity to receive what is being described in a completely open and receptive way without grasping for intellectual understanding. As Candice says humorously, "Intellectual understanding is the booby prize!" Above all, what is written here is not meant for mere speculation; rather, it is an introduction to the instinctive recognition of open intelligence *in one's own experience*.

Each chapter begins with an introduction and explanation of the subject of the chapter, followed by questions and answers that help clarify open intelligence and illustrate its applicability and practicality in everyday life. After the initial introduction to the main ideas of "open intelligence," "relying on open intelligence," and "data" in Chapter One, the chapters may be read in any order without following a particular sequence.

Within each chapter is the key point and pivotal instruction of the Balanced View Training: to rely on open intelligence for short moments, repeated many times, until it becomes continuous. This key point along with practical instruction is repeated again and again, in countless different ways, in order to speak to all kinds of readers.

This book is a compilation of transcriptions taken from Candice's talks, edited by volunteers from around the world who, along with Candice, did every bit of the work in the yearlong process of bringing this book to publication. The recording of hundreds of talks, posting them on the Internet as free downloads, transcribing more than 100 of those talks which resulted in over 1,600 pages of text, compiling, editing, proofreading and re-editing were all carried out by grateful people whose main interest is to make available to everyone what has been so beneficial to them.

Scott M.
Skåne, Sweden
March 2008

Author's Introduction

We are happy to be able to offer this book to our friends spread out across the globe. It is a book that will change the way you look at yourself and the world. It will bring great ease and comfort to your mind and body and make your relationships much more interesting and enjoyable. In this book you will find one simple change in the use of the mind that brings about mental and emotional stability, insight, compassion and skillful ways of living life. When I was a young woman I began using this simple change in my own life, and it has given me a life of joy, friendship and the ability to be of benefit to the world.

I'd like to share with you how this book about one simple change came about. As a child I wondered at the fact that everything seemed to be connected. When I was aware of this profound connection, I felt carefree and joyful and I liked the world and everyone in it! I could see that it was impossible to take any one thing, remove it from the whole and make it into an entirely different and separate thing. This insight fascinated me from early on. It had a deep meaning for me, and I wanted to be able to easily describe the insight; yet, whenever I tried, I was at a loss for words.

I had heard the word "indivisible" used, and I felt that the concept of indivisibility applied to my experience of the world. I asked my mother what indivisible meant, and she showed me how to find the word in the dictionary. The definition I found was: "incapable of undergoing division." It was very exciting to me that there was a word for this insight I had had and that the definition for this word was so readily available for anyone who just looked in a dictionary.

I became interested in all kinds of writing that described the indivisible nature of everything, because whenever I read books that attempted to describe indivisibility, the words in the books seemed to elicit in me the instinctive realization of this special way of looking at things. I wanted that experience to be permanent in myself, and I wanted to be able to share that experience with others. I searched for a book that was completely filled with writing that directly evoked that experience, but I never found one. I knew that if such a book actually existed, it would be of great fortune to everyone. It seemed that if people related to one another in this special way, there could be really great communication and a feeling of friendship among everyone in the world.

Growing up, I was taught many things that I was told would lead to happiness. Yet, all of them seemed difficult to learn when compared to the instinctive sense of happiness that was associated with the indivisibility of everything. I tried many activities that were supposed to help bring about well-being and self-respect, such as: education, religion, community service, compassionate action, work, family life, friends, intimate relationships, food, money, leisure pursuits and so forth. I used psychological, spiritual, medical and mental methods to try to change my thoughts and emotions into better thoughts and emotions. I looked for the right people and right situations to bring about happiness.

No matter how hard I tried to be happy through these means, happiness was always just out of reach. The benefit from all these activities and situations never compared to the soothing energy of deep understanding that came from knowing that everything is inseparable. I knew there was something untapped within me, but I didn't know how to find that innate resource.

Then something amazing happened—my life fell apart at the seams! As I struggled to make sense of unexpected and violent events that I faced, I couldn't get back on track with my old way of living. My best ideas failed me. Filled with intense emotions, thoughts and sensations, I felt that I could not face life with the tools I had used. Old ideas availed me nothing. I simply could not rely on any external or internal strategy that I had employed, and I could not stop the thoughts and emotions that were racing through my mind.

Filled with fear of the future, bewildered by the past and desperate in the present, suddenly I realized that all of the turmoil—the thoughts, emotions, sensations and other experiences—were appearing within an open, soothing and indivisible space of relief. I found that by the power of resting as that relief for short moments, repeated many times, I gradually began to identify with inherent relief and serenity—rather than with the turmoil. Increasingly, I realized the turmoil was actually the dynamic energy of a vast indivisible space, an open intelligence that was not limited to me or my experiences.

In fact, everything whatsoever was simply the unconfined creativity of this indivisible intelligence. By persevering in my simple practice, I found a wellspring of natural warmth, connection and compassion arising in my thoughts, emotions and actions, along with insights into the nature of existence. Along the way life got better and better, and my abilities to contribute to the benefit of all flourished. All this came about through the simple practice of relying on open intelligence for short moments, repeated many times, until it became continuous.

As I began to share my experience of short moments, many times with others, their lives began changing dramatically for the better. My life became filled with the purpose of sharing with other people this one simple change in the use of the mind. This change is the basis of the ability to solve all problems. Many of the people who experienced similar results in their lives joined together with me to start the Balanced View movement, which has now spread all over the world like the warm rays of the ever-shining sun!

My youthful vision of friendship and good communication among the people of the world is becoming a reality! Finally, we have not just one book, but many books that beautifully describe the indivisibility of everything, and this is one of them!

Last of all I would like to say, if you dream big dreams, know that you can make them real! All the power you need to fulfill your vision will be found in short moments, repeated many times, until it becomes obvious at all times.

I am deeply appreciative of the kindness and mastery of Scott M. who led the skilled and dedicated team from throughout the world that transcribed, compiled and edited the talks in this book. I would also like to specifically thank a friend who would like to remain anonymous, Robin G., Simon H., Matt L., Keith R., and Swami S., who along with many others contributed so much to preparing this book for publication.

I am continually grateful to Heather B., Mia C., Kathy R. and Jochen R. for their loving friendship and beneficial training and management activities that are of great support to me every moment of every day. The Balanced View trainers and participants are carrying the message of one simple change around the world, and due to them the friendly faces of Balanced View are everywhere.

ONE SIMPLE CHANGE MAKES LIFE EASY

CHAPTER ONE

We invite you on a marvelous journey into a vast resource of peace, happiness and skillfulness that exists within you. It's a journey that only you can take—no one else can do it for you. However, within the covers of this book you'll find a constant friend and guide along the way, exact directions and instructions, and a global community of support for adopting the one simple change that makes life easy. Reading this book and putting its key points into practice will give you a life you never dreamt possible, no matter how good your life already is!

When starting out on a journey, it's important to know the language that will be used in the country we'll be visiting. For the purposes of this book, a simple language is used throughout, and that language will be defined in this chapter. Once you're familiar with the language, you'll find it very easy to find your way in our journey together.

I'd like to share another travel tip: as you read this book, don't try to understand it or memorize what is written here. Just put the one simple change into practice in an easygoing way. By the time you reach the end of the book, it's very likely you'll notice that, simply by reading the book, you'll be able to follow its instructions. So, just relax and enjoy our journey!

Now, let's take a look at the language we'll use in our travels by talking about the words and phrases "mind," "open intelligence," "relying on open intelligence," "to empower" and "to rest," along with "datum," and "data." We'll look at how the words are used in this book and how they are connected to the one simple change we're making.

First of all, we can say that basically there are two approaches to the use of the human mind. In the first approach, the focus of the mind's activity is placed on its contents. Another term for the content of the mind is "data." Data (one datum or several data) are anything that occurs in the mind. It can be a thought, emotion, sensation or intuition, and it can relate to inner or outer events; it is anything that can be seen, felt, enacted, intuited or experienced in any other way. Open intelligence is either involved in data, or it is naturally at ease. When open intelligence is involved in data, we forget how to relax and how to rely on open intelligence.

In the second approach to the use of the mind, the focus is placed on one simple change—relaxing the mind rather than focusing on all the streams of data. In this approach all data are seen as appearances of open intelligence, and it is this open intelligence that is the basis of mind. If you're wondering what open intelligence is, just stop thinking for a moment. That absence of thought is what open intelligence is! It is like the clear sky! You are still alert, cognizant and aware, even though there is no thinking. However, whether there is lots of thinking or no thinking, it takes open intelligence to be aware of both.

So, the same open intelligence that's present when you stop thinking is also present in every thought. Over time, by the power of sustaining open intelligence for short moments, many times, confidence in open intelligence is nurtured until it becomes permanent and continuous at all times and in all situations—including the times when many thoughts are arising.

When the focus of the mind is placed on its contents, then our thoughts, emotions, speech and activities will be directed to our own needs and our striving to be good, comfortable, successful, kind and happy. Even when we do things for others, it may seem like an effort, and it may be difficult to maintain a giving attitude without becoming resentful or expecting something in return. None of us likes that feeling!

The conventional beliefs about the mind regard it as being located in the brain and governed by the workings of the brain. This belief assumes that the mind depends on a combination of a person's outlook, personal psychology, environment and biochemistry. In the context of this belief system, the mind is seen as sometimes being capable of providing happiness and other times not. When we view the mind in this way, we may often feel at its whim, wanting to be in control of it, but realizing we really aren't. Sometimes the mind may seem like a foe we need to conquer.

When the mind is used to focus on data, our scope of intelligence is restricted to those data. We assume that they make up our identity; in other words, we believe our identity is comprised of the accumulation of thoughts, emotions and experiences over the course of our life.

It is likely we have thought that there was no choice but to focus on our data, and we may have been unaware of any other possibility. We may not have known that the fundamental nature of the mind is open intelligence, and that we can rely on that to develop a balanced view of all the data that occur within it. When we choose to maintain open intelligence rather than following after or blocking data, we experience a relief from our usual thought processes.

By repeatedly relying on open intelligence for short moments, many times, our attentiveness to the presence of open intelligence increases. More and more, we experience warmth, ease, compassion, a balanced outlook, innovative thinking, creativity and an exceptional ability to make good decisions and solve problems. A simple word for this is wisdom. Our thoughts, emotions, speech and actions begin to spontaneously focus on the welfare and benefit of everyone, not just on ourselves. This innate ability to be at ease, wise, balanced and compassionate is discovered when we relax the mind's focus on data. As the mind relaxes into open intelligence, data are recognized to be the dynamic energy of open intelligence. Another term for this is "rest," which is also used in the text.

Data and open intelligence can be likened to a breeze blowing through the air. The breeze and the air are inseparable and both are air. When a breeze blows, it is the dynamic energy of air. When data appear, they are the dynamic energy of open intelligence. Like the color blue is inseparable from the sky, data are inseparable from open intelligence. We come to realize that no datum has an origin independent of open intelligence.

Open intelligence is hot, pure and luminous. Because it is hot, it shines forth and outshines data, all at once. Because it is hot, it burns all data and points of view. Similarly, the hot sun shines forth within pure space, pouring forth radiant energy and outshining it all at once—pure, hot and outshining, pure benefit spontaneously burning off each moment.

Amazingly, when we look for the mind all we can definitively state as our direct experience of the mind is that we are aware of data. When we examine the mind in this way, we discover that open intelligence is the constant in all data, including the datum of mind. Each appearance in the mind is distinct and clear, yet cannot be found to have an origin or substance other than open intelligence. When we look at the mind in this way, we see that, rather than there being a mind that is a storage device for perceptions, the mind is nothing other than open intelligence itself, which is inclusive of all data.

All of the appearances in open intelligence are like a mirage or hologram, vivid in their own right, but without an origin other than open intelligence. There are two aspects of data: one aspect being a description or label and the other being the forever empty, always abiding and empowering aspect that is implicit in this open intelligence that is the basis of all data. If we do not understand these two aspects, we will consider data streams to have far more significance than they actually do.

When our conventional belief systems and assumptions about mind are at play, we divide our data into positive, negative and neutral categories. We are constantly trying to improve our thoughts, emotions, speech and actions in order to make them positive rather than negative. It is believed that being a good person comes from the effort involved in organizing our data into what would be considered "good" by most people.

It is certainly worthwhile to be a good and kind person, but the actual basis for ultimate goodness in human beings is the innate wisdom quality of the mind—open intelligence. "Innate" means it requires no thought or other effort; it is already naturally present within us. We find that ultimate wisdom and skillful means are already present in open intelligence. This may be very hard for us to understand at first, but understanding will come with growing confidence in the direct experience of open intelligence.

We have learned data from other people from the moment we were born, and the tendency has been to collapse our perceptions of people and circumstances into these data sets. This collapsing happens so fast that it is hard to see it happening. Almost immediately, and certainly over time, the data we assume to be true become *the entire focus of our attention*—the reality we seem to know. They limit what is possible in our life, robbing us of permanent recognition of happiness, joy, pleasure, friendliness, creativity, productivity, cooperation and effectiveness.

All data are related to open intelligence in the same way that a mirage or a hologram is related to space. Even though a mirage or hologram may look very real and seems to be vividly apparent, it has no nature that is independent of its source in space. Likewise, even though data may seem very real, they have no nature or power of their own that is independent of open intelligence. For open intelligence to become fully evident, we must commit to seeing data as having no independent nature.

Open intelligence contains all data. Just as colors are inseparable from a rainbow, data are inseparable from open intelligence. When data streams arise, let them be and do not cling to them. They are like the flight path of a bird in the sky. The bird's flight path vanishes without a trace, and each previous datum vanishes without effect. Do not attempt to prolong a datum by pursuing, avoiding or replacing it. The bird's future flight path is yet nonexistent—so you don't need to anticipate the next datum. The present flight path of the bird is indivisible from open sky, and the present data has an open natural presence that is indivisible from open intelligence. Leave it alone and refrain from trying to change it in some way.

As data appear, rely on open intelligence! This is the essential practice during daily activities. If one doesn't follow after a datum and doesn't develop a story about it, the datum is naturally released in open intelligence.

We will now examine the most important choice we have to make in each moment of life: the choice of how we use our intelligence. If we choose to use our intelligence to describe everything, we get lost in descriptions, and we find ourselves on a roller coaster ride of thoughts, emotions and other experiences. If we choose instead to let open intelligence simply be for brief moments, we increasingly enjoy soothing energy and a balanced view. Simply stated, relying on open intelligence is recognition of open intelligence, and constant distraction by data is non-recognition of open intelligence.

On our journey together, the cultivation of open intelligence is referred to as "relying on open intelligence," "resting as open intelligence" or "empowering open intelligence". To rely on open intelligence or to empower open intelligence is to cultivate many moments of open intelligence, many times, until it becomes obvious and continuous. When we stop the constant thinking about data and simply rely on open intelligence, we experience powerful wisdom. We realize that all data have their origin in open intelligence and that no data can be found to exist in their own right.

Rest is best, because we directly experience freedom from worry and concern. We're better able to be of benefit to ourselves, our family, community and world. When we rely on open intelligence in a natural way, we tap into our innate strengths, gifts and talents and contribute them for the benefit of all.

To rely on open intelligence or not: that is the question!

Here is a very practical suggestion: at the very moment data form, let your open intelligence remain open and allow your perception to be serene and spacious. That *is* open intelligence; that is a view which has no point from which to view. By the power of simply relying on open intelligence, the experience becomes increasingly obvious, and data vanish naturally.

Because of the long-held habit of not recognizing open intelligence, the brief moments of open intelligence may not last long at first. In other words, the brief moment of open intelligence may almost immediately slip away. There may be no stability. That is why it is important to rely on open intelligence for short moments, repeated many times, until it becomes obvious at all times. Rather than sitting for long periods only a few times a day, it is better to rely on open intelligence for short moments throughout the day, repeated again and again.

By repeating the recognition of open intelligence, we grow used to it. "Many times" means that we need to grow more and more confident in ordinary open intelligence. This is the key point in how to rely on open intelligence for short moments, many times. By persisting in this one simple change in the use of the mind, we see benefits from the outset. The first time we make the choice to rely on open intelligence rather than getting lost in thinking about our mental, physical and emotional states, we sense the power of the complete relief to be found in relying on the power of open intelligence.

It makes no difference what data arise: in the moment of relying on open intelligence, it is impossible for there not to be a soothing openness in which they vanish naturally, leaving no trace, like a line drawn in water. At that point, in the wake of their vanishing, identify open intelligence, relaxed and enormously potent. In letting data be by relying on open intelligence, mental and emotional stability, insightfulness and skillful qualities and activities become increasingly evident.

What begins as brief moments of open intelligence starts to last for longer periods of time. By the power of relying on open intelligence, it grows to last a full day, weeks, months, years and then an entire lifetime. The very first moment of open intelligence already has the full-blown result of relief, compassion and self-benefit. By acknowledging open intelligence again and again, ups and downs and disturbing states diminish and then resolve completely.

If we apply ourselves to sincerely relying on open intelligence, there comes a time when we discover complete mental and emotional stability. When we experience this, life suddenly becomes a lot easier. We realize that this amazing open intelligence isn't out of reach at all. Simply allow open intelligence to be sustained. When it's totally easy and simple to recognize the power of open intelligence in all daily activities, we become confident in open intelligence, and eventually it remains stable.

Relying on open intelligence for short moments, repeated many times, until it becomes continuous is to briefly return to open intelligence again and again, because it is this non-distraction that brings us all the way to complete wisdom, love and tremendous beneficial energy.

If we utilize this one simple change in the use of the mind that is found in relying on open intelligence, we will prove to ourselves that it is powerful beyond measure. It is the primary skill we need in life to ensure our well-being in all situations.

When the sun rises at daybreak, we don't have to wait for it to be warm and brilliant. The midday sun may be stronger than the early morning sun, but all of its warming and illuminating qualities are present from the very first moment, even if they may not be fully apparent. It's the same with relying on open intelligence. From the beginning, its power of wisdom is naturally present. What is essential is to maintain open intelligence in order to attain stability.

It is crucial to understand that open intelligence is endowed with perfect qualities. By the single power of relying on open intelligence, all faults are exhausted and all qualities are naturally perfected.

Because the non-recognition of open intelligence is momentary, it can be cleared away and seen through by the simple power of relying on open intelligence. Wisdom and skillful ways of living life become obvious at all times, and it's very important to understand this. Simply sustain open intelligence. Until open intelligence is fully evident at all times, maintain moments of open intelligence that are spacious like the sky.

I'd like to share with you briefly about the global support system that is available for people who are relying on open intelligence. Balanced View is a worldwide movement of people offering 24/7 mutual support for relying on open intelligence. This support is given face-to-face, via email, on the Internet and by telephone. We are not alone. When we build confidence in Balanced View's Four Mainstays, which are: 1. relying on open intelligence, 2. the trainer, 3. the training, and 4. the community of people throughout the world who rely on open intelligence, we can know that we will increasingly experience the soothing energy of open intelligence, and we will never be fooled by appearances of data, not during our life and not upon our death.

Well, there you have it! We have learned the language that will be used on our journey, so we're ready to go!

BE GENTLE WITH YOURSELF
CHAPTER TWO

"The essence of your own being doesn't need anything to prop it up—it simply is, so relax and enjoy! Please don't be unkind to yourself any longer. I really ask you this from my heart."

Powerful urges and emotions arise in us; they just come and then they go. Even though their labels are often vivid, distinct and powerful, they have no independent existence outside of open intelligence. These things appear to be so real and compelling and seem to be reasons for us to feel shame, humiliation, guilt and fear, but the truth is that we have a choice as to how we relate to all of them. We can either get involved in them—feeling limited by their labels—or we can simply rely on open intelligence as they appear and pass away.

Many of us spend our whole life as if on trial for our data streams. It's as if we were sitting in the witness stand, and we look out and see that we are also the prosecutor, the defense attorney, the judge and the jury all at once! However, it's not necessary to continually be interrogating ourselves about everything we have said and done. We have learned over the years to focus on these data sets and identify with them, but by doing so, we've kept ourselves in a prison. Yet, there's no need to worry. We've always been completely exonerated, because none of this data about which we've been questioning ourselves has an independent nature. When we simply rely on open intelligence for short moments, repeated many times, this becomes obvious.

The truth is, we don't need to change anything. There are people on death row who are relying on open intelligence, and they've been able to completely come to terms with everything that has gone on in their lives. They have found a way to live a life of total freedom and stability in that monastery called prison. If we think that our thoughts, emotions, experiences and circumstances need to be changed in order to realize who we are, or if we think that the projections of our own minds need to be changed, we are in shackles. *Nothing* needs to be changed. The natural state, the ease of our own being, is already guaranteed to everyone.

It is by allowing everything to be *as it is* that we open up to a profound wisdom that has been unknown to us. This wisdom is powerfully responsive in all situations. It is the wisdom of a balanced view that is not dependent on descriptive frameworks.

I invite all of you to put a complete stop to the addiction to labeling each and every occurrence. When we persist in labeling ourselves and others, we engage in a machine-like war within ourselves. In doing so we judge certain of our appearances to be good and others to be bad, and we become like robots sorting thoughts: "These are the good ones, and these are the bad ones; I've got to get more good ones, and I've got to get rid of the bad ones. I've got to show everybody else what my good ones are, so they will accept me, and then maybe I can think that I am acceptable." Beyond all the extremes, beyond the labels of good and bad, is wisdom. Wisdom does not need anything to be good; it is already wholly positive in and of itself.

Come to a complete stop and enrich yourself and the whole world with the open intelligence that's at the basis of everything. No one is dependent on any label to *be*. Being *is*, regardless of labels. The only self-essence of any label is forever flawless open intelligence, so why not look at everything from the vantage of open intelligence rather than through the foggy filters of labels? The essence of your own being doesn't need anything to prop it up; it simply is, so relax and enjoy! Please don't be mean to yourself any longer. I really ask you this from my heart.

We may all have had thoughts come up like, "Oh, will I ever be happy? Will I ever be able to overcome the things that have bothered me? Will I ever be able to get over the things that people have done to me?" Know that it's possible to rely on open intelligence whatever the appearance might be. Don't ever settle for any label about anything. To hold to any idea like, "This is the way it has always been, and this is the way it is going to be from now on," is so totally limiting. When we rely on the natural ease of being, we discover that every single moment is the supreme moment of complete spaciousness that has never been tied to anything. It's completely pure, entirely restful, and is filled with an energy beyond anything that can ever be cooked up through data.

Through sustaining open intelligence we find that we live our life in a happy, friendly way, taking good care of ourselves and others. We don't yell and scream at ourselves about our thoughts and feelings, and when we don't do that to ourselves anymore, we don't do it to others either. Even if someone has done something hideous, when we look at them we recognize first and foremost that they've acted out of their data streams, just as we have all our lives. We can understand that if we had the same data, we would have behaved exactly as they did.

If in our relationships we choose to scream and yell and to shame and blame people, well, that's just one way of going about things, but it's not the only way. When we're profoundly at ease, we find an immense force and power within us that allows us to take action that is freed of that kind of expression. It's an action that is penetrating and incisive and cuts through everything. Who knows what that action might be? It might be a kind word, a small act of caring, some simple expression of love, or it might be solving the problem of world hunger or getting clean water for everybody.

Whatever it is, it will be done with laser-like clarity that's completely free from judgments and limiting data. The emotions will do whatever they do, but they're not the source of our response. Wisdom is the source. All of this happens naturally and spontaneously without any contrivance or artifice at all. When we take it upon ourselves to act as nature does, then we begin to see the truly natural order of everything, and we are able to live and respond appropriately to our own individual life and to the lives of everyone else.

I would ask you once again to be gentle with yourselves and others. When we can look at people in this gentle way, we know what makes them tick, because we've learned what makes us tick. Does that mean that we just sit back and let people murder and maim and do whatever they want to do? No, it doesn't mean that at all. Open intelligence overcomes all negativity with the balanced view of wisdom. This means that our primary relationship with everyone is from the self-perfect nature of open intelligence, because through relying on open intelligence we've come to see that we are all part of the natural order of everything. To realize this does not require exertion. Everything is completely at ease, no matter what it is.

As the ease of our own being becomes more and more obvious to us, then we know what love is. Love and ease are equal and synonymous. Love is our true nature. We were meant to love others and ourselves without excluding anything. Nothing needs to be manipulated, coaxed to another level or changed. Many of us have been taught that we need to improve ourselves throughout our lives and that we're going to have to work hard at it because our basic nature is flawed. These are things I learned too, but I finally found something much different to be true: I found that open intelligence has never been flawed in any way and that short moments of open intelligence, repeated again and again, become continuous.

The original purity of everything supersedes all ideas about anything. No one is marked with any kind of original sin or karma. Go to the ground of your own being for a brief moment—the complete ease that is the entire basic space of every thought, emotion and experience—and you'll know that all of those ideas, like original sin and karma, don't apply to your most basic nature and they never have. The pure intelligence of everything *as it is*, is completely pure, like space. Rest in that and your intelligence will be penetrating, wholly positive and inconceivably beneficial.

When we substantialize ourselves as a personal identity and don't have familiarity with the authentic source of intelligence, discord and great discomfort are created. Once we substantialize ourselves and substantialize everyone else, we are at war internally, and we create war with others. There can never be peace in the world until there's peace within. Only when we as human beings elect to be at peace with all our mental and emotional appearances and end the war within can we express peace as a species. Of course, that would be wonderful, and we'd all love to see that, but where does it begin? It doesn't begin with diplomacy between nations, and it can't be accomplished through political ideology. It begins with individual human beings saying, "This is who I really am, and I'm going to take responsibility for living as that. I'm going to find this peace within myself by relying on open intelligence and hold myself to account for embodying that peace on a daily basis."

I can guarantee that, from that resolve, something truly amazing will open up. When we rest as the wisdom that's the basis of everything, we end the war within ourselves, and we become naturally compassionate towards others in an uncontrived way—a way that we don't have to cultivate and that naturally spills over to everyone. We see everyone more and more through the eyes of kindness.

Another way of describing this is to say that when we rest, we are resting as love. Love is already within us; it's what we really are, and this connects us with everyone and everything. In love there is no separation, and it's in this love that there is a haven of complete and immense safety and comfort. From the beginning of our lives we've looked for safety, comfort, and love from our caregivers, our homes, and outer circumstances, but we were never really able to find safety or comfort that we could ultimately count on. Pretty soon we started to look to other places, like romance, food, money, work and so on, but the safety and comfort somehow always escaped our grasp. Through relying on open intelligence we discover that the nature of our own being is the absolute safety and absolute love that we've been seeking. Until we rest in that basis, life will be fraught with uncertainty.

Whatever we are looking for anywhere else, it already exists within us. It's only by relying on open intelligence repeatedly, over and over again, that we gain familiarity with it, and we find the real safety and comfort we've always been looking for. No matter where we are searching, unless we know this underlying basis that is the utterly safe haven of rest, we just can't find a truly safe place anywhere.

Q: *I feel that so many organizations, governments, and political leaders have betrayed my trust that it's hard for me not to scream and yell about the things they've done. It seems to me that if we're dealing with unjust and corrupt people and organizations, a gentle and benevolent approach like you're advocating will never work. Could you comment on that?*

A: Whatever we buy into, that is what becomes real to us. We can be very limited by the belief systems and assumptions we have about life. We appraise the world and all beings in it as being objects that are either beneficial or harmful to us, and we're convinced that these objects have the power to affect our thoughts and emotions. Based on that conviction, if an organization or a government acts in a certain way, then that action will seem to have the power to affect our thinking and emotional states. We might feel either hopeful or afraid, depending on what the government is doing and what our belief systems and assumptions are about that government.

If there's only this one way of looking at things, then our experience will be very frustrating; we'll be at the mercy of events beyond our control. In the scenario I have just described, it's our thoughts that have created our experience of the world. We know that different people experiencing the same situation will have a wide range of responses depending on their own thoughts and emotions. One person can be in a concentration camp and be terrified, overwhelmed and unable to cope, and another person in the same situation can develop great compassion and be of great benefit to everyone. One person sees a horrible situation as totally harmful, while another person sees it as actually being of benefit in some way.

Let's say two people have great wealth. One person might be totally paranoid and would withdraw from the world and try to protect and hoard everything she has. Another person in the same situation might be very contented and always looking for ways to use her resources to benefit others. These different reactions are based on the thoughts and emotions that comprise what most people think of as their mind.

When we're looking through this limited filter of thoughts and emotions, it's like looking through a low-powered telescope that can only vaguely see what's going on in a certain section of the sky. On the other hand, with a high-powered telescope looking at the same area, one can see the entire panorama in all its vividness. Rather than prizing the ability to describe, explain and experience—the small telescope, as it were—what we're beginning to see in the world today is the advent of people who are more focused on actually getting familiar with the ground of being itself. They're more interested in seeing what things look like through the much higher-powered telescope of open intelligence, rather than just explaining, describing and categorizing things. This is a radical and revolutionary step for humankind.

When we talk about any of these things—life, being, explaining, describing, experiencing—what is it that's actually aware of all those things? That which is aware is the basic space of everything. It's aware of all data, all belief systems and all assumptions, and yet is unaffected by any of them. This is what should be known and experienced, rather than being mired only in thoughts and emotions.

Q: In the end it seems that there's nothing that can really be done about the fear I so often feel, because it just comes up when it will.

A: Fear has no power to confuse us whatsoever, because it has no independent nature. It's really nothing but the dynamic energy of open intelligence. It's like a star shooting across an empty sky, leaving no trace. If we elaborate on the fear and give it power, then it *will* have power. If we don't rest and instead we try to apply an antidote to the fear, then that gives the fear more power. Conversely, if we rest when the fear comes up, it will vanish on its own, and that's how we know the fear has no real power. Fear is nothing, really. One of the signs of accomplishment is fearlessness. This does not mean that fear never appears in open intelligence; it means that when fear or anything else appears, there is fearlessness. Fear and fearlessness are not two.

Q: I'm seeing more and more how one of the fundamental issues in people's lives is another type of fear—fear of rejection. It seems to come up very, very strongly, and I wonder if fear of rejection might be resolved through relying on open intelligence.

A: When we take ourselves to be a personal identity, we are substantializing ourselves with our data, so that we seem like something solid and stable. We take ourselves to be an individual defined by our data. Once we've established ourselves as someone in that regard, then we will also establish everyone else as an "other" to that self. Once that structure is in place, we begin to fear that others will reject our data, because our data are what we take ourselves to be. I would say that this is something common to almost everyone. We're afraid that the data of others won't match up with our data and that they're going to reject us. Of course, we'll never find anyone whose data exactly matches up with ours.

Human beings are pack animals, so to be ostracized from the pack is the ultimate rejection. As long as we think we are somebody, this kind of fear will be going on. But it's really no big deal. When it comes up, rely on open intelligence and what we need to know will be known. Fear of rejection is definitely something to go beyond. It is extremely limiting to continually hope that people won't reject us and fear that they will, or hope that we'll fit in and fear that we won't.

What we're really hoping is that junior high school will never reoccur! We don't want to ever again experience the kind of rejection we felt from other out-of-control adolescents who were joining cliques, saying that we weren't in their cliques, and then saying all kinds of mean things to each other and to us. That's a hideously painful time, and we're always hoping that it won't happen again, but we're subtly afraid that it will. This is all part of taking ourselves to be our data and taking other people to be their data, too.

The act of either rejecting or accepting people is an entirely dualistic behavior. Human beings have created many institutions where there is no openness and where situations of fear are created. No matter what kind of organization we join, there is always the subtle underlying assumption that if we don't toe the line we can be thrown out. It's impossible for people who are truly living in open intelligence to ever perpetuate those kinds of institutions. We are fully capable of creating institutions where people know they are welcome lifelong. These kinds of institutions are purely democratic, nonhierarchical and require few rules. Their guidelines simply serve the group unity and purpose. Rather than imposing restrictions, these are organizations where mutual support and success are fostered in everyone. That's what we're doing in Balanced View.

If I worried about whether or not people rejected me, I could never give these talks, because there are all kinds of opinions about me and what the Balanced View Training has to say. But open intelligence is beyond all conventional attachments of every kind. For me, there isn't any thought about personal things like being accepted or rejected by other people or by institutions. There's just the fervent passion to cultivate a world in which there is immediate benefit for everyone through the power of gaining confidence in open intelligence. Remember, short moments, repeated many times, become continuous.

OBEDIENCE TO THE UNENFORCEABLE
CHAPTER THREE

"Obedience to the unenforceable is found in open intelligence. It is acting according to the non-action of effortless wisdom that is conclusively for the benefit of all in every conceivable way."

There's nothing whatsoever that needs to be done about anything in order to be aware and wise. Enjoy the ease of your own being *as it is,* in which nothing need be done and nothing needs to change. However you're living your life and whatever the circumstances of your life may be, they're the perfect circumstances for gaining confidence in open intelligence. Whatever your perception of your situation may be, that situation is indivisible from open intelligence. All is known clearly and directly in the intelligence that is the basis of everything.

The perception called "you" is a datum inseparable from open intelligence, just as the appearance of everything else is a datum inseparable from open intelligence. There's no entity or force that can somehow do anything to keep anyone away from open intelligence. It is simply untrue that there are any obstacles between you and open intelligence.

Please don't worry about all the concepts and the difficult ways of doing things you may have taken on because of obedience to one philosophy or another. If you want to be obedient, be obedient to the unenforceable! Obedience to the unenforceable: that is the supreme and ultimate obedience and the only real obedience there is. Otherwise, there's obedience to the attempt to sort out and rearrange all our thoughts, emotions and experiences. When we spend our lives trying to rearrange everything in order to be happy, it's like trying to put together a one trillion-piece jigsaw puzzle of the cloudless sky. In other words, nothing will come from it, and the process will be exhausting and frustrating and will never lead anywhere.

Now, for many of us, what we've in fact been practicing is obedience to the enforceable, which is the assumption that our thoughts, emotions and experiences can force us to feel one way or another. Obedience to the enforceable means that we obey our thoughts and emotions according to whatever their label may be. I'll give a personal example of this: I was told that my name was Candice and that I was a girl, so I began practicing obedience to having that name and being that gender. Then other characteristics and qualities were added over time to describe me, and those became my belief systems as well. I was born into a Catholic family, so I started practicing obedience to the idea that I was a Catholic, and that there was a God and that he needed to be feared. I learned that this absolute being was keeping a scorecard and on that scorecard were lists of my good and bad attributes. Of course, in my mind the list for the bad things was much longer, because I could never get rid of the negative side that always seemed to be there!

I also learned obedience to other things, like taking myself to be of a certain race and that I was an American and that I had a certain type of intelligence and emotional makeup. As I grew older more and more belief systems were added on: political views, psychology, philosophy and many others. I practiced obedience to all those things with great fervor until I was in my late twenties, at which point I looked around and just didn't know where to go from there. I had collected so many belief systems in creating my identity that I was dizzied by them all.

I finally got into a situation in my life where things started to go in a way I hadn't expected, and I didn't know what to do. The obedience I had to all those belief systems didn't help me at all. I could find nothing in this data that could support or sustain me. I looked to one datum, and it wouldn't help; I would look to another, and it wouldn't help. In addition to the belief systems, I had even added in a few other antidotes to take the edge off when I needed relief. I would have a drink, smoke marijuana, socialize or immerse myself in work, but none of that helped either. It didn't matter where I sought my solace; at that point in my life none of the antidotes I'd previously relied on gave any relief whatsoever.

When I realized that relief was not to be found in any of these beliefs, I crashed. Suddenly my life looked completely bleak, and the years ahead didn't look like they would be any better. I got into an extended state of total hopelessness, but in that complete hopelessness and despair I somehow realized that all of the intense emotions and disturbing states actually had the same underlying basis, a basis that wasn't affected by those emotions. I didn't really have a concept to describe it then, but I knew that when I rested my mind for short moments, repeated many times, I felt the total presence of relief. When any of these inflammatory appearances would emerge, I would rely on the open intelligence which is the basis from which they had sprung. Over time the reliance on open intelligence became more and more continuous, until it was permanent at all times with no division between what appeared and the open intelligence in which it had appeared.

Anyone who becomes totally familiar with open intelligence as it is being described here says exactly the same thing, namely, that open intelligence simply *is*. It's not generated by anything. It is non-produced; it is unborn; it is indescribable; yet, it is naturally present. That recognition brings with it the true humility that is the obedience to the unenforceable, which is obedience to the love dwelling in every heart. This is not some kind of nihilistic philosophy that says that everything comes from nothing and leads to nothing, so we can do whatever we want to do. It isn't that at all. We must act as though our conduct were before the highest judge of open intelligence.

This is very important. "Acting as if before the highest judge" is another way of expressing obedience to the unenforceable. The appearances are all equal, but that doesn't mean that we merely act according to the appearances; we act in accordance with the underlying principle of unity. We act according to the non-action of effortless wisdom that benefits all in every conceivable way.

Q: *You are saying that our behavior should be as if standing before the highest judge, but I know very well that often in the past I have not acted in that way. In light of what you're describing, what is the best way for me to make amends for the harm I've caused others?*

A: If we feel guilty about harm we've caused, then through relying on open intelligence we can make a very powerful change. Instead of going into all the stories of guilt and blame, we rely on open intelligence. If we have harmed others, we will know best what kind of amends need to be made if we are relying on open intelligence.

There are a couple of good ways to make amends with people whom we've harmed through our actions. First, within ourselves we can say, "I'm truly sorry that I did this," because we've recognized the harm we caused and don't want to repeat it. A very simple and direct action is then to say to the person, "I'm sorry that this occurred, and I promise you it won't happen again." A lot of times in the past we might have said we were sorry, but then we continued doing the same things over and over again. For example, we might have been perpetually late, and every time we were late, we said we were sorry, but then we persisted in always being late! Rather than carrying on with behaviors for which we have to continually apologize, we should choose to make a direct change: when we make an appointment for a certain time, we arrive at or before the appointed hour.

The change we're trying to make may require a very high level of commitment. If we're very serious, we might say, "I vow that I will never do this again, even if my life is in jeopardy." Why won't we ever do it again? Because by the power of relying on open intelligence, we naturally want to benefit ourselves and others. That's what our vow is: to unflinchingly rely on open intelligence so that we do not cause harm to others. Then when we speak to the other person, we can do so having really looked into this matter very deeply, and we can say with utmost sincerity that we're really sorry this has happened and promise that it won't happen again. We've already decided within ourselves that it's not going to happen again; therefore, with full confidence we can promise them it won't happen again. This is really very powerful.

Relying on open intelligence means being fully relational. There is nothing to defend against or protect, so these responses come about naturally. We can follow through on our resolve easily and naturally, and we don't need to belabor things at all. When we learn how to make direct changes, we never have to muck around in guilt or blame again.

Q: *I have been struggling with some negative behaviors that stem from how I was in the past. I find that I sometimes still act inappropriately and do things that harm myself and other people.*

A: When you begin relying on open intelligence, this kind of coarse conduct just gradually gets ironed out, and the edge to everything softens, but the progress is usually gradual. One of the illustrations that has been used traditionally is the potter's wheel. If you're making a clay pot, you pump a pedal with your foot that makes the potter's wheel spin, and even after you stop pumping, the wheel keeps on going for a while before it finally stops.

Simply remain at rest, empowering yourself for short moments, repeated many times, allowing everything to be *as it is*. Be filled with the joy and gratitude of having made the choice to relax your perceptions. Relying on open intelligence is such a relief and boon for your life. It's like finding a huge treasure hidden in your house! Imagine having a huge pile of gold, but never having been able to recognize it, because you didn't know what gold was. You thought you were in poverty, but then all of a sudden when you're able to identify the gold, you realize, "Wow, I'm very wealthy!" The treasure of open intelligence has never been anywhere else; it is always right here, fully present within all appearances.

Q: *Guilt and blame about things that have happened seem to loom so large in my life. Could you say something about this?*

A: Let's take a little poll on suffering right now. How many people here have felt guilty? *(All the people in the audience raise their hands.)* How many people have blamed other people or themselves for their problems? *(All the hands go up.)* Okay, so you see, we are all in the same boat! Doesn't it feel good to see that you aren't the only one? When we're only swimming around in our own suffering, then it seems like we must be the only ones who have felt guilty or have blamed ourselves and others. It's important for us to come together and acknowledge how much we have in common.

We can suffer terribly for the guilt we feel within ourselves. We may actually feel guilty for things that other people have done to us, and we carry around this incredibly painful guilt all our lives. We feel that we must have done something wrong to make them harm us. This idea of being responsible for the harm someone else has caused is a very big source of hidden guilt in many people

What do we do when we start to see all this data? What we can do is to rely on open intelligence without elaborating on the data. Maybe we feel guilty for harm we've caused other people, but we're going to go nowhere in the resolution of that by thinking about it all the time or harboring intense emotional states related to that thinking. Only in relying on open intelligence when these feelings arise is it possible to go beyond all guilt and blame; otherwise, our whole life will be based on guilt and blame. Open intelligence is the essence of our being, but the only way to recognize this is to rely on it, and it alone, when these data come up.

Many actions of our life may be a playing out of guilt and blame in a strange way that we don't even perceive, because we're blind to it. This is one of the important things about the Twelve Empowerments Training, which allows us to become familiar enough with our own data that we're not blindsided by them anymore. When they come up, we can rely on open intelligence, and gradually the guilt and blame take on an amusing tone. Instead of their crushing us as if we had Mt. Everest on our chest, our lifelong burden of guilt and blame is lifted.

Q: Something very harmful was done to me at a young age, and I find it extremely hard to forgive. I don't want to carry the burden of the blame anymore, but I still can't bring myself to forgive the person.

A: Often we have a thought or a memory that appears involving a hurtful image of something that happened or was done to us, and then maybe the next thought comes up, "Oh, that was horrible, but I need to forgive." All these are just data. It is only in relying on open intelligence that true forgiveness comes about. I can barely utter the word "forgiveness" now, because there has never been anyone to forgive, and there's no one to do the forgiving. Whatever it is, all is already forgiven. We can only go beyond the seeming solidity of all the ideas that we have by relying on open intelligence and realizing that they're already undone. They certainly can't be undone through toying around with them.

Believing that we have to change our thoughts about another person in order to find a resolution to the situation is a total detour. We've tried all of these things: negotiating, forgiving, rationalizing, justifying, analyzing and so on. Why not instead go for the ultimate negotiation, where there aren't any parties to negotiate! That is the single nondual expanse of peaceful intelligence and freedom—and it's right here! To play around in the swamp of negotiating and justifying is like getting drunk or stoned; it's just another contrived way of adjusting things that avoids the super-completeness of open intelligence. Just rest in the essence of your own being and let everything be *as it is*, and you'll know everything that is to be known about everything. Do you want to know a bunch of conventional ideas, or do you want to be able to see as the flawless knower sees?

When we ease into the naturally settled reality of our own being, we remain empowered, despite all the appearances that arise. Through the empowerment that comes from resting with all the appearances, a complete compassion for others and ourselves comes about. We see the turmoil we've put ourselves through by making up such big stories about everything we think and feel. It's in that kind of compassion for ourselves that we have compassion for other people. True compassion can't come about in any other way. If we make amends or direct changes with another person from complete wisdom and love, we'll know what to do and how to act, which is a far better course than relying on pop psychology, psychiatry, self-help books, cultivating positive behaviors or anything else.

Q: So many negative things have occurred in my life that I feel were beyond my control. I've gotten into a kind of mindset where I expect these negative things to happen, and I find it very difficult to give up this way of thinking.

A: If we think, "Certain things have happened to me and things like that are going to keep happening to me," then we're making ourselves a victim of all the data we have about ourselves. First we believe we have a personal identity, and then we believe that the well-being of that personal identity is dependent on certain things. For example, we feel dependent on whether we have a good night's sleep and whether we have good dreams and no nightmares, or whether our day is filled with pleasant thoughts, emotions and activities, or whether people treat us in a pleasant manner or not. We subtly or overtly base our well-being on all these things.

I always recommend that people simply give up their right to be a victim of their data. If we keep it very simple, we can say that at any moment in our lives we're either choosing to go with our data or we're empowered by them. Rather than getting into all these trips about blaming other people, parents, spouses or negative events, if we just say, "My data are my data," then there's no one to blame. It's up to us as to how we respond to the contents of our minds. But if we don't want to make that choice, and we want to go on with our painful stories, then that's what we choose. In that moment we've chosen to be a victim of our painful stories, and that's just the way it is.

No matter what situation we are in, as long as we are following after data, there will be things that we will want to change, and there will be people we like and people we don't like. We will want to get the people we like around us and get the people we don't like away from us. To live in this way means that our life has become a prison. Who made it into a prison? We did! No one else ever makes our life into a prison. It's up to each of us to not become a victim of our thoughts, emotions and opinions. When we treat our thoughts and emotions as enemies, then we're at war with ourselves, and I think we can all agree that's not a nice situation to be in.

If we are able to rest and not be at war with our thoughts and emotions, we'll no longer collapse into this idea of a "poor me" who is a victim of suffering. In open intelligence we realize that we're really free of the perception of suffering, even though suffering appears. This is completely beyond what can be understood through dualistic thinking.

Dualistic thinking is based on the idea that either we're suffering or we're not, and that through different strategies suffering will come to an end. But when we rely on open intelligence, we find something very different. We find first of all that we can be completely free of our mental afflictions, even as they continue to arise. We find that we're more at peace with all of the mental and physical afflictive states that previously caused us so many problems.

What was afflictive is no longer afflictive. I didn't say that what was afflictive disappears or we get rid of it or it goes somewhere else. When we rely on open intelligence we no longer see afflictive states as something that can alter our well-being. That's real freedom. In relying on unalterable open intelligence, it becomes more and more obvious to us that what appears in open intelligence, as it only is open intelligence, cannot alter open intelligence. No matter what appears, it's a vivid appearance of open intelligence. It doesn't matter whether it's a thought, an emotion, a sensation, a serious bodily illness or injury or even death. Whatever it is, we know we're going to be okay.

Q: *I have real difficulties dealing with the problems of everyday life. I get frustrated and angry when things don't go my way. Can you say something about that?*

A: Yes, I can illustrate an extreme example of what you've described. If we've trained ourselves to be uptight and tense, and somebody hits our car and directs an obscene gesture at us, well, if we have a gun, we might take it out and start shooting! It doesn't have to be that excessive; there can be a variety of responses to the frustration and anger. We might choose to give the other driver the same obscene gesture, or say something threatening, or we might try to hit him in return. The other extreme might be that we're overwhelmed and we break down crying and pull over on the side of the road. "Oh, no, not again! Now my car has been damaged, I can't drive it anymore! Boo-hoo, poor me."

There's a wide range of responses depending on our own temperament or disposition. We can go from one extreme to the other: from being a total victim to being the perpetrator of further violence and assault. To indulge in either extreme is to do violence to ourselves and potentially to others. We've become tense and uptight by training ourselves to have all these responses. When we rely on open intelligence we don't need to be a victim or a perpetrator. We give up all our descriptions about who we've taken ourselves to be, and we get familiar with what's at the basis of it all. In that we have a much more balanced view, and we can say, "Wow, look what I've put myself through most of my life. I thought I had to have all these data to prove who I am, but I see now that I'd much rather be at ease!"

This becomes clearer and clearer. Then we start to see what other people are putting themselves through by believing in all their data. We look around at our family members and friends, and we see how much better off they'd be if they were relying on open intelligence. We're not criticizing, but it's sad to see how people hurt themselves by trying to substantialize their personal identities with data.

They may not listen to what we have to say about relying on open intelligence, but that's okay. That's simply the way it is. It's their choice—just like it's our choice. Regarding those who don't want to rely on open intelligence, this isn't an opportunity for position-taking or for us to say, "I'm relying on open intelligence and you're not!"

We know we're maintaining open intelligence when we can look at everyone with compassionate eyes and we don't have to force our opinions on anybody. That's obedience to the unenforceable.

LOVE AND RELATIONSHIPS
CHAPTER FOUR

"True relationship comes when we can be with others without being ruled by our data. It means living in the oneness we all share, the open intelligence which includes and transcends all differences and sees everyone as its own self."

Our natural state is to love and be loved. However, the only way to truly love is to enter the total love of one's own pure being and to live in that. It is this love that allows us to accept everything about ourselves just as we are, letting us see the inherent perfection in all that appears without needing to change any of it. When we are in tune with the perfection of our own being, we will see that same perfection in everything, and unconditional love will naturally flow. This is how we are able to truly love ourselves and thereby love others. Until then, all the talk about love is just a story.

Often we look for love by trying to contrive what looks like love and by arranging loving appearances, but this rarely leads to anything like true love. How can we know what love is unless we're familiar with our own open intelligence, which is the source of true love? Until we gain confidence in our true nature, we'll have a description or some ideas about love but never know what love truly is.

Often we try to love by imitating what we *think* love is, including doing certain things we hope will bring us love. Implicit in this is the hope that others will love us and the fear that they will not. In that case the entire relationship is based on hope and fear: we are hoping that love will happen and fearing that it won't. We feel that we're lacking love, and we need the other person to love us so we can get the love we want. What's more, we make our love conditional upon their love by thinking that unless they love us and show their love in certain ways, we won't be able to love them. Well, that's a total misunderstanding of what love truly is.

When we begin to gain familiarity with open intelligence, our relationships with people change, because our relationships become unconditional. Having found wholeness within ourselves, we're no longer looking for someone else to fill a void, and our love will flow from that place of wholeness without needing to ask anything in return.

As we continue to empower ourselves, we find in a very natural way that the relationships we've had all along no longer look the way they once did. For example, with our family of origin we may have had a lot of psychological labeling about who did what to whom and how we ended up being such-and-such because of what they did. When we gain confidence in open intelligence, we discover the aspect of ourselves that has never been hurt by anyone or any experience. We then start to see these same people in a new way: "Wow, what do you know—they're just like me!"

When we no longer need to blame anyone, we find tremendous compassion and a connection that we've never had before. Previously we may have felt that we needed something from people, but now we know that we don't. Maybe we thought they owed us something, but now we know they don't. In fact, we don't need anything from anyone to make ourselves whole, because we already are whole.

This principle holds true in all relationships, whether they're long term intimate relationships or brief encounters we have while walking down the street. We don't require anything from anyone, nor do we need for people to match up with our ideas of who we think they are or should be, and therefore we're able to see everything and everyone as equal and perfect in their own way. This doesn't mean that we act foolishly; rather, our actions flow from total wisdom. We enter into some situations and not into others. This happens in an effortless way. We're not locked into fixed ideas like, "That person is bad," or "I always do this," or "I couldn't possibly do that." We see things clearly as they are, and no matter what happens we rest, and from rest we know what to do. That is the mastery over the illusion of data, wherein all data are outshone by open intelligence. This mastery leads to a joyous and enormously beneficial life.

Until then life is fraught with uncertainty because of the perceived need to maintain certain relationships, ways of being and approaches to life in order to feel comfortable and safe. It's only when comfort and safety are thrown completely out the window and everything is allowed to go pell-mell and helter-skelter that the natural order of things is recognized and everything is seen to be timelessly free. Only then is true stability gained.

When we're resting as love, we come to see how everything within us is equal and fully pervaded with love. All our thoughts, emotions and experiences are the equalness of this love. When we know this about ourselves, then we automatically know this about other people, too. We know that they experience the same things we do and are made of the same essence we are. This recognition is very, very important, because it allows us to love in an extremely powerful way without any conditions. When we love ourselves and others in this way, then our relationships are simply about being of benefit to each other. We find there's a free, natural relationality that is entirely joyous, filled with love and always fresh. When there's that kind of freedom in a relationship, it's a real delight.

When we become established in open intelligence, we see how to relate to everyone and everything in an easy and natural way. When we rest with all the circumstantial appearances in our own mind, we come to understand ourselves and others completely. One instantaneous and immediate benefit of that understanding is that we have an intuitive knowledge of everyone else. We see that the people whom we had thought to be wrong, bad or better than us are really not at all different from ourselves. We come to deeply and compassionately understand others. We can see that just as we had been taking ourselves to be all our data, other people have been doing the same thing, and we know how painful that is.

Naturally and spontaneously we learn to relate to ourselves in a way that's completely easeful and non-harming, and we then know how to relate to others in that way as well. The more we rely on open intelligence for short moments, repeated many times, the more likely it is that we'll be able to make positive changes in our relationships that might have seemed impossible before. We may have had very acrimonious relationships with others for decades, but through relying on open intelligence, we find that we're looking at exactly the same person who's doing exactly the same thing they've always done that was so irritating, annoying and just plain wrong—and now none of it matters. We're able to be with them in an easeful way while at the same time knowing exactly what to do and how to act.

When we see who we are, then we see who everyone is, and we feel close to everyone in a natural way. We find that we're willing to be emotionally intimate with others—not out of some kind of contrived effort, but in a very natural way. When there's no need to try to change oneself anymore, then there's no need to try to change anyone else, even though we may have been trying our whole lives to change other people to make the world all right. Some of us have really been trying to do that, haven't we? However, when we don't need to change people anymore, then we can enjoy them thoroughly, no matter who they are.

In the past we may have been accustomed to forming relationships with partners, husbands, wives, friends and co-workers based entirely on matching data sets. We think, "These are my data; let me know what your data are, and if your data match my data, then we can decide if there's a relationship." Typically we only want to have people as our friends who agree with our data. If we decide to get married or partner with someone, not only do we want to have someone who agrees with our data, we want someone who *loves* our data sets. However, the infatuation with one another's data generally only lasts for a short while. Have you noticed that? After some time we'll want to change their data and they'll want to change ours.

Most of us have seen this played out in romantic relationships, and many people have seen it happen several times over the years! When we first get together with a romantic partner, everything is fantastic. It feels so good. We think there will never be anything better. We feel like we're the luckiest person on earth. We want to be together with our beloved all the time, and we don't want to spend a moment apart. We see our beloved and feel *sure* they're the one for us. No one has ever been so wonderful!

We have all these tremendous feelings coming up in us, and we think it's because of the other person, but that's where our error lies. We think that this intense love is due to the object of our love, rather than recognizing its source within ourselves. We then run to the object of our love, cling to it and say, "Be with me forever, and I will feel this love forever!" But what happens? Since we haven't recognized its true source, after some time the love starts to disappear, and because we've attributed the arising of the love to the other person, when it disappears we blame the disappearance on the other person and ask them to change in some way. In all likelihood they'll respond by blaming us and asking us to change. Well, this is all just too painful to bear. We usually try to regain the original experience of love somehow, but we find that no matter what we do, it's impossible to regain the intense feelings of love we had in the beginning.

These are very painful data, in which we attribute external causes and results to everything that happens. We say to the other person, "Well, I think you need to change." However, what's really behind that is that we want the love to return, and we think their behavior is an obstacle to that. In a kind of ambivalent, mixed-up way we're saying, "If you change, then the love will return. If you stop talking that way to me, or if you'll just put a towel down when you get out of the shower so I don't have to walk through that puddle every time you take a shower, or if you would just peel the potatoes my way instead of your way, then the love will return." We all know what this is like, because we've been through it. This kind of behavior is epidemic, isn't it?

When we look at it in such a clear way, it becomes humorous, but when we're lost in it, it's not humorous at all. Expecting relationships to provide the undying love we seek is really a dead end—whether it's a relationship with an intimate partner or a child or whoever it might be. The love we seek is already within us; in fact, it is the fundamental condition of what we are. When we live in the pure open intelligence that is always present within us, we'll be able to love unconditionally, no matter how our partner or others behave.

We all want to experience this love; somehow we know that it is our birthright, but if we don't feel it within ourselves, then we'll always be looking for it. We'll look for it in our personal relationships, in the organizations we join and in the connections we have with the world around us, but because we look outside ourselves our hopes of finding it are dashed time after time.

We need to recognize that when we fall in love and have that tremendous opening that love brings, the love we're experiencing is not created by an object outside ourselves. That love is our true nature, and it is always within us. To fall in love is a very powerful experience, because it gives us a direct introduction to the true nature of our own being. This is the magical thing about falling in love: it introduces us to who we really are. When we fall in love, everything is so great and everyone looks so wonderful. Well, when we rely on open intelligence, that same feeling is available all the time!

When we completely rely on open intelligence, then our clear seeing starts to penetrate everything, and we see that love is not created by something outside ourselves, but is what we are. Forever free open intelligence has never been made into anything, and yet includes everything. If we relax, the complete indivisibility of everything and the love inherent in it become more and more obvious to us. There's nothing sweeter than effortlessly resting as love, seeing that love in everyone and every experience, and letting perfect love flow through us to all. That is what is offered through the way of rest.

Q: I'm having a lot of trouble relating to my partner who is often so incredibly unreliable and inconsiderate. For instance, three times in a row he failed to turn up for an engagement with me. I sometimes just want to say, "Screw you!" to him and be done with the whole thing! What can I do about such strong negative emotions towards my partner?

A: First of all, if you think a thought like, "Screw you!" regarding your partner, remember that it's just another datum. It's not really a meaningful statement about anyone or anything; it's an ephemeral datum that's equal to every other datum. It's not a judgment set in stone; it's a passing wisp of nothing. Like a line drawn in water, it will disappear of its own accord, and the open intelligence that is the reality of both you and your partner remains unaffected. So, you don't have to beat yourself up about having that thought.

Often people think that when they rely on open intelligence, they'll never have thoughts like "screw you," and they'll never say things like that again. They think their words and thoughts will be always rosy and sweet. But this is just more splintering and fragmenting of everything. All words are completely equal, no matter what they are.

As you begin to rely on open intelligence more and more, you might eventually have moments when your mind is raging with everything you've ever wanted to say: "You total idiot! I can't stand living with you! I'm going stark-raving mad because of all these things you've done to me!" Or, you might all of a sudden be flooded with every mental picture you've ever had of doing harm to people, or you might have sexual fantasies that you've been trying to hold at bay and never wanted to think about.

All these thoughts could be flashing through your mind, but to the extent that you're established in open intelligence, you'll be laughing, because you realize that all of them are completely equal. You may have been trying to selectively hold all these terrible things away from "the pristine niceness of open intelligence;" yet, you see that they're all equal and ultimately have no capacity at all to cause you or anyone else harm or pain. This is the birth of compassion. Seeing that all data and all conduct are equal opens the floodgates of love, wisdom and energy. This understanding ensures that we can move beyond a lifestyle of petty emotional reactivity.

A lot of us not only feel victimized by people but also by circumstances in general. We think that certain things are probably going to happen to us that will cause us to suffer, and so we end up creating suffering for ourselves, usually on a daily basis. When we think something is happening to us that makes us suffer, then we are indeed a victim—of our own thoughts! We've made ourselves a victim to all this data we have about ourselves. First we believe we have a personal self, then we believe that the well-being of that self is dependent on other circumstances: whether people treat us nicely and respectfully, whether they turn up for their engagements with us and whether events go according to our wishes. We subtly or overtly base our well-being on all these circumstances. But when we begin to enjoy the all-encompassing empowerment of great benefit and the wonderful feeling of relief that comes with that, then we start to see that we're not at the whim of anything.

We gain a tremendous indwelling confidence; we know that we're all right with whatever appears. It doesn't matter whether it's a thought, emotion, sensation, serious illness, injury or even death. Whatever it is, we know we're going to be okay; we know our true being is changeless, timeless and forever free. We come to experience that all data that appear within open intelligence naturally vanish of their own accord, causing no harm and leaving no trace—and that includes the datum of death. Data are their own undoing and are free in their own place. Nothing needs to be said, done or noticed about them. In fact there's no one to notice them! There's only open intelligence with its own appearances. One instant it's the clarity of being somebody, the next instant it's the noticing and the next instant it's the object being noticed, but all these are merely thoughts within open intelligence. When we gain familiarity with that, then indwelling confidence and certainty come about, and we're able to be in all circumstances without impediment. We find we no longer need to avoid relationships with others, for everyone is seen as equal; we're established in the perfect love that is our true connection with everyone.

Q: I'm interested that you mentioned avoiding relationships, because I feel I do that much of the time. Can you speak a little more about that?

A: True relationship comes when we can be with others without being ruled by our data. It means living in the oneness we all share—the intelligence that includes and transcends all differences and sees everyone as its own self. Unconditional love and infinite respect for everyone naturally arise when we rely on open intelligence. That is real relationship. If we are degrading or demeaning people—ignoring, criticizing, hating them—or gossiping about them, being patronizing towards them or excluding them, any of these could be considered avoidance of relationship.

Taking our data to be real limits recognition of open intelligence, and this limited recognition of open intelligence can affect our relationships with other people. By holding to some data and rejecting others, we end up excluding and judging other people. When we rely on open intelligence, we no longer need to do that. Everyone is included in the limitless circle of our love. In the past, we may have caused harm to others based on holding to our data, whether it was with our parents, siblings, friends, extended family or co-workers. In the Twelve Empowerments Training there is a wonderful opportunity to look into how we have been harmful and how we can make direct changes in relationships so that we no longer harm ourselves or others. We see directly how we've used our data to avoid relationships with others, and then we commit to making positive changes in those relationships. The Twelve Empowerments are a tremendous support.

Q: I know that these days there's a lot of talk about the unity of humankind and the coming together of all people, and I wonder if you have any thoughts as to whether there can ever be true unity among nations and the various peoples of the world.

A: Something that's tremendously important to all of us today is this idea of the unity of everyone. "We're all one" is common parlance these days, and that's good. Lots of songs have lyrics based on it, and lots of people talk about it. Along with that idea, there is also often a belief that there's going to be this special date in the future when the world will experience a dramatic event and everyone will be unified.

We all hunger for this oneness and for world peace. We want it so much, and we don't just want to talk about it; we really want to know the reality of it. We know it's true, we know we're all one, but we want that oneness to come about in our own experience in a permanent and decisive way, rather than just as occasional thoughts, lines from songs or warm and fuzzy feelings of oneness which arise for a moment and then rapidly fade and disappear. We want the *real* oneness, the oneness of complete, unbridled wisdom and compassion. We want that to be a lived and direct experience for ourselves.

That oneness can only come about through the power of completely empowering the mind with open intelligence for short moments, repeated many times, until it becomes continuous and obvious. This enables seeing the essential equality of everything that appears within our own mind. That's the true oneness we're seeking, and the only oneness there is. There's absolutely no other oneness possible. Since the true nature of the mind is all-encompassing open intelligence, all phenomena, all circumstances and all people in the world really exist only within our mind, so when we're established in the truth that all appearances are of the same indivisible essence, that is true oneness. Then, it doesn't matter who we are, where we are, or who we're with. Wherever we are, it's absolutely equal.

There are people who are in prison, facing execution or being tortured who are able to maintain complete equanimity even in those extreme circumstances. I've seen this in my own experience in a very traumatic situation. Even though the situation was such that the thoughts and emotions related to the event could have tortured me for the whole of my life, because I was able to rest, there was complete equanimity.

Even in the case of a physical assault, ultimately the perpetrator, the victim and the crime are all one, as there is no division anywhere. The unified field of open intelligence, which is our true identity and the true nature of all phenomena, remains unaffected by any event, no matter how horrific it might be. When you're in tune with that oneness, people may attack you and hurl insults at you, and you'll just stand there with a heart full of compassion; you'll be able to smile and know exactly how to respond in a way that is free of emotionally charged reactivity. At other times, you may do nothing. Who knows what will happen, but you'll know what to do, and whatever you do, it'll be an appropriate action.

All appearances are outshone by the clear light of open intelligence. Establishment in open intelligence provides the optimal power that a human being can ever have. It is this clear light of open intelligence that sees everything as one—as equal and even—in all circumstances. Then there's a free flow of action that is really non-action, which pours from wisdom in an effortless way, manifesting as true compassion for all beings.

When the ability to rely on open intelligence is gained by more people around the world, then increasingly humanity will be able to manifest the unity of all nations and peoples that we all long to see. But there's no need to wait for oneness. It's here right now. Short moments of open intelligence, repeated many times, become continuous.

SEX AND DESIRE
CHAPTER FIVE

"Whether we are sexually active or not, we are in the perfect circumstance for relying on open intelligence. Relying on open intelligence has never been bound by any conventional designations, because open intelligence is the root of all designations."

A fundamental aspect of the Balanced View Training is complete acceptance of sexuality and the whole realm of the senses. Sexual desire is not something that is other than what is totally pure. In ever-clean open intelligence, there has never been anything unclean, and there's no part of the body that is unclean. Everything, no matter what, is primordially pure. Whether it is a movement of sexual desire in the body or thoughts or emotions of any kind associated with that, they're all primordially pure. They have never deviated for an instant from the basic space of open intelligence in which they appear.

Nonetheless, it's important for human beings to make wise choices regarding sexuality and relationships. If we only mix our thoughts, emotions and sensations together and make a decision based on them, there won't be clear seeing. When we empower ourselves with open intelligence, we'll see thoughts, emotions and desires for what they truly are, and we'll be able to act wisely and in a way that benefits all beings.

If we choose to be sexually active, then everything about that activity—the seeing, tasting, touching, hearing and smelling—can be experienced as primordially pure and delightful. One can enjoy any activity in which one engages as the free-form play of total purity, total pleasure and unconditional love without needing to change or censor anything. That makes an act of intimacy very special and extraordinary. When we rely on open intelligence, we come to intuitively know about our body and how to take care of our body, and we know about our emotional states and how to take care of them, too. We'll also know how to care for the emotional states of others.

It is incredible to rely on open intelligence and to get to know about all the data we have around desire, whether it's sexual craving or any other form of longing. All expressions of desire are vivid appearances of forever empty open intelligence. However, if we take them to be something in themselves, then we may end up creating all kinds of stories about them, and we'll find ourselves obsessing about them in one way or another. When we rely on the power of open intelligence, we have a choice about what we do in life. We no longer feel like we're controlled by all our data. When we are established in wholeness and timeless freedom, we're beyond the belief system of cause and effect. We no longer buy into that conventional belief, because we see that the reality of who we are is untouched by cause and effect. It's very, very powerful to get to know ourselves in this way, and when we do, then we understand the power of choice like never before.

I've used sexual desire as an example, because I've never met anyone without sexual desire, but this aspect of choice applies to whatever desire we are dealing with. We all have desires in our lives: for sex, companionship, money, food, housing, success, respect and so many other things as well. Perhaps in the past we've had a strong desire come up in us, such as desire for money, and we felt that we couldn't control ourselves. We had to go and make a lot of money, and even if we succeeded in making a lot of money we still wanted more. The same is often true with sexual desire; we may have sought more and more sexual experience and never attained what we thought was full satisfaction. Due to intense sexual desire we may have acted in ways that hurt ourselves and others and persisted in those behaviors despite the harm they were causing.

Food, money, sex, work, leisure and relationships—we never seem to have enough of them, and no matter how much we have of any of these, they never fully satisfy our craving for more. Eventually we come to realize that these things never lead to ultimate fulfillment. I'm speaking from shared human experience, in that we all seek a sense of pleasure and satisfaction, but most often we're not able to find it.

Most of us have been taught that sexual desire is something in and of itself and that it has power over us. We believe in that power, and to a large extent humanity lives in subservience to the power we have invested in sexual desire. If we consider the problem of overpopulation, many solutions have been proposed, but the world's population continues to increase. There are many population control methods—birth control pills, condoms, abstinence and so many other things—but have any of these ever been fully effective? No. Why? Because we love to be sexually engaged with each other! It's a totally natural impulse, and no method of stabilizing population growth can be fully effective as long as it's only a matter of using one datum to control another datum.

As a species we haven't yet discovered our inherent ability to be the masters of our desire. For the survival of the human race, it is now vitally important that we understand that this intense biological urge has no independent nature and that it is merely another datum appearing and disappearing within the infinite expanse of pure intelligence.

This is not to say that we shouldn't be sexually active, but that the expression of the sexual nature needs to come from wisdom, rather than from craving. There is no need to give directions or admonishments for everyone to follow; open intelligence has its own inherent moral code, and open intelligence sees itself in all. When we rely on open intelligence we'll know what we need for ourselves and what is right for us, and then right action will naturally ensue. We will know what to do in an unerring way without thinking about it, and whatever we choose to do with our sexuality will be beneficial.

When strong desire of any kind arises, the wise approach is to rely on open intelligence, seeing the desire as open intelligence, until the desire is directly perceived to *be* open intelligence. When we're able to do that, this very powerful force of craving will be directly transmuted into the well-being that is the essence of open intelligence. We don't need to change the thoughts, the desires or the afflictive states at all. We don't need to push them away or reject them, seek anything in them or act them out. All we need to do is rely on open intelligence, and the thoughts and emotions will gradually undo themselves, and in their undoing is revealed complete well-being. Only in this way can we really come to understand everything about ourselves.

This is not a method for eliminating sexual desire or a path to "becoming pure," because everything about us is already primordially pure. To try to neutralize sexual desire or remove it from our being would be to devitalize ourselves and take away the tremendous energy of a potently beneficial force. We may choose to be celibate or live in solitude, but that shouldn't be an antidote to sexual desire or a way of repressing desire. If we have chosen to be celibate or live in solitude as a means to avoid or neutralize sexual desire, then it's really helpful to rest as the desire and discover the inherently pure and potently beneficial energy of desire. If we then want to choose celibacy, that's fine—it's a perfectly valid lifestyle—but it wouldn't be wise to see the neutralization of desire as something that's purer than sexual desire.

Whether we are sexually active or not, we are in the perfect circumstance for relying on open intelligence. Relying on open intelligence has never been bound by any conventional designations, because open intelligence is the root of all designations. When we rely on open intelligence regardless of circumstance, then we begin to definitively realize that we are not dependent on anything. If we believe we require conditions in order to rely on open intelligence, then we've instantly created more duality. We may think that we're not going to be a good enough person to know open intelligence unless we are celibate or chaste, but this is just one more conventional designation.

When we get familiar with ourselves as open intelligence, then we see everything clearly. We are able, perhaps for the first time, to really be with people in a natural way that is based entirely on caring, concern and love. The more human beings rely on open intelligence, the more that love and caring will inform everything about human life on Earth, whether in relationships, families, institutions or the societies we live in.

Q: I want to ask you about casual sexual encounters. Up until now I would usually have some desires and then simply act on them just to have some fun. At this point I can see more and more that this is not the right path for me. Could you please give me some guidance about how to deal with this habit of indulging in casual sex?

A: That's a good question. Sex is of interest to almost everybody, because we're all sexual beings, after all. We have all kinds of information available these days about our sexual nature and how we should behave sexually and what our thoughts and emotions should be pre-sex, during sex and post-sex. We have data that are part of popular culture, and there are many moralistic data and social injunctions, which vary from culture to culture and which govern our feelings about our sexual nature. We are told about what kind of sexual desires we should and shouldn't have and how we should or shouldn't act them out with ourselves and with other people. Unfortunately, many people never truly come to understand their sexual nature beyond these mere conventions.

There's a lot of focus in Western culture in particular on the urge to act. Through successive generations, those urges to act have been liberated from strict moral constraints and have become much more freewheeling. Today people in Western culture start having sexual relationships much earlier in life and have sexual relationships with many more people during their lifetime.

In my own life, when I was ten or eleven, I hadn't been exposed to MTV or the Internet, as these things didn't exist then. I wasn't thinking about being sexually active with other people, but I *was* thinking about being sexually active with myself. Of course, I wasn't hearing anything about that from anyone. Very young people nowadays are exposed to many more kinds of sexual ideas than I was when I was young, but there isn't a wise forum for seeking guidance or a venue to speak openly about the tumultuous thoughts and emotions that go along with those ideas.

The sexual nature awakens in us when we're little babies, and when we innocently start to play with our genitals we are many times told in no uncertain terms to not do that. Later when we get to be teenagers and those intense feelings come totally alive, we're told that those feelings and the activities associated with them are to be avoided. So, we have these powerful erotic movements within our bodies, and most of us are told to not explore them with ourselves or with others. There is also a tremendous amount of shame, repression and avoidance associated with these feelings, thoughts and fantasies.

The strong movement of sexual energy that comes up for young people is just the energy of initiation into adulthood—that tremendous energy latent within the body which, when aligned with our true being, can be of great benefit to ourselves and others. This energy is most noticeable at that time of life, because it comes when young people are separating out from the confines of the family, and part of that separation is in the form of this tremendous energy to know and express themselves. This energy is occurring spontaneously within a context of all-encompassing perfection and wisdom, but if it's not properly understood, it will not be recognized as such.

We often develop very ambivalent belief systems about our sexual nature, which means that we love it, but at the same time we have all these doubts, worries and guilt feelings about it. We may have learned that only certain kinds of sexual lifestyles are appropriate. We may have learned that we have to be married in order to have a sexual relationship and that we should get married and then stay with that person forever and that sex in that context—and *only* in that context—will be okay. When we're in a sexual relationship, a lot of us think that it has to be a certain way, like for example, that there has to be an orgasm, or it is preferable if both people have an orgasm at the same time, and if that doesn't happen then that's not okay. We may have learned to be troubled by the sexual fantasies we have or that they have to be of a certain kind or else we'll feel that we've gone beyond what is acceptable.

We might also hear about casual sex, and we might think, "Oh, that sounds *good*, I'm going to try that!" but that doesn't really resolve the conflict either. We still have a great deal of ambivalence, and now we've just added casual sex into the mix. Our sexual longings haven't gone away; they're always circling around within the same ambivalent belief systems, leaving us unsatisfied and searching for more. This is a big problem for many people these days.

When we learn to rely on the power of open intelligence, a vast context opens up within us, which allows us to get some breathing room. By empowering ourselves with open intelligence, we find freedom from the compulsion to act on every desire. As we begin to see the equalness and primordial purity of all appearances, then the moral judgments, fixed ideas and belief systems we may have held about sex begin to loosen.

The more we let go of these strict belief systems, the more we can discover the inherent perfection within our sexuality and enjoy our sexual nature in such a way that it brings us closer to our truly beneficial nature.

Instead of sex being at odds with what we consider holy, we can discover sex itself to be holy—and a doorway into our own super-complete wholeness. We are then empowered to make wise choices. In a very easygoing and natural way we can decide how any kind of sexual activity will benefit others and benefit us. This lets us be more relaxed in any kind of sexual activity we choose, and this will bring deeper levels of enjoyment, intimacy and satisfaction for our partners and us.

Unless we empower ourselves completely, we can't really make wise decisions about sex, food, money, work, relationships or anything else. The more we sustain open intelligence, the more likely we are to be very careful and wise about the relationships we enter into, whether they're sexual relationships or of any other kind. When we rest, then inseparable from that rest is the desire to be of benefit. It's just an innate part of the natural workings of our mind and body. Rather than just entering into situations pell-mell, we relax, take our time and are much more careful. Before taking any action, we're much more likely to be asking ourselves: "How is this going to affect me and how is it going to affect the other person?" When we start asking that question at each juncture in our life, we will know that we are really on the right track.

You're a young man, and I've never been a young man myself, but I've heard that young men have a lot of sexual urges. Well, guess what, women do too! But it's important to understand that these urges are only urges—they're not any kind of command to do anything. Sexual urges do not have an independent nature that can force anyone to act. Maybe this is news to some of us, but sexual urges are not substantial in their own right. Like all other phenomena, they have no power over us. They are simply data occurring in the vast expanse of open intelligence.

Many of us learn that our sexual urges have power over us and that we either need to act on them or stop them. However, whether it is the sexual urge itself, a compulsion to act on the sexual urge or the drive to stop the urge, all those data are equal and none of them have power of their own. What's needed is to rely on the open intelligence in which those data appear and disappear and find our true power to act there. If we continue to act on every sexual impulse we have or if we continue trying to control or repress those impulses in some way, then we can never know the real nature of our sexuality or ourselves.

The more familiar we are with the empowering essence of all data, the more we will recognize them as aspects of open intelligence. If we feel that we have to modify or act on whatever comes up, then we can never know the essence of all phenomena, which is open intelligence itself. It's a really exciting part of the open intelligence adventure to let our data be whatever they are without needing to modify them or act on them.

When we are relying on open intelligence, whatever kind of sexual relationships we have can really become exalted. I don't mean exalted in some sort of corny, over-spiritualized way, but in a very natural, completely profound and easy way. Sex is meant to be totally natural and enjoyable. If we gain familiarity with and confidence in open intelligence, then we will know what we should do. We will be wise, loving and careful, and our sexual relationships will reflect that wisdom and care.

To allow all data to be as they are is so incredibly freeing. Rather than restricting or confining the expression of our sexual nature, relying on open intelligence makes the expression much more spacious and open, in a way that could never have been imagined, conceived or contrived. When our confidence in open intelligence is profound, there is simply a great honor and respect for everyone, including ourselves.

Come to know these wonderful expressions of human living as they are. They are expressions of open intelligence; they're not something about which we need to feel ambivalent or guilty. All the appearances of open intelligence are primordially pure. If we rely on open intelligence while exploring our sexual nature, we come up with a direct and firsthand experience that there really is no division between the appearances and open intelligence. If we're having sex with someone, we rely on open intelligence while doing so. Whether we are being sexual with ourselves or someone else, we come to really see that all of these thoughts, emotions and sensations of the body are truly inseparable from the limitless, primordially pure intelligence that is our true nature.

Q: I have been wondering about the role of appropriate limits and boundaries and what my preferences should be in terms of the way that my sexual energy is being used as I rely more and more on open intelligence.

A: It is important to know how to act and what to do in a very natural and uncontrived way. This can only come about with confidence in open intelligence and its power of wisdom. Once you try to set a "limit" or a "boundary," then you have a whole belief system about limits and boundaries. If you are relying on the open intelligence that is innate in everything, you don't have to build a system to describe it. You continue to rely on open intelligence, see all as open intelligence and from that place of wisdom let what happens happen. This makes things very easy. If you start to build a language system to describe what is going on, then you will be reading books about limits and boundaries, blogging with people who are into limits and boundaries and meditating on limits and boundaries. And what will you end up with? Limits and boundaries!

If you rely on open intelligence, then you will know what to do. Before I had this shift twenty-seven years ago, I didn't know what I should do with my sexual energy, but as I grew more familiar with open intelligence a profound change in my relationship with sexuality naturally came about of its own accord. That transformation was altogether organic and uncontrived; it had nothing to do with setting boundaries or limits.

When you are relying on open intelligence, then you are relying on wisdom no matter what appears. One of the things you learn very quickly is that there are certain appearances that can blindside you; that means that you become totally involved in whatever is appearing and you can't even think about relying on open intelligence. It happens so fast that you don't know what's happening, and if you're not careful you can be swept away into compulsive action that's not rooted in wisdom. This is very common, and it creates problems for many people.

The Balanced View Training has a system of support 24/7 to help when such moments occur, and this comes in the form of the Four Mainstays: relying on open intelligence, the trainer, the training and the community. Balanced View's Twelve Empowerments is a twelve-day training that is specifically designed to show you in detail what your data are so you will be able to see in advance where you are likely to be blindsided. Most human beings have areas where they are easily blindsided, such as sex, food, money, relationships, leisure, power and work. These are very natural parts of human life. When we clearly see how those desires play out within us and we find the wisdom that is indestructible and unaffected by desire or any other viewpoint, then it makes it much easier to rely on open intelligence. When you have carefully examined your data and have found support in relying on open intelligence, then instead of being blindsided you remain easeful and clear without even trying to do so. This is extraordinarily helpful.

A Balanced View
CHAPTER SIX

"All kinds of seemingly opposing things can come up—illness, death, disaster, terrorism, praise, success and joy, but "great equanimity" means being at ease in the face of all these appearances. When nothing can affect our well-being, then we truly have a choice in life."

From the vantage of relying on open intelligence, we have an all-encompassing view, with which we can see things as they truly are. From an airplane flying at 30,000 feet we can see with a completeness that's not possible from the ground. In a similar way, from the all-embracing vision of open intelligence we have a much broader outlook regarding all experience. We see that there's no need to hold to any datum whatsoever, because all data are completely equal. The capacity to see things in that way is called "the balanced view."

Open intelligence and all the data contained within it are a seamless expanse. Even though data appear within open intelligence, open intelligence remains *as it is*—unchanged by whatever appears and never having been made into anything. One experiences the balanced view through clear seeing that is completely wide-open, spacious and carefree in every moment. This view provides the capacity to choose among the many different options that are available and to understand which will be the most beneficial to all beings.

No matter how any appearance is described, it is timelessly free and unobstructed. When we return again and again to open intelligence as the basis of everything that appears, then more and more we have complete equanimity regardless of what's happening. With the freedom of complete perceptual openness in the direct encounter with any appearance, we see that appearances have never taken hold. If there is an arising of a strong appearance—like panic for example—we see that the panic and the complete ease of being are not two, just like thought and no-thought are not two. As we rely on open intelligence more and more, then less and less do we see two anywhere.

In relying on open intelligence for short moments many times, equanimity becomes all-pervasive, night and day. All kinds of seemingly opposing things can come up—illness, death, disaster, terrorism, praise, success and joy, but "great equanimity" means being at ease in the face of all these appearances. When nothing can affect our well-being, then we truly have a choice in life.

Rather than training our minds to always take a position or have an opinion about what appears, we empower ourselves with the great equality of everything. The more we do so, the more there will be a naturally occurring warm sense of well-being that pervades everything. Things that once ruffled our feathers won't ruffle them anymore.

This isn't just some abstract philosophy that we read about in a book and then memorize. Rather, it's a decisive experience that expresses itself in a practical way in our lives. No matter what the descriptions are, they all have their basis in the primordial purity of everything just *as it is*. If we are looking for a description, why not that one? It's very important for all of us as human beings to come together in this relaxed way, where we can look each other straight in the eye without needing to drag along all our descriptions of past, present and future.

What do we really want? Do we want to have a big pile of beliefs, or do we want the relief that's at the basis of everything? No matter who we are and how negative our circumstances might be and whether we've done horrible things in our lives or great things, we can get to know the fundamental nature of reality and return to that again and again.

So, if we hear that our lover doesn't want to be with us anymore or that we have a terminal illness and that we are going to die or suddenly we're faced with some other very challenging situation, when the relaxed naturalness of our own being is understood as the basis of all appearances, then we're able to be in all these situations without impediment.

Q: Would this great equanimity apply for you in an extreme situation? To compare, say, the birth of your child with the death of your child, would those two be equal?

A: At the deepest level, yes, they would be. "Great equanimity" doesn't mean that one is thoughtless or emotionless. It means that all appearances are seen as equal and that the basis of appearances is equanimity. It's not like taking a big band-aid of equanimity and applying it when bad situations occur. The nature of open intelligence is complete equanimity, so that whatever appears that equanimity is present as the appearance. The force of ever-present open intelligence is present in and as the appearance without distraction. Open intelligence is not an observer of something else; it pervades the single nondual expanse of equalness.

Q: So could that equanimity include the emotion of joy at birth and grief at death?

A: Absolutely.

Q: It doesn't exclude the feeling of sorrow or grief?

A: Not at all. It's equally embracing and all-inclusive and allows the free rein of everything.

Q: That's hard for me to understand.

A: Yes, it can't be understood with the intellect. It's completely beyond thinking or doing anything about it to try to make it come about. When we rely on that which is the source of joy and grief, birth and death, then we have complete freedom.

Q: How can I continue to rely on open intelligence while being in pain?

A: The essence of everything, even pain, is open intelligence. Rather than trying to describe everything that's going on and then worrying about what's going to happen or whether you're on the right course of treatment, continue to abide as the essence of that pain—even though it may seem difficult to do so. That's the greatest chance you have of healing yourself. When you empower the already healed well-being that is the essence of pain and sickness, that's the best medicine!

Looking at the experience of pain in a practical way, we can see that when there is acute pain, like say, when we have a severe headache, usually the sensations of pain are in fact fleeting. It may seem like we've had a bad headache the whole day, but when we rely on open intelligence we start to realize that there are lots of different sensations that go with having a headache and that they come and go. There isn't a headache absolutely present every single instant. There are gaps, and there are also different descriptions of the pain, such as low, moderate or intense. As we rely more and more on open intelligence, we become much more aware of how these descriptions come into being, and we also find that they no longer rule us as they once did.

As we get older we may have a lot more disturbing things going on with our bodies. A lot of you are young, but listen up, because I'm a little older! Just sit here for a minute and notice every little ache and pain you have. By the time you're my age, those aches and pains will be many orders of magnitude greater! If you haven't gained confidence in the great equanimity of open intelligence, then any of the disturbances you have within you now are going to be even more exacerbated. You probably don't think about the end of your life or dying very much because you're so young, but when you get to be in your late fifties, then the horizon gets closer and you know that the body is going to start falling apart. Don't describe these things—which means don't give them a label—and you will be able to resolve issues that may come up for you, either now or later in life as you are aging.

Q: *I'm presently in the process of leaving a community with which I've had a long affiliation, and I'm being criticized greatly by the people for my decision. When I didn't respond to their criticism at first, they then started being even more vehement in their condemnation. It may be because I've begun relying on open intelligence that the criticism hasn't stung me as much as it would have earlier.*

A: Sometimes when we've been around a group of people who are accustomed to seeing us react in a certain way, they'll have a certain expectation about how we'll respond when they criticize us. However, when we don't respond in the expected way, they may feel the need to be even more extreme. "Well, if we can't get her going with these things, let's try something even harsher!" Some people will love us and say lots of nice things, and other people will dislike us and say all kinds of cruel, nasty, mean things, but whatever way it is, that's just the way it is. It's all timelessly free.

Now, regarding the situation you're describing, it's really amazing. At one time, if you had heard negative things about yourself, you would have found it very difficult to bear. You might have ended up totally devastated, but now here you are feeling quite at ease about the whole circumstance! There's no need to react or respond in any way. One goes about one's business, whatever it is. Whatever appears, just let it be. Whatever happens, just rely on open intelligence. Equanimity is the ability to be at ease in all situations without impediment, including situations where you're being criticized unfairly!

Q: I find it very disturbing to watch the news on TV, because the things one sees can be so horrible. But even if I avoid watching the news media or reading newspapers, I'm still around people who do, and they're always talking about these disturbing things, and I find that my mind becomes so unsettled. Is there anything I can do about this?

A: Just relax and take care of yourself as you are. It doesn't matter what people shout and scream about. Whatever the newspapers, television or the movies are shouting and screaming about, it's all a fantasy world. It can't affect us unless we let it do so. If we're watching the television news and getting all whipped up into the negativity that's so prevalent there, then that's our choice. But if we just watch all of what comes before us and we completely relax with no need to hold on to any of these descriptions, we get to know who we really are. Nothing can disturb the peace inherent in our true nature.

I live in a small beach town in California, and every year someone comes down at low tide and builds an incredibly intricate sculpture out of sand. It has every detail and nuance of the most elaborate statues you'd ever see in marble or gold, and great care is taken for many, many hours in building it. Then slowly and relentlessly the tide comes up and totally washes away this beautiful work of art.

Similarly, no matter what appears, it will change and eventually vanish naturally. The law of impermanence applies to everything. What hasn't yet appeared will appear, and whatever appears will disappear. The things that were going on at one time have all vanished, and now there are other things appearing. The whole world could blow itself up in an instant, but indestructible open intelligence would still be, so why not get familiar with that? When you know that, where is the need for fear?

Q: *With all the things going on, especially since 9/11, I feel a great deal of anxiety on a regular basis. I've heard about being comfortable with insecurity, but what would you suggest when one feels overwhelming fear about what might happen?*

A: The unpredictable, magnificent display will just do what it will, and so we might as well relax and enjoy the ride, because we really never know what is coming next! No matter how safe we think our country is, we don't know what's around the corner. A threat could come in any form—an attack by an enemy, political or religious persecution, social injustice, an earthquake, civil war, our own death or someone else's death.

Whatever happens, happens, but when we rely on open intelligence, we can just let it happen! We don't need to think, "Oh no, I don't want this to happen. I want my life to be different!" Well, if missiles are landing around us and other countries are invading, guess what, we won't be able to change that. We might as well know how to rely on open intelligence, because then we'll have peace of mind no matter what's happening outside. Then we'll know what to do in the situation, and we'll be able to respond from wisdom, rather than freaking out and getting all involved in our emotional states.

Believe me, anything can and will happen. If we're living our life based on data, then it's going to be very difficult and painful for us when those unexpected things occur. However, if we're relying on open intelligence, then we're able to see it all as an incredible display. Instead of all the experiences of life being enemies or something that we have to be afraid of, we see everything as an ally. Recognizing appearances as supportive of gaining confidence in open intelligence is a way of committing to open intelligence. It means that we say to ourselves, "I'm going to acknowledge open intelligence as the fundamental ground of my being. That's what my life's about, and I'll never give up!" What does "never giving up" mean exactly? It means that no matter what happens, the emphasis is going to be on open intelligence rather than on the appearances.

Q: I heard you mention in a talk on the Internet about the fact that at some point in our practice, everything could just sort of blow up and that we might have a really tumultuous time where all of our thoughts would be going crazy. Could you explain more exactly what it is you're speaking about?

A: If we've been intense practitioners for some time, we may think that all of the negative thoughts and emotions have been renounced or left behind. We may think that we're beyond them, and that if such things appeared in our minds it would represent a regression for us. However, as long as we're thinking in that way, we're avoiding the timeless freedom of open intelligence.

At some point we have to be able to leave all the position-taking behind, throw away the meditation cushion and throw away all philosophies—including our own philosophies! It's then that the great equanimity comes about. When we're able to see everything as absolutely equal and give up our habit of trying to repress and control the contents of our minds, that's the moment when—*boom*—everything that we've been trying to hold at bay comes rushing in.

There may be a point, no matter how much practice we've done, when the shit is going to hit the fan, so to speak! Every great being who's ever achieved the potent powers of the clear light of wisdom says the same thing: no matter how long we sit on our cushion in meditative absorption, eventually everything's going to fall apart. We see this happening very publicly with many important figures in the spiritual world today, don't we? All of a sudden these internal upheavals have happened, and many of them weren't prepared.

It may be that all kinds of crazy thoughts will occur to us, and we can't believe we're having these kinds of thoughts. All the things we've been pushing away—such as sexual fantasies that we're sure can't be included in spiritual practice—will all come flooding in. Even if we've gotten into some kind of extreme state, like emptiness, no-self, no-thought, impartiality or neutrality, and we've been able to hold on to that state for a long time, suddenly these thoughts can start bombarding us, and then the state we've been holding on to will be gone.

Now, that's a very graphic description, isn't it? Despite all our attempts to control the contents of our mind by neutralizing negative states, suddenly there isn't any control. Everything's flying all over the place! But then what? If we're prepared in that moment to handle it on our own, to rely on open intelligence and let the appearances come and go, then there will just be great laughter! This is described in all of the great traditions: the indestructible, unchanging laughter that comes from the recognition of everything *as it is*. We'll see that everything is equal and there is nothing to fear in any appearance. The open intelligence underlying pious thoughts and lustful, hateful thoughts is identical. It is in realizing the great equality of all appearances that the true warmth of uncontrived compassion is unleashed. It remains hidden until the equalness of all appearances is realized.

You won't be able to predict what will happen in these upheavals, but when they come you'll either know what to do or you won't. If you have had good instruction, then you'll be prepared, and you can just be with it and laugh. If you don't know what to do, then it's time to rely on your trainer, because that's what trainers are for. They are there to support you in these frightening moments when the whole system of the mind begins to crumble. They're going to know what's happening when all the confines of concepts are completely shattered. Many of us have heard of the letting go of belief systems and assumptions and the shattering of all concepts. Well, this is what the shattering of all concepts means. It isn't like taking a teensy-weensy hammer and smashing the word "concepts." It's wild, energetic, free and beyond anything that could ever be imagined. So, if this hasn't occurred for you, get ready by gaining confidence in open intelligence!

SKILLFUL MEANS
CHAPTER SEVEN

"I have found conclusively in my own experience that love always brings about the most fruitful results. Love needs no other means—love alone is the most sublime and skillful of means. One could say that love is the ultimate skillful means for creating peace and well-being in our lives, in our communities and on the Earth."

What I'm interested in is the down-to-earth expression of open intelligence that genuinely benefits people. I'm not interested in mere philosophy that has no practical application, nor am I interested in writing great treatises that no one can understand. I want to share what's most essential and valuable in life in a very direct and practical way so that people all over the world will be helped. I'm interested in daily life as it's lived by people everywhere with beating hearts and breathing lungs.

Teachers can only teach in an authoritative and persuasive way if their teaching is based on their own lived experience; mere theoretical or hypothetical knowledge doesn't have the power to transform. It's very, very important to know the distinction between instruction that's based on the teacher's direct experience and instruction that's merely theoretical. When a teacher's wisdom is clearly and directly communicated, then people who are open to that wisdom can quickly recognize and realize it in themselves. A teacher who has the direct experience of resting imperturbably will be able to use the skillful means inherent in open intelligence to introduce a student to a direct experience of open intelligence.

There are many teachers and teachings all over the world, and the use of skillful means can take many different forms. Skillful means may appear stern or severe in certain circumstances—or graceful and kind in other circumstances. However, if their use is entirely based in open intelligence, their application will be unerring in any given situation.

A teacher who has realized the basic goodness of open intelligence can easily recognize the data of those who have come to them for instruction—even the subtlest data, about which the individuals themselves may not be aware. In helping people move beyond those data, some teachers work in ways that sometimes seem very harsh, but that isn't the approach taken in Balanced View. We've found another way that works incredibly well, and that is the way of love.

Of course, love can take many forms. Even if a teacher's speech is fiery in its expression, if it is offered in love, then it can be received as love if the person has the willingness to do so. If a direct message needs to be delivered that has some bite to it, the love can be so evident that the bite won't even be noticed. The message will be undeniably loving, even though it might look like a fireball! Love such as this is always wildly compassionate, and it always maintains a wholesome connection with everything and everyone, everywhere.

Love overcomes all. I knew this even before I had this incredible shift twenty-seven years ago. As a mother raising three children, it was impossible for me to ever demean or spank them. I knew that I only wanted to love them unconditionally. Of course, as their mother I could see where they needed to change their relationships to their data, but there was a way to do that without engaging in hurtful behavior. I have found conclusively in my own experience that love always brings about the most fruitful results. Love needs no other means—love alone is the most sublime and skillful of means. One could say that love is the ultimate skillful means for creating peace and well-being in our lives, in our communities and in the entire world.

In teachings and communities based on love and made up of people who are devoted to realizing their true nature, genuine warmth and caring are always in evidence. When new people come to such a community, they are welcomed with kindness and warmheartedness. There is no false hierarchy or attempts to exclude or isolate anyone. In a community of such people, the qualities come also in the form of the tremendous love manifested by the teacher and the members of the community. These qualities are the product of a great resolve to embody love and to live in love and to never stray from that ideal. That love is the teacher's primary skillful means.

As people have grown up, they have gained a certain self-identity by being exposed to the data of their family and community. We all have ingrained ways of living that are usually modeled on what we have seen in other people. We've taken ourselves to be our data, and we've taken others to be their data, and this creates duality, judgment and suffering. However, when we meet people who are relying on open intelligence without being distracted by data, we suddenly realize within ourselves, "Wow! They're not focusing on their data, and I don't have to either!" This is one example of what it means to be introduced to open intelligence, and this can come through direct contact with a teacher or through contact with a community where powerful open intelligence is in full evidence.

Through relying on open intelligence we come to see that the conventional identity we've taken ourselves to be is not our true identity. We grow more familiar with the wisdom identity that is naturally present and complete in itself. When the teacher's skillful means and wisdom are fully present, this wisdom identity can easily and expertly be revealed to others.

When we begin to discover this whole new way of being, we might feel a bit disoriented at times and may not always know how to act at first. But through relying on open intelligence for short moments, repeated many times, wisdom gradually begins to manifest, together with the skillful means to be totally relaxed and competent in all situations. We'll have a totally relaxed mind and body in all situations, whether or not thoughts are present.

In living a life based on the ongoing recognition of everyday open intelligence, there is a supreme boldness in every moment. There aren't any scripts for the way one's responses to life will unfold. Whatever one says is said without forethought and with no need to worry. We no longer waste our mental and emotional energy on thoughts such as, "Oh, what are they going to think about me?" or "How is this going to make me look?" because there's no referencing back to a personal identity. There's just an effortlessly relaxed natural presence and the supreme boldness of speaking authentically.

One is able to spontaneously respond to everything in an effortless way, because there's no longer any fear based on anxious anticipation. Many people find that their fears just drop away. It's seen so clearly that fear is nothing but a passing datum within open intelligence and as such has no independent nature and no meaning of its own. It's actually just a form of pure intelligence itself—an ephemeral, vivid appearance within the timeless wisdom that is our true nature. Whatever comes up is seen to be perfect *as it is*, and the proper response arises naturally, no matter how challenging the situation may be.

For a person who is completely relying on open intelligence, no merit or virtue need be accumulated, for neither of these applies to what is already super-complete. An authentic or pure teaching never veers from this conclusion and never adds anything that requires improvement of a flawed self. It asserts that there is only one self, and it is limitless, indivisible, timelessly free and inherently perfect. It doesn't say that we must develop merit or virtue or perform different activities in order to be pure enough to understand and realize our true nature; it says our true nature is already realized! Furthermore, the authentic, direct teachings say that there is only one method, and that is to rely on open intelligence in a completely uncontrived way until it becomes continuous. This may be stated in more than one way, but the essence of the teaching is always the same. The ideal disposition of a person who wants to rely on open intelligence is to simply be open enough to listen to the teachings and to practice reliance on open intelligence on an ongoing basis. That's all; it's really no big deal.

In many paths, preliminary practices are recommended to cultivate merit and virtue and to bring about a purification of body, mind and speech. At the same time, it is essential for us to know what their exact purpose is, for without the correct understanding such practices can be a detour. The true purpose of any practice is to reveal flawless, stainless wisdom. Once that occurs, wisdom body, wisdom speech, wisdom mind and wisdom qualities and activities will all be naturally present. There's nothing to be purified, so the true purpose of preliminary practices is to show that everything about our body, speech, mind, qualities and activities is already and forever flawlessly pure. When the teacher's skillful means and wisdom are such that this can be clearly and directly communicated, then the inherent purity of everything becomes obvious very quickly to people who are interested and open.

Some people might think that they have to go to India or Tibet or some special holy place in order to find the proper circumstance to be at peace, but wherever we go, there we are! We carry our data with us, and they will create our experience no matter where we may be. What's needed is complete perceptual openness in all experience, and that can be found anywhere. To say that one experience or place is better than another is to cut ourselves off from true skillful means and wisdom. To say that some things are better and some worse is just a conventional idea, and conventional ways of approaching life need to be looked at with a discerning eye, because they're unlikely to lead to real freedom or peace.

The absolute simplicity of everything *as it is*, is completely uncontained by any philosophical constructs or frameworks. When we hear about how great and exalted we are as human beings, a door is opened, and when we walk through that door, there's no turning back. There is nowhere to go back to and no one to go back. We say, "Wow, what I've found within myself is so amazing!" and we naturally want to share the ease and wellbeing we've found with everyone. It's this complete ease of being inherent in relying on open intelligence that brings an incredible shine to the skin and a smile to the face. We cheer up!

If we expose ourselves to unerring instructions that are precise and specific—with even the slightest bit of an open mind, coupled with the commitment to returning to open intelligence—we'll come to recognize the fully evident nature of our own self. It's very important to have unerring instruction that quickly brings about the decisive experience of the true nature of our own being. Unerring instruction leads to the swift accomplishment of timeless open intelligence and the dawning of the powers of potent benefit. The instruction I'm speaking about here is not the conventional worldly knowledge. I'm speaking about the open intelligence that appears in the mind stream of certain individuals at a certain time and provides a teaching that is absolutely perfect for those living in that era. This teaching rapidly leads to the dawning of open intelligence and is always spoken in a language that people of that era can easily understand.

With this teaching there's no effort to be made and no tricks or gimmicks to be employed. All one need do is rely on open intelligence for short moments, repeated many times, until it becomes obvious at all times. That's it. There's no need to do anything else or rely on anything else. In relying on open intelligence we finally find what we had sought through all the practices we've ever done. No matter what we may have been seeking from various practices or activities in the world, we'll find the true happiness and well-being we're looking for in relying on open intelligence.

Q: I know that in many traditions the guru's grace is one of the most important blessings offered to a disciple. Is the guru's grace something that you think is important to seek out or wish for?

A: When we completely rely on open intelligence, we abide *as* grace. What is most important is to get a firsthand experience of the grace of complete ease of being. One meaning of "guru" is dispeller of darkness. The way to make best use of the guru or teacher is to empower the clear light of open intelligence in which both you and the teacher appear. Open intelligence is the guru's true form.

If we want to be totally devoted to the guru or teacher and not spend a moment away from him or her, we can do that, but it's not necessary and not everyone will want to do that. There are many beliefs and practices that may have been very successful in the past but which just aren't working in the same way anymore. It's up to us to discover new ways of culling the essence from those traditional practices and then to apply that essence in ways that work in the modern world. When we hear a term like "guru's grace," it means different things to different people depending on their data. There are many people today who when they hear the word "guru" or anything about having a guru or relying on the guru's grace are going to immediately run in the opposite direction!

However, if we talk about getting ongoing support from a Balanced View trainer and the training, this is something people can more readily understand. To rely on the support of a trainer is actually the same as taking refuge in the guru's grace, but "relying on the support of a trainer" is an expression that may be more inviting to people. Whatever is being offered, it's important that it be available to everyone. The true guru's grace is universal and touches everyone impartially, and to allow that grace to reach people all over the world is more important than anything else. There is wisdom and skillful means in using language that a majority of people can easily relate to.

Q: I know that I should have compassion for people who do things that harm themselves and others, but at the same time, I think I should at least point out to them how their behavior is affecting other people. What's the best approach to doing this?

A: When we come to see that all of our own appearances are nothing but open intelligence, then we naturally find compassion for ourselves and for everyone. Compassion never needs to be cultivated or developed; it's inherent in open intelligence and can only be found in open intelligence. If it's cultivated, then it may just be a contrivance. When we discover true compassion in ourselves, we find that it arises in us naturally, so we don't have to get it from anywhere. With that discovery we're able to see clearly what other people are thinking and feeling. We can see where they are holding on to data, and we know how painful that is. In the situation you described, one approach might be to directly point out the person's faults, but uninvited advice is often not very helpful. You could walk up and say, "Hey, I see what's going on with you, and I'm going to tell you about it!" However, in Balanced View we haven't found that to be a particularly effective method.

If people ask me for help and invite me to look into their data with them, then I'll do that, but otherwise I don't intrude in that way. There are much easier and more useful ways to help someone than pointing something out without having first been asked to do so. When we get familiar with the open intelligence at the basis of everything, there are many skillful means of opening up a place of receptivity in people. For instance, we can patiently and lovingly be with the person, accepting them as they are. This often helps loosen up things in them, and a place of empowerment appears where before there had only been clinging to data. When that occurs, they'll naturally be more prepared to look objectively and openly at themselves and their behavior.

If I see something in someone that I think they might need help with, rather than speaking to the person individually I might just speak about the situation they are facing in a talk to a group in which they are included—knowing that the person in question will hear what I have said. Afterwards, I can see whether the person has heard it properly and taken it in. This way, all the people listening can benefit from the instruction, because we all share so many of the same data. In this particular method we are all indivisible, but no one is invisible!

There are plenty of people who are ready to rely on open intelligence and who want support in doing so, and those people will probably be open to hearing what you have to say. However, if you speak to those who are ambivalent or not interested, then you'll probably find only resistance, and it's quite likely that neither you nor they will benefit from the conversation. Using discrimination in who you speak to just makes things so much easier. Rest is best. Just relax!

A NEW WAY OF BEING
CHAPTER EIGHT

"When we get familiar with that which is aware of all these concepts—yet remains untouched by any concepts—then we place ourselves directly in the position of being, which isn't a position at all. Being does not have an address or location."

In any era in which human beings have lived, there have been people who have yearned to understand life in a profound way. However, as long as anyone is trying to understand life within the context of thought alone, they will never be able to grasp the unknowable essence that is beyond thought. If people are only experiencing life through the different modalities of thought, the unknowable will always remain beyond their grasp.

To believe that our intelligence is comprised only of our thoughts and emotions is really very primitive, and this assumption limits the understanding we can have about our intelligence. If we believe that intelligence is a byproduct of a biological creation called a human being, then we will be limited by that belief system. The assumption is, "I am intelligent because I have a human body; I'll have this intelligence as long as I am alive, and at death that intelligence will no longer exist."

When we are locked within these mental structures, we will always be referring whatever happens back to our individual selves. Everything is seen as occurring to a "me" as the subject within a subject-object relationship. Even if we're dealing with other so-called subjects, we will actually be seeing them as objects. The other people in the world are objectified and appraised as to how they will be beneficial to us or not beneficial to us, and we'll look at everything as somehow having the power to affect our thoughts and emotions.

Why should we be limited to a scenario that contends that we are separate, individual subjects? Why should we assume that the subject-object relationship absolutely exists and that reality is made up of matter and can be described by perceptions? Looking at everything as solid and existing in its own right is one way of looking at things, but it's not likely to reveal our true nature. It would be like looking only at one tiny piece of a gigantic puzzle and trying to assess the whole puzzle from that one piece.

If we want to know the essence of life and intelligence, then we have to get familiar with their flawless knower. When we get familiar with that which is aware of all these concepts—yet remains untouched by any concepts—then we place ourselves directly in the position of *being*, which isn't a position at all. Being does not have an address or location. Open intelligence may be experienced within the human body, but the human body is not the source location for open intelligence. Open intelligence is universal—in fact, it's beyond the universe. It's the basic space in which the entire universe appears.

When we talk about anything at all—life, intelligence, experiencing, being—we must know what is actually *aware* of all those things. Open intelligence is the flawless knower that is aware of everything; it's inseparable from the ground intelligence of everything. This ground of being is aware of all data, all belief systems and assumptions and sees all data as itself. This ground of being is what is seeing, knowing, explaining, describing, experiencing and being.

We may have accepted a belief system that understands us as a subject that is perceiving objects, but when we just relax and examine *what's looking*, then we see that there is only open intelligence encompassing all of this data. That open intelligence is the basis of what we take ourselves to be. When we become familiar with the ground of being, then we see everything *as it is*. We see the wide range of reality *as it is*, without any investment in trying to pin down reality as being any one thing. We see every appearance as temporary and fleeting, and less and less is there a fixed stability to everything. When we become familiar with open intelligence as the ground of everything, then our range of experience is radically altered.

If we acknowledge our thoughts and emotions over and over again as being significant in their own right, then we'll be ignoring the basis of the thought itself, which is open intelligence—the ground of being. It's always present, but we don't notice that it's there. However, if we simply rely on the equilibrium of what's looking, then we can allow all the unpredictable thoughts and emotions to be whatever they are, without getting overwhelmed by their apparent significance.

We drain ourselves of our life energy when we persist in holding to the importance of something that doesn't have an independent nature. Whether we label impressions of the mind as "anger," "joy," "good" or "bad," they all appear in the same basic space of open intelligence and are made only of that space.

We want to go right to the source of what's looking, rather than looking for something outside ourselves. As long as we're constantly seeking wisdom—rather than relying on what's looking—for that long we won't find it, because it's what's looking that is wise.

Many of us have spent much of our lives seeking in one way or another. We may have been seeking answers, seeking relief from suffering or seeking some sort of mental freedom. We may not have even described it as "seeking," but we felt somehow that there was something more to be had or known. No matter how we have expressed this seeking, it all comes down to that urge to freedom. In fact, every single moment of our life is an expression of the urge to freedom. We have a great urgency within everything that we think, feel and do, and that urgency is none other than the urge to absolute freedom. That is always what we're looking for, but unless we know how to truly relax our mind, we'll never have more than a few fleeting moments of freedom in our lives.

Even the most violent and heinous actions are in fact expressions of this same urge to freedom. People are all looking for ways to relieve their anxiety in all that they do and think. We've learned through long practice to take our thoughts, emotional states and experiences to be real and substantial. As a result we try to find the thoughts, emotions and experiences that will give us relief—however confused the attempt may be. For most people though, the attempt to relieve anxiety never really works. At best the attempts only neutralize data but don't give any sustained feeling of freedom or relief. This is why so many people end up feeling frustrated and confused.

Even the spiritual search is for the most part entangled with attempts to change one datum into another, and the result is that the seeker can't really recognize any freedom in the seeking. However, in relying on open intelligence, all conventional frameworks are gone beyond. The Balanced View Training reveals that nothing about our data need be changed; there is just the basic space of open intelligence, the natural order of everything that sees through all conventional frameworks.

We've tried to get out of our negative thoughts and into positive thoughts. We've tried to get out of our negative emotions and into positive emotions. We've tried to get out of our negative experiences and into positive experiences. We've tried to get out of our negative relationships and into positive relationships. The intent of what we call spiritual seeking is usually to try to get into some kind of a state and get out of an opposing state, and as long as we're trying to get into a certain state and get out of another state, whether we call it spiritual seeking or anything else, we're simply shuffling back and forth.

The key distinction between this shuffling back and forth and what is presented in the Balanced View Training is that by the power of relying on open intelligence, what we're looking for is immediately revealed. In other words, relax everything you take yourself to be, relax all ideas of who you think you are and *(snaps her fingers)* it's just right here.

The ground of pure open intelligence that has never been opposed by anything is known only in that complete relaxation. You can call it awareness, clarity, the universal ground, conscious intelligence, pure intelligence or open intelligence; it's the unopposed ground of everything that is. When we relax as that, then we see that it knows itself. We find that the ground of being is self-knowing. All phenomena are in fact the self-knowing of the unopposed ground.

In a very practical way we can bring that understanding into our own experience by relying on open intelligence for short moments, many times, until it becomes continuous. And what does that mean? It means that whatever our thoughts are, whether they're describing emotions, sensations, experiences, people, places, things or whatever they are, we repeatedly relax for short moments until that relaxed ground of being becomes obvious at all times. It's as simple as that.

We have the Four Mainstays for support: 1. relying on open intelligence; 2. the trainer; 3. the training media; 4. the community. These together are the most powerful instruction about living that can ever be practiced.

When a thought appears, just relax, without any effort whatsoever to correct what appears. In this way, you will soon come to know that everything that appears exists only within open intelligence. I don't mean open intelligence as merely a human phenomenon, but open intelligence as the center and matrix of the universe.

Open intelligence is pristine, spacious and clear like the cloudless sky, and therefore the nature of all thoughts, emotions and experiences is also sky-like and infinite, for they appear within open intelligence and are made only of open intelligence. When we rely on open intelligence we're able to see that.

Everything within the vast expanse of the ground of being is completely at ease. All appearances come from ease and return to ease, and the coming and going are completely at ease too. When we relax we enjoy that natural ease of open intelligence that is identical with who we are. It doesn't matter what color our skin is, what gender we are or whether we are smart or not—this ease is completely available and accessible to everyone equally. Whoever one may be as a human being, it is possible to enjoy the complete ease of being in all circumstances.

To perceive all experiences as open intelligence is to realize the meaning of rich and vital openness. The open intelligence I am describing does not move anywhere or alter in any way. Take a moment now and relax as the true nature of your own mind, the open intelligence that is changeless and unmoving. It has no color, shape or substance that can be found anywhere.

When you arrive at the open intelligence that has no color or shape, look for a center or circumference. Does that intelligence have a center or circumference, or is it limitless and wide-open like space? Now look around a little. Is what's looking moving anywhere? The things you're seeing may be changing, but is there anything changing in what's looking? Is there an inside and an outside that is divided by the skin line? Are there many objects outside yourself, or are all of these things actually appearances *within* open intelligence?

Finding no distinction between inside and outside, you arrive at open intelligence, which is vast as the sky. You also arrive at what open intelligence entails, which is the ability to engage in life in a way that is thoroughly enjoyable and completely beneficial for yourself and others.

If you've ever wondered what open intelligence is, it is just this. You recognize open intelligence when you allow all that appears to be *as it is*. You find that open intelligence has no outside or inside, no dimension and no characteristics that can be substantiated.

To facilitate this understanding, first ask: where do appearances come from, where are they now and where do they go? The appearing, the staying, the going—that is all open intelligence, too. There is never any transition or change. During your examination you will see that just as mist arises out of the air and dissolves back into air, appearances are the magical display of open intelligence, arising in open intelligence and vanishing back into it. They are illuminations of open intelligence—that and nothing more. Appearances and open intelligence are completely synonymous.

Last night I had an interesting conversation. I was talking with an Indian swami who has lived in Rishikesh for a long time, and he was lamenting the changes in the area. He said, "When I came here to Rishikesh so long ago, it was just a small place with a tremendous spiritual atmosphere, and everyone here was either a sage or a seeker. Now everything has changed, and all these people who come here don't care about seeking at all; they just want to have a good time. Wouldn't you agree that the River Ganges and this holy place are very special, and isn't it terrible what is happening here these days?"

I replied, "You know, every place is special, and no matter what appears anywhere, the law of impermanence always applies. What has appeared will eventually vanish, and what hasn't yet appeared will come to appear. All of these things that were going on here at one time are disappearing and other things are appearing. When things are changing as dramatically as they are today, it is just another expression of the immutable law of change and impermanence."

The conversation made me think about the new holy river where spiritual seekers are gathering today. Do you know what that river is? The Internet! The holy river of the Internet is an incredible manifestation that can connect human beings everywhere, and it's flowing throughout the world.

Technology has gone a long way towards bringing about a foundation for global unity. Today we can go to remote parts of Tibet and find monks with cell phones! A marvelous web of communication has come about, and it's all part of the holy river where the whole human race can gather.

For a very long time direct teachings—like those of Balanced View—have been very difficult to receive. They were taught by only a few people, and many of the teachers were inaccessible. Seekers had to go and find a teacher to instruct them, and often they had to prove themselves in some way in order to get the teachings.

But things have changed in the modern world. The tradition of sages and seekers coming together is very significant, but we don't need to hold on to any traditional idea about how things must be or look. Wisdom has never gotten stuck anywhere. It doesn't get stuck in historical circumstances, historical figures or traditions. We don't need to be fixed in any of our belief systems, no matter how elevated we believe them to be, or how many people might believe in them. All we need do is relax in the open intelligence that's always present. It's beyond all conventional descriptions of this or that, and it's always right here.

Q: This reference you made to the Internet really intrigues me. I know the Internet is a lot of things, but I'd never thought of it as a "holy river"! Could you maybe go into that a bit more?

A: Well, first of all, the Internet and computers are a great metaphor for the appearance and disappearance of data within the basic space of open intelligence. For example, digital information moves around in the form of ones and zeros, and those ones and zeros form an image on a computer monitor that seems to be real. I'm sure that many of us have gone to a web site and gotten completely engrossed in it for hours at a time, but the thing that we're so enthralled with is nothing but a collection of ones and zeros appearing and disappearing on the computer screen!

Another example of this effect is a pointillist painting. Pointillism is a style of painting where the artist paints a scene, not by using brushstrokes, but by applying thousands and thousands of tiny points of color with the tip of the brush. When the painting is looked at from afar, one sees a fantastic picture of a landscape or a human face, but if one comes very close one sees that the painting is just a bunch of dots which, as a whole, create an image.

Whether it is pointillism or the bits and bytes of computerized representations, we're looking at a bunch of dots, which can be compared to data within open intelligence. If we insist that there is an inherent reality to the image we are seeing, our understanding will be very limited. If, however, we're able to recognize that the image on the computer screen, the pointillist painting or the perceptions of our senses are made up of data and nothing more, then we've increased our capacity to recognize the open intelligence which underlies all data. We've increased our capacity to know what is really at the basis of perceptions.

Another thing to consider in following this metaphor is how the Internet is completely open and how it came about through radically unconventional ways of thinking. The rapid growth of the Internet into a huge global phenomenon didn't come about as a result of the efforts of a government or a large organization; it was a grassroots effort that came from many, many people who were able to make a leap into thinking in a new way. The Web was developed by grassroots users who wanted to ensure that information be free. Open source applications such as the Linux operating system and the Web encyclopedia Wikipedia emerged that could be altered by their users. This represented a tremendous challenge to the long-held assumption that an application had to be strictly controlled within an authority structure.

Early pioneers of the Internet predicted that hundreds of millions of people would have a personal computer and that the Internet would spread all over the world. Most people scoffed and said that this would never happen. The conventional thinking was that most people wouldn't buy computers and wouldn't pay for Internet access. Well, now we see what's happened! Fifteen years after those predictions, far more than the predicted number of people own computers or computing devices, and access to the Internet is available all over the world.

Similarly, we are now at a time when more and more people will be getting familiar with open intelligence. Like the Web, Linux and Wikipedia, Balanced View is a grassroots movement. This movement makes the skillful means of open intelligence available to everyone. We must do this for ourselves as individuals and for our species as well, because if we don't, we may be on our way out as a species. We need to develop a balanced view in order to survive.

As I see it, one scenario would be that only a fraction of humanity—say a billion or so—will get familiar with open intelligence. The best-case scenario would be that everyone would be able to do so, because the direct instructions on how to become familiar with open intelligence are now so directly accessible. One might think that this is an outrageous prediction, but didn't it sound outrageous fifteen years ago when those few people were predicting that the Internet would eventually be available to hundreds of millions of people?

We are now a global human culture with the capacity to freely share information all around the world. As a result we're developing a more standardized way of communicating. We have language systems that are getting more and more blended and cultural expressions that are becoming more and more common to all. We're also beginning to see standardization to some degree in the language and concepts we have for discovering the nature of existence. This is comparable to millions of people using the same website, such as Google, for example. Everyone who uses Google has a basic understanding about it that is held in common with other people who use it.

Due to some extent to the standardization of global culture, teachings that were once limited to a specific culture or tradition are now being made accessible to much of humanity. Direct instructions for how to become familiar with open intelligence are now available to anyone with access to an Internet connection. The Balanced View Training is designed to be user-friendly for the modern person. They relate to the experience of a broad range of people and are not culturally based or beholden to a specific tradition. The training can now easily spread around the world, not only due to the Internet, but also because it is communicated in a modern language and directly meets the needs of the people of this age.

AFFLICTIVE STATES
CHAPTER NINE

"In maintaining open intelligence we discover the lack of separation between happiness and suffering. What that means in a practical way is that, whether there's happiness or whether there's suffering, we can be totally at ease and serene."

The term "afflictive states" refers to thoughts, emotions and sensations that are experienced as disturbing. Many of us have felt overwhelmed at times by deeply distressing states. We can't stand the pain and suffering, and we keep looking for a way out of the torment of these afflictive states, but it may be that a way out has never been described to us in a simple way.

When we rely on open intelligence, we find our way out. We discover our essence, which is unaffected by any kind of emotional state. When we look with discrimination, we can see that whatever happens in our life—even if in the moment it seems like a terrible tragedy—really cannot alter or change open intelligence at all. Open intelligence is absolutely constant; it never changes. In this discovery we find true freedom and tremendous compassion for ourselves and others. We find the effortless wisdom to know how to take care of ourselves and the planet we live on. We discover our basic human goodness. This is what the Balanced View Training offers.

Mastery of afflictive states doesn't come from cultivating positive states or transforming negative states into positive states. True mastery comes from relaxing the mind in the open intelligence that is its essence and then seeing whatever appears as a form of that intelligence. Our mind is naturally wise and helpful and is inseparable from limitless, timeless, pure open intelligence. When we try to micro-manage the mind by attempting to modify or censor what occurs in it, we cut ourselves off from our inherently peaceful, happy and beneficial nature. All appearances, whether we describe them as afflictive, negative or positive, are only the dynamic energy of open intelligence and nothing more.

Since they're made of the same open intelligence, all appearances are equal, and since they're evanescent, mirage-like appearances that have no independent reality, there's nothing to be gained or lost from them. Rather than resisting or desiring these appearances or trying to change them in any way, we simply relax as they arise, and we recognize in each appearance the pure open intelligence which is the essence of our own being.

In maintaining open intelligence, all data are resolved—but not through making negative data into positive data. Nothing about ourselves needs to be changed! Now, when we first hear that we don't need to get rid of negative thoughts and emotions, many people think, "How can that be? If I just let my thoughts and emotions run wild, I'll turn into a barbarian!" But as we begin to develop confidence in open intelligence, far from turning into a barbarian, we discover the deep peacefulness that is our inherent nature—and as we continue to relax, we begin to manifest the profound wisdom that comes from being undistracted by anything that appears. All the thoughts and emotions will be whatever they are, but they will not disturb us any longer.

When I speak about extremely afflictive states, I'm not talking as a philosopher; I'm talking as someone who has experienced very difficult and disturbing emotional states. For years I tried to overcome my afflictive thoughts and emotions through all kinds of means: achievements, philosophy, psychology, intellectual understanding, prayer, socializing, sex, alcohol and marijuana, to name the main ones. However, when I got into a particularly disturbing situation twenty-seven years ago, none of those approaches worked anymore. I was in a state of incredible fear and I couldn't find comfort in any of the belief systems or remedies I'd previously relied on. I found no relief in anything I'd ever learned, in any self-help technique or in any person I knew.

In the midst of that crisis I somehow discovered that all the painful emotional states had as their underlying basis a vast, infinite pure space that is completely free from suffering. At the time I didn't know exactly how to describe that realization; I just knew that to rest in that space brought instantaneous relief from the pain. In fact, the more I rested there, the more I saw that it gave the same relief in all experiences, whether positive or negative. The relief wasn't separate from what appeared; it was the root of the appearance and included the appearance. The more I rested as that relief, the more a warm sense of well-being began to pervade everything. Gradually I discovered the ability to be in all situations without impediment and remain in complete ease no matter what was occurring. This was the seed that has now grown into the Balanced View Training.

Balanced View teaches that thoughts and emotions don't have an independent existence; they're nothing but ephemeral appearances within open intelligence and have no power of their own. Most of us have learned to use our mind in a very limited way to describe ourselves and what's going on in the world. But when we have only this limited relationship with the mind, we won't have the zest or energy for the marvelous contributions we're capable of making to the world and to ourselves. Even if we outwardly seem to be very accomplished people, we'll be withering on the vine compared to what we could be if we weren't trying to micro-manage all our thoughts and emotions. If we spend our lives battling with our thoughts and emotions as if they had an independent nature, we'll never see them for what they truly are.

In boxing, two fighters try to pummel each other into unconsciousness. Well, when we spend our lives immersed in the grueling practice of trying to get rid of afflictive states, it's like having a boxing match with our minds! Taking our thoughts and emotions to be enemies that we're afraid of, we feel that we need to beat them into submission, always afraid that if we don't they're going to wear us down with their jabs day after day and finally knock us out for good!

To analyze thoughts and emotions, reject them or try to fix them with different approaches serves only to strengthen their apparent reality. We've really been boxing only with shadows, but every attempt to change or improve our thoughts only gives the shadows more seeming substance.

We're always looking for something that's going to make us feel better. In wanting to improve ourselves, we might say, "Tomorrow I'm going to be a good person. I'm *not* going to get mad and blow my top!" Then the next day comes, and we just can't keep the thoughts and emotions in place, and the top blows off, right in the boss's face! We want to achieve freedom from negative thoughts and emotions by reshaping them into positive thoughts and emotions, but this really can't be done permanently. Thoughts and emotions are inherently spontaneous and unpredictable. Trying to control them is like trying to hold on to the reflection of the moon in a pond. There's nothing to hold on to—and there's no "you" to do the holding! Both the subject and the object are like a mirage.

Perhaps we'll buy a self-help book that tells us how to deal with depression and low self-esteem. We'll feel happy and hopeful for a while, but when we set the book aside, what happens? The old negative thoughts just come rushing back in. So, we pick up another self-help book that has other solutions, and the same thing happens again, because we're simply applying one datum to change another. It's a fruitless endeavor, and it never really works.

We should be aware that it's not only the negative thoughts and emotions that are disturbing—*all* thoughts and emotions are in a sense disturbing if we don't recognize that at their basis they're all vivid appearances of open intelligence. We try to keep the ones we like, but we can't. And we try to get rid of the ones we don't like, but we can't do that either, so both ways it's painful!

In maintaining open intelligence we discover the lack of separation between happiness and suffering. We see that, whether there's happiness or whether there's suffering, we can be totally at ease and serene. How? We rely on open intelligence that is the fundamental nature of both happiness and suffering, and there we discover real peace. We find the ease of being that is unaffected by any emotional state. This means we'll have many new options in life; we don't need to cling to old assumptions concerning happiness and suffering when they come up in us. We have a much more profound understanding that, however our own joys or sufferings might appear, their underlying basis is the same.

In the beginning, for most people it's easier to momentarily rely on open intelligence when positive and neutral data appear and more difficult to rely on open intelligence when negative data are present. As we practice relying on open intelligence with positive and neutral states, our ability to do so increases. Eventually we'll be able to rely more and more on open intelligence with the negative states as well. When negative states arise, it can be very difficult at first to enjoy the ease of our being, because everything in us is screaming, "No, no! This can't *possibly* be open intelligence!" It might even seem completely impossible to rely on open intelligence with states such as panic, anger, hatred, confusion and jealousy, but that doesn't mean it *is* impossible. We've just trained ourselves to believe that these emotions are a threat. But in relying on open intelligence we can understand the non-threatening nature of the afflictive emotions. By repeatedly relying on clarity for short moments, we support ourselves in maintaining open intelligence even when afflictive states appear.

A lot of times we've looked for ways to get rid of our afflictive states through antidotes. However, even if we find a way to drown the afflictive states for a while with a bottle of vodka, or by smoking a joint, or taking an ecstasy pill—when it wears off, what happens? The afflictive states simply come flooding back. Maybe the antidotes we use aren't as extreme as the ones I just mentioned. Instead of taking drugs or getting drunk, perhaps we watch television all day, look at pornography, play endless electronic games, sleep or eat too much. Or perhaps we call friends and gossip, work extra long hours or engage in other activities that distract us from our pain. Whatever the modes of escape may be, they're all antidotes and none of them can fully resolve our negative thoughts and emotions.

No matter how bound up you are in any of these afflictive states, I would urge you to avoid using antidotes and instead to just relax and rely on open intelligence. If you feel like you're really in the grip of something, reach out for support from the Four Mainstays, and then do your best to rely on open intelligence and get to know the essence of who you are. Empower the relaxed nature of your own being, see everything as an expression of that pure being, and whatever is appearing will naturally resolve itself.

One could continue to give meaning and significance to the stories we have, but why bother? One story generates another. All the stories about our perceived deficiencies start getting fired up. "I'm not good enough," or "I don't want to fall in love because then that person might abandon me," or "I can't get the job I really want because I'm not competent enough," or "I can't do what I really want because I don't have enough money." The more we limit ourselves with such stories, the more suffering they generate. We can also use our stories to try to grasp for more peace of mind, but this only increases the restlessness of our mind. Using stories to try to settle the mind is like trying to diminish the bubbles in a bubble bath by using a mixer to stir up the water!

Many people believe that they're subject to moods and that moods are created by thoughts, and therefore thoughts hold a terrible power over their lives. These different moods come into our minds like gloomy weather patterns, and as a result our own well-being suffers. Then we make sure others suffer as well! Right? We might wake up in the morning with the thought, "I'm such a rotten person that I'm definitely going to have a crummy day!" We then respond to that thought as if it had complete power over us, and lo and behold, we find it comes true! And then we inflict our crummy mood on whomever we see!

In a mood-based life, every day is like a roller coaster ride of ups and downs. We have happy thoughts at the top of the roller coaster, and then we have a sad thought and all of a sudden the roller coaster plummets! By staying on this roller coaster and believing every shift of mood reflects who we are, we become blind to our deepest inner reality, which is never affected by any mood, thought or emotion. Encased in fear and pain, we become numb to our own suffering and the suffering of others.

The truth is that thoughts and emotions never have the power to rule us. It's only the way we react to them that seems to vest them with power. The underlying basis of all thoughts and emotions is the clear light of open intelligence, the completely relaxed essence of mind that's always at ease. Open intelligence is synonymous with wisdom, love and energy. Through empowering the essence of our being, our life is infused with those qualities, and we find we always know what to do and how to act.

We all have a choice about how we use our minds: either to try to change the thoughts and emotions that appear within the mind, or to empower the pure being that is the mind's basic space—our own native super-intelligence. To understand this is very important, because the first way leads to confusion and suffering, while the second way leads to real freedom. Relying on open intelligence takes us outside the parameters of a mood-based life, into the discovery of unending open intelligence that is our true nature.

If we spend our whole life giving meaning to our thoughts and emotions, our lips will freeze into a frown and all the light will go out of our eyes. It won't be long before we'll be sitting in the dining hall at a senior care facility complaining about our arthritis and poor bowel movements and pointing out everybody's faults. "Oh, will you look at the blue hair on that one! And that lady over there is the one who cheated at bingo!" Nothing will change; but now we'll be 80 years old, our bodies will be falling apart and we'll continue to be lost in all these stories.

True well-being doesn't come from a process of selection where we say, "This is what is good about me, and this is what is bad." We are not divided into one part that's fundamentally flawed and sinful and another part called "open intelligence" that's wonderful and pure. Many of us have been raised to believe that we are sinners and that we're inherently flawed in some way, but at some point we have to realize that those ideas are completely untrue and have no power. Otherwise, we'll be in prison for life, whether we're living as a monk, a housewife, a corporate executive or a prisoner at San Quentin. The real prison bars are in the mind! Freedom from imprisonment is found when we recognize that the afflictive states are *already* free, because their sole essence is open intelligence.

Because we take ourselves to be a personal identity that is destroyed at death, anything that seems threatening to that personal identity makes us feel very vulnerable. We may be afraid of earthquakes, tornadoes, political turmoil, violence and terrorism, because these things threaten our bodily existence. The only way to resolve the grip of fear is to come to know that we are not ultimately dependent on anything for our existence, not even the survival of the body. The fears many of us have—getting seriously ill, growing old, dying, not having enough money, being subjected to the negative opinions of others—all drop away if we maintain open intelligence, because open intelligence can never be hurt in the least by any outcome. When we see that nothing can affect our well-being, not even death, then we truly have a choice in life. We're no longer collapsed into an idea of a "poor me" who's a victim of suffering; we're free to live as the limitless, timeless beings we truly are.

Whether you've done all sorts of horrible things in your life or you are a paragon of saintly virtue, this moment is equal for everyone. A room can be dark for a very long time, but the moment the light switch is flipped on, the darkness disappears instantaneously. So, relax, smile and enjoy yourself! That's how you're meant to be in all situations. When these stormy afflictive states come up, relax completely; there's nothing you need to do about them. They disperse in and of themselves, like the flight path of a bird in the sky and have never for a moment been separate from pure open intelligence. If you rely on open intelligence for short moments, repeated many times, you will see that this is the case.

Q: This is the first time I've heard the term "afflictive states," and I'm not sure to what exactly you are referring when you use the term. Could you maybe give some specific examples of emotions or states that you consider afflictive?

A: Sure, I'd be happy to make this as clear as possible. The term "afflictive states" refers to thoughts, emotions and sensations that are experienced as disturbing. The first category of afflictive states includes all the thoughts and emotional states related to desire. We really need to understand the importance of desire in the human experience. There's nothing wrong with desire in itself, because the ultimate desire is to get to know ourselves as open intelligence. Desire, or yearning, generally means the longing for things such as good health, staying young, food, money, sex, work, relationships, leisure or whatever it might be.

Desire comes coupled with the belief that by getting what we desire we will have well-being. Holding to this belief leads to an endless no-win cycle of continuing to desire—yet never fully attaining well-being. Even though over and over again our experience is that the desire does not bring us what we're seeking, we continue to desire anyway. We could say that the blind repetition of desiring is a form of insanity, because we're doing the same thing over and over again—and yet expecting different results.

The second primary afflictive state is aggression, which could also be called anger or hate. Anger or hate towards people, places or things is a form of aggression that we see played out in families, communities, nations, and in the world. Many times though aggression is not only directed towards outward objects but also inwardly towards ourselves. We're engaging in anger and hatred by hating our own thoughts, emotions and sensations and feeling that we need to change them. As a result we may be angry at ourselves, and this only leads to anger towards others.

The third primary afflictive state includes conceit, smugness, pride and arrogance, which are traits that lead people to have exaggerated estimations of themselves and their opinions. When we are overcome by pride and arrogance, we think that we know what is right, and if others disagree with us we're convinced that the other person must be wrong. We express and defend these very strong opinions in such a way that we do not honor or acknowledge the opinions of others.

Close-mindedness, which is traditionally called ignorance, is the fourth primary afflictive state. When we are close-minded, we cut ourselves off from the recognition of open intelligence. We say, "There might be open intelligence, but I don't want to go there. I want to continue to indulge or avoid all my thoughts, emotions and sensations." Unless we can rely on open intelligence in the face of conceit, pride or arrogance, we'll never be able to accept the contributions and suggestions of the trainer, the training and the community in which we involve ourselves. To accept the contributions of the trainer means that we accept that there is another person just like us who is already relying on open intelligence, and because they have tapped into open intelligence they can skillfully share with us how to rely on open intelligence just as they do.

The last afflictive state is envy and jealousy. Envy could be defined as spite and resentment at seeing the successes of another, and jealousy as mental uneasiness from suspicion or fear of rivalry. It is really a hell realm to continually be circling around in our own thoughts, emotions and experiences, taking them to be real and trying to do something about them. When we're constantly trying to indulge, avoid or replace thoughts and emotions with something better, we can never get out of this realm. Wow, these disturbing states are looking kind of bleak, aren't they!

The very, very important point to make about afflictive states is for us *to not reject what is appearing*. To not reject afflictive states means that when they come up, we rely on open intelligence rather than acting on them or wanting them to go away.

Relying on open intelligence is not an avoidance or a rejection of something, and it is not suppression or repression. Afflictive states and the power of wisdom are one and the same. Even though that might seem inconceivable at present, by the power of relying on open intelligence we prove it to ourselves. We come to see in our own experience that with all these exceedingly troublesome states like fear, anger, aggression, envy, jealousy, conceit, pride or desire, there is really nothing there—just as there's really nothing substantial in a mirage. However, we'll never see that as long as we indulge, avoid or reject what is appearing.

When we rest as these afflictive states and do not reject them, they dissolve into themselves, and when they dissolve into themselves they become something wonderful instead of something terrible. Like a lotus blooming out of the mud, that doesn't have a speck of mud on it, so too, out of these totally afflictive states appears this totally magnificent power of wisdom, totally untainted in any way by the seemingly negative appearances.

When afflictive states are left unrejected they become spacious and expansive, because the nature of intelligence is completely open and unobstructed. When they come up and we rely on open intelligence, then we allow the openness that is inherent in disturbing emotions to become evident. Aren't openness, good cheer and warmheartedness towards others a greater benefit to us than feeling tormented by disturbing states?

By relying on open intelligence, rather than engaging in afflictive states, we begin to feel more and more compassion, until we feel compassion all the time. Rather than acting on afflictive states, when they come up we empower ourselves with open intelligence, and loving-kindness appears from within them. Our mind becomes totally clear, and everything we see becomes luminous and radiant. When disturbing states are left unrejected, they dissolve back into themselves, and appearing from within these states is a balanced view that produces insight about how to skillfully handle all situations.

When we rely on open intelligence for short moments, repeated many times, all of these states dissolve into themselves, and what appears from within them is bliss, compassion, loving-kindness, lucidity and a balanced view. This is amazing! This is the true meaning of nonduality. Bliss, compassion, loving-kindness, clarity and a balanced view are the fundamental condition of afflictive states.

A Beautiful Death
CHAPTER TEN

"When we gain familiarity with open intelligence, then we have nothing to fear; even a terminal illness won't be daunting for us. We are able to be without impediment, whatever the situation is."

What appearance could be more demanding of us than death? Death is inevitable, and no one is left unaffected. A fundamental human dilemma is that throughout all of our life we know we will eventually die. In acknowledging this universal condition, we develop great sensitivity and compassion for ourselves and for everyone else, because we know that everyone dies, and not just us.

Yet, we should know in a profound way that birth, life and death are all timelessly free appearances of a more fundamental condition. When we become familiar with the reality that all the appearances, including death, are wide-open and have never been made into anything with an independent nature, then when death comes we are ready, and we won't be so troubled by it. Death can then be an easygoing and carefree moment that is complete and identical to any other.

When we maintain open intelligence in the direct experience of any circumstance during our lifetime, it is a preparation for the final experience of death. By the power of sustaining open intelligence, without attempting to correct appearances, all the experiences we encounter in life are a practice for that ultimate experience. Unless we know that dying is just part of the living process, we can be really startled and confused when death appears.

If we're angry and upset that we're dying and we elaborate on that anger, then we'll attempt to cling to life. If we try to avoid death and all the feelings that go along with dying, then we'll be absolutely miserable. If we aren't familiar with open intelligence, then as we are dying we might become frightened and grab on to the data of clinging to life. We would then be desperately holding on to life rather than seeing that we're on the verge of encountering the last experience we will ever have—death. If, however, we become familiar with instantaneous open intelligence during our lives, then when it is present so beautifully and obviously at death, that obvious and empowering open intelligence will be recognized for what it is.

Some years ago my beloved younger sister died of cancer. Her doctors had told her that she had only two months to live, and she informed the whole family about the prognosis. When any family receives news like this, each person has their own response. The news can in some ways force them to look more deeply at who they are, or at least who they take themselves to be, and who they take their dying family member to be. This occurred for the people in my family and for my sister as well.

Fortunately, my sister's practice of relying on open intelligence was something that she could rely on to support her in preparing for her death. She really came to terms with the fact that this was the end of her life and that she was dying. As it became clear that the end was near, she called us to come and be with her. When she died the family was beside the bed gathered around her. I was in the bed with her holding her hand, and when she took her final breath I could feel her last pulse. She'd been quietly suffering, but along with the suffering there was a sense of great relief and profound peace of mind in her.

With her last breath her face went from being calm with no smile to having the most incredible smile I've ever seen in my life. She was smiling as though she had seen the most beautiful vision one could imagine. Several hours after her death, that smile was still there. She was in a state of utter lucidity and peace—that natural state of utter lucidity that is totally beyond the body.

When we die, if we've previously recognized the reality of what we are, we just slip effortlessly into that natural state of utter lucidity. This lucidity was so clear in her because she was able to accept her death so gracefully due to her practice of gaining confidence in open intelligence. She was so well prepared that her death brought complete relief and the resolution of all data, including those she had had about death.

The simplicity and beauty of her death had an immense power and affected the entire family in a wonderful way. The way she died was actually a form of loving communication, and it had a significant and lasting effect on every one of us. The result was that all the data we had about the others in the family—our judgments and opinions of each other and whom we had taken each other to be based on our past histories—were dissolved.

Sometimes we take people to be their past, and we keep trying to define them with that yardstick. To make ourselves feel more comfortable we need for them to be something we can label, but this prevents us from seeing them as they really are. When my sister died, we were so profoundly touched by witnessing her death, and all of those judgments were erased in each one of us. The subtle and overt tensions, negative patterns and arguments and analysis were dissolved, and our relationships were brought to a new level.

When we talk about the importance of death, it's really essential for us to realize that death is something that we can and should become acquainted with before we die. My sister had gotten to know herself very deeply through her practice of relying on open intelligence. In the Balanced View Training we become familiar with ourselves through a very similar practice, which is the gradual familiarization with ourselves as open intelligence. Increasingly we become familiar with our true identity—the fundamentally perfect condition that is the nature of everything. That open intelligence is the basis and essence of all our data, including our data about death.

When we die, there is the instantaneous open intelligence that is forever present as well as a complete loss of the memory of life and the absence of any longing to return.

When we gain familiarity with open intelligence, then we have nothing to fear; even a terminal illness won't be daunting for us. We're able to be without impediment, whatever the situation is. This increasing familiarity with open intelligence will carry us through all the doctor's appointments, all the worries about the changes in our lives because of sickness and aging and all the concerns about dying.

The attitude we have towards death either gives us freedom in our life or lack of freedom. If we have the idea that death is the end of us, then we'll consider death to be an enemy, and it will be something that we're scared to death of! We won't want it to happen, because we think it means the end; but thinking that death is the end is just an assumption about the way things are.

At death it is only data that change. There is no other change. If we want to know what it's like to die, then we need only to go to sleep tonight. When we go to sleep, our conceptual framework changes from something in the waking state that seems kind of manageable to something in the dream state that is phantasmagoric where all sorts of images start to appear.

In a similar way, when we're dying the grip loosens and we can no longer keep control of all our experiences in any sort of ordered way. If we have had some practice during our life of not trying to arrange the display of our thoughts, emotions and experiences, then when we die we will not be dismayed by the disorder we may experience.

When we're alive we have certain types of thoughts and emotions, but when we're in the process of dying, those radically alter. We don't have the same kinds of experiences; instead, we have unpredictable experiences that we've never had before. One of the things that will happen is that the different sensory mechanisms of our body will shut down. The eyesight, the ability to feel tactile sensations, the ability to smell things or to hear or respond to what's being said—all of these will go one by one. Finally the breathing and the heartbeat will also stop.

We may have emotions that are new to us regarding the experience of death. We may have thoughts like, "I have eaten my last meal! I will never see my loved ones again! I am going somewhere and no one is going with me!" If throughout our lives we've been indulging, renouncing or replacing our data in order to feel better, then we won't have the mental energy to do that any longer. Our supposed ability to think our way into well-being or control our thoughts will also be lost. Unless we've learned to rely on open intelligence, none of the strategies we've cultivated during our lifetime for handling disturbing thoughts and emotions will help us when we die.

These are the kind of very powerful thoughts, emotions and experiences we'll have, and it's quite possible that they'll be far more afflictive than anything we've ever experienced before. But if we are relying on open intelligence, it's likely we'll be able to let these things be as they are. We're only distracted when we think something needs to be done about what's appearing. All the thoughts, emotions and sensations that appear at death—we can let them be what they are. Any thought or emotion will disappear in and of itself like a line drawn in water. The appearances have no power whatsoever to affect us unless we let them.

If we haven't relied on open intelligence, the process of death can be very frightening, because it seems that it's all over for us. There can be a desperate struggle to hold on to life.

Alternatively, we may be relieved to know that our suffering will end. If, however, we are relying on open intelligence rather than getting lost in the data of dying, then all of our experiences and reactions can be easefully released. We will be empowering the peacefulness of everything just *as it is*.

Open intelligence never changes and is ever present as that which knows all these things that are occurring—not only during the process of death, but during the process of life as well. Open intelligence is that which knows death, but death does not affect open intelligence, just as birth doesn't. We might believe that open intelligence depends on the Earth, sun, time, space or life in order to be present. However, open intelligence is not dependent on anything in order to be naturally present—not the heartbeat, the breath, the warmth of the body or even the universe. When the heartbeat, the breath and the warmth of the body all go and the universe is no more, open intelligence *is*.

The more we empower open intelligence completely, the more we arrive at an experiential realization of this fundamental nature of open intelligence that is beyond all conceptual and intellectual categories. If through relying on open intelligence we have familiarized ourselves with the process of death, then we will be able to be completely at peace when it occurs. When open intelligence gets so brilliant that it outshines everything—including the life and death of the physical body—we'll be able to be totally relaxed and have the complete enjoyment of our true body, which is the body of open intelligence.

Abidance as open intelligence isn't some kind of strange state that only applies to certain people. It is the natural state of all human beings, and the more familiar we are with it, the more comfortable we can be in all circumstances—including the circumstance of death.

Q: In a lot of teachings today we hear about being "unborn." What does that mean exactly in relation to what you are talking about?

A: Most of us take ourselves to be an entity that is destructible, namely the body, and we think that open intelligence is generated by this entity. We assume we are born and that we're going to die. The idea of being born is indoctrinated from early on. Most parents will say after their child is born, "Here is our baby! We are so glad she was born!" and this idea that we were born is constantly being reinforced in us. Death is also very much in the background of everything all the time, because what comes with this idea of being born is the idea that we will die. Once we learn that we are this destructible body, we feel that we can be destroyed in the finality of death. At the same time, we may have some unconscious data that subtly avoid that finality, such as: "Everyone else will die, but I won't. Somehow I am going to escape. Others might get terribly ill, but I won't. I won't age, and I won't die."

In a lot of teachings something may be said about our being "unborn." This proposition goes against everything we've heard so far. First we heard that we're born, and suddenly we hear that we're unborn! What to make of that? The truth is that "being born" is an extreme vantage just as "being unborn" is. What we emphasize in the Balanced View Training is that the unborn and the born are not two. What is it that's aware of either being born or unborn? What we think about as unborn and born has never been separate, and both concepts are due to open intelligence.

This understanding cannot be arrived at through intellectual speculation, but only through the practical experience of completely relaxing body and mind in all circumstances. As complete confidence is gained in open intelligence, perfect mental stability and mental clarity become obvious. I'm not suggesting just sitting around in an easy chair all the time, but rather that we completely relax body and mind in all situations, no matter what may be appearing. Only through profoundly remaining in the fundamental condition can these concepts be understood.

Most of us go through life fearing death, because we believe that we've been born and we'll die and also that we're something solid, stable and finite that will end at death. However, what we call "I" has no independent nature—its only nature is the fundamental condition underlying everything.

Q: I grew up in the sort of religious background that has horrific versions of what can happen after death. I find it really hard to be at ease with these old ideas that I want to be free of, but which seem to still have a hold on me.

A: Some traditions have very complex descriptions of the states after death; but whatever those descriptions are, the key instruction is just to rely on open intelligence in the direct encounter with all that appears. Know that they are just appearances of open intelligence. No matter what the appearance is, just relax.

As I said earlier, when the physical death of the body occurs, all kinds of appearances can and do arise that we have never seen before. A lot of these appearances have to do with our belief systems. If we have a strong belief in horrible things happening after death, then it's possible that we'll have such data when we die. I'm not saying that these things will happen for everyone, but many people have extremely fixed beliefs about such things, so when they undergo a death experience, then all the belief systems that they've had may be in evidence.

If we're living our whole life focused on ideas of who we take ourselves to be, we're always trying to keep the lid on all the things we don't want to think about—all the negative data, thoughts and emotions. When we begin to rely on open intelligence, what happens? The lid is off! Once the lid is off, all the appearances start to appear everywhere like fireworks in the sky. However, if we've gained familiarity with open intelligence, this won't be a problem for us. When all the negative data arise, we can rely on open intelligence for short moments, repeatedly, until it becomes continuous. This is the pivotal instruction.

Q: I recognize that most people either have a very fearful relationship with death or they choose to ignore it as best they can, but I know in my own life that I want to understand that death is very much a part of life. Can you give some more down-to-earth examples so I can follow what you're saying?

A: There are many examples for what I am speaking about. For instance, I am always amazed at how many people come out here to the seaside and buy a house right on the edge of an eroding cliff! Haven't they seen that the cliff is gradually being worn away and that eventually their house may fall into the ocean? They seem to feel that they are somehow outside of the processes of nature.

When we're at complete ease within ourselves, we know that we are part of nature. We can look at a house on the edge of an eroding cliff and go, "Ah ha, that eroding cliff is just like me; I am eroding every moment too. That house on the cliff isn't going to be there long, and neither will I!" When we are able to greet all the unthinkable things like death and destruction with ease, then we feel totally comfortable and at ease with ourselves, and we feel like this with everyone else, too. We just fit into nature and into the all-together, and we don't feel any separation from anything.

How about the flowers in the garden? The reason we love flowers is because they're a beautiful reflection of who we are. Coming out of a rich, vigorous emptiness, we're like seeds that sprout, go through their stages of growth and flowering glory, then gradually age, rot, are composted and then disappear into the earth again. This is what sparks our interests in the flowers we enjoy—they're a precise reflection of ourselves. We don't cling to the rose and say, "Please don't go. I can't stand it if you leave me!" We know that the rose will fade and die, and this is just the way it is for the rose and for us.

All the thoughts that appear and events that occur happen as naturally as the flowers in the garden. They're like a shooting star in the night sky and are their own undoing. Nothing can be done to either encourage or prevent them. Even if we really love certain people very much, someday we'll leave them behind—either we'll die or they'll die. When we are entirely at ease, then that completely restful nature of our own being will be naturally present no matter what's going on—whether we're with the people we love or the animals we love or the flowers we love.

I have one final story that may help give us quite a different perspective. There was once a very great teacher who was teaching, among other things, that one had to leave the world, live in a cave and sit in meditative absorption for many years in order to realize the ultimate.

At some point, though, he said to himself, "This isn't it." This great man saw that the ultimate was not something to be acquired, but something that was ever-present and that there was no destination and no one going there. He was able to go far beyond what he had previously taught, and he escaped from the cage of his philosophy.

As he was dying he was completely at ease, and he was able to say, "My delight in death is far, far greater than the delight of traders at making vast fortunes at sea or those who are proud of their victory in battle or of those sages who have entered the rapture of perfect absorption. So, just as a traveller who sets out on the road when it is time, I will not remain in this world any longer, but will go to dwell in the stronghold of the great bliss of deathlessness." Now, that is certainly a beautiful and comforting perspective about death!

PRACTICES
CHAPTER ELEVEN

"There are different kinds of practices that are appropriate for different people, so in that sense there is no practice that is inherently right or wrong. A correct understanding is that everything is perfect all at once, just as it is. This is the attitude of the wholesome goodness of open intelligence, the totally balanced view."

The easiest and most direct of all practices is to rely on open intelligence and to return to that repeatedly. Relying on open intelligence is something that anyone can do; it is absolutely accessible and available to everyone, and it isn't dependent on special circumstances. No matter what happens, we can be at ease with all appearances, simply seeing all appearances as passing forms of open intelligence. In this way we overcome all potential obstacles by not seeing anything as an obstacle. Nothing need be an impediment or pose a threat. We pull out all the stops and we are at full throttle! With that kind of enthusiasm we are at ease with anything that comes up.

People sometimes assume that "being at ease" means that we don't need to do anything but sit under a tree, but it doesn't mean that. Whether we're sitting, working incredibly hard or engaging in all sorts of activities, we maintain open intelligence as we do those things. In whatever way we go about our lives, we rest imperturbably. Perhaps we've been ceaselessly meditating for years or doing incredible practices throughout our lives, or we've been very busy with our business, career or family. These are all perfect opportunities to empower ourselves, and as such we can continue with them while relying on open intelligence. Nothing need be excluded. The result of maintaining open intelligence will always be increased efficiency, kindness, peace of mind and beneficial activities. Eventually it will lead to complete mental stability.

If we are drawn to sustaining open intelligence, then that is right for us. If we don't feel drawn to it, then it probably isn't right for us at this point. Many people live their whole life without ever knowing about open intelligence, so just to have the chance to know about it is incredible. However, this doesn't mean that maintaining open intelligence is right and other things are wrong. Whatever practice one may be doing, I would suggest that a person choose a practice and then commit to it one hundred percent. Only you can decide what is a match for you; but whatever it is, once again, commit to it one hundred percent.

There are different kinds of practices that are appropriate for different people, so in that sense there is no practice that is inherently right or wrong. One of the wonderful things about the wholly positive intelligence that unifies everything is that whatever teaching any person wants or needs, it will appear for them in one way or another. There are so many types of practices, observances and ways of being, and they are a perfect expression for whoever is participating in them. A correct understanding is that everything is perfect all at once, just *as it is*. This is the attitude of the wholesome goodness of open intelligence, the totally balanced view.

Yet, if we're sustaining open intelligence and combining that with a practice that assumes that there is a subject who is headed towards a destination of open intelligence, then that would be mixing two things that don't go together, like oil and water. With relying on open intelligence, there is no destination and no one going anywhere. Timelessly free pure open intelligence is already right here, and we've never been separate from it. There is nothing to realize or to attain, and no practice is needed to get us to where we already are. When we are totally at ease, we get familiar with what has always been.

We can be involved in any practice—mantra repetition, selfless service, meditation, chanting, devotion or anything else—as long as we don't think it's leading somewhere. If we think we are a seeker doing practices to get to a destination, then we are missing the pure open intelligence that is already here and already free. If practices are done with the idea that they are leading to a destination, they will actually strengthen our identification with a limited personal identity, and no matter how many practices we do with that attitude, the destination of the complete well-being of open intelligence will remain out of reach.

Q: *I see a lot of people these days proselytizing about their religion. They have a lot of conviction about their faith and they feel like they have to convert other people. I personally don't like proselytizing, but at the same time I know that people like my parents are suffering and that they would benefit from this training. What am I to do in a case like this?*

A: Once we have seen our own suffering, we really see the suffering of others, not just in an intellectual way but in a completely clear and heartfelt way. We may very much want to do something for other people, and there is no rule about what to do or what to say. It just happens spontaneously. One approach is to wait for an opening and then speak to them in an appropriate way, but even better than that is the power of your own example.

If someone sees a change in you, they might say, "What happened? I notice something different about you. You seem to be so much more at ease." There's no need to force a message on people or to say anything that is uninvited or unwelcome. That would probably only be a turn-off for them, but if your parents see a change in you and are interested to know more about how you changed, they will come to you on their own. In that case, there would be attraction rather than promotion.

Q: Is there any benefit in being with others who are relying on open intelligence, or is it more or less an individual affair?

A: First of all, open intelligence is equal everywhere and with everyone, and there is no ramping up of open intelligence that is due to being in certain locations. At the same time, it is very natural and beneficial for us as human beings to come together with others who are committed to the same things we are.

In Balanced View we have the Four Mainstays, which provide ultimate and unerring support for the instinctive recognition of open intelligence in one's own direct experience. The Four Mainstays are the simple practice of short moments of open intelligence, the training, the trainers and the worldwide community.

The Four Mainstays are like four legs of a chair. The chair must have all four legs; otherwise, it is of no use. If a chair has less than four legs, it will take a great deal of energy to sit in it and it will be of no real support. It will be more effort than it is worth to try to sit in the chair. When the chair has all four legs, we can rely on it without any effort, without anything needing to be done. The chair is available and we can count on it.

All Four Mainstays are required for radical empowerment of the individual and for radical empowerment of all of society. The Four Mainstays elicit the very powerful open intelligence of human society. This is a simple, straightforward and practical human matter. If we have friends who are living in the same way we are, it makes it a lot easier, because they can give us understanding and support. The community of people relying on open intelligence reinforces and reaffirms our choice to live as open intelligence. We utilize the open intelligence inherent in the Four Mainstays to empower our actions for creating revolutionary change in human society.

Q: *It sounds great to be able to just be there relying on open intelligence, but what if I had five kids to feed? I can't just sit there satisfied with my own individual situation.*

A: Well, are you talking about yourself or a hypothetical example? Why don't we talk about a real person? I have a husband, three kids and eight grandchildren! The advice is exactly the same whether you have five kids to feed or not: to rely on open intelligence and to do it repeatedly, whatever the circumstantial data of one's life may be. Whatever it is you're doing and whatever is happening in your life, that's a perfect circumstance for gaining confidence in open intelligence. Short moments, repeated many times, become continuous and obvious.

Q: *Devotion is very important in my life, but I don't hear you using that word. Could you speak about devotion, and more specifically about the devotion of the heart, and whether one needs to cultivate this type of devotion?*

A: In relying on open intelligence, devotion just naturally comes about. I don't know anything about cultivating devotion, because that isn't something that I ever did. What did happen was that I realized that the underlying basis of all my zillions of data streams was timeless freedom. I realized that this freedom was inseparable from this data and that all my data were equal. I became incredibly devoted to that—completely and utterly devoted to that. Out of that sprang devotion to everyone. Devotion to everyone is what my life has been about, so I have a very large family! If you feel the devotional impulse, consider yourself very lucky and take advantage of it, because it is a way to really enjoy the pure pleasure of true relationship.

When people talk about the devotion of the heart, the "heart" is not a location in the body. The heart is the essence of everything *as it is*. Inseparable from open intelligence is the heart; inseparable from open intelligence is love and inseparable from open intelligence is God. In this Training we use the words "open intelligence" instead of "God" or "consciousness" because open intelligence are words that beings can easily understand. If people familiarize themselves with open intelligence, then they know that by which all is known.

When we rely on open intelligence for short moments, repeated many times, we rest as love, we rest as the heart, we rest as wisdom and we rest as devotion to everything *as it is*. When we hear these terms like the heart or devotion, then we need to know what they truly are. Devotion in the ultimate sense is the complete heart devotion to the essence of our own being—the unmitigated, relentless heart devotion that can't be turned on or off. It is natural to us, and we recognize it when we rely on open intelligence. This is very, very beautiful.

Q: Could you speak about the need for prayer?

A: This is a question that is asked from time to time and is something that I've thought about very much throughout my life. The word "prayer" means "petition," but if you want to practice prayer, it is important to know what the *ultimate* petition would be. Praying to know yourself as open intelligence is a prayer worth praying. In that prayer, you are really praying to yourself!

Now, for most people the idea of praying to oneself is a little scary! We look at our lives and we think, "She said that when I pray, I'm praying to myself. That's a little daunting considering my track record!" However, we're not praying to ourselves as our conjured-up personal identity; we're praying to ourselves as the natural order of everything—the super-intelligence that's at the root of every single one of our thoughts and actions. We're praying to that which causes a flower to bloom. Isn't that a beautiful and inspiring idea? Isn't that just gorgeous to even consider!

No matter what kind of concept you've had of some kind of divinity or divine being, it's all right, but keep in mind that anything you can conceptualize is a datum that appears within open intelligence. By recognizing open intelligence, we know that which is the genesis of everything. It is the all-creating monarch of all concepts of divinity—and their opposites. All these concepts are equal, and they are superseded by the profound wisdom that is at the core of every appearance.

Q: What are your views concerning vegetarianism? Does one need to become a vegetarian in order to more readily recognize open intelligence?

A: When I was a young woman, I guess I'd heard of vegetarianism, but I wasn't a vegetarian. I'd also heard of meditation, but I'd never meditated. I might have heard of people called gurus, but it never occurred to me that they would be anyone I would meet. I might have read something about nonduality, but it wasn't anything that I really wanted to explore or think about.

What I did know in my own experience was that there was an indivisible ground of love in everything and that human beings are inherently perfect. I had known that since I was a child, so I didn't need any scientific explanations or philosophy books to tell me that.

The massive shift I experienced twenty-seven years ago was an opening up or refinement of my perception, where I was able to see everything as completely indivisible. From that point on, doing anything to achieve something looked totally unnecessary—like for example becoming a vegetarian in order to achieve the refined perception of open intelligence. It was obvious that it just wasn't crucial. Sitting on a cushion and watching thoughts, emotions and sensations arise and fall in order to get to a goal—that didn't make much sense to me either.

When the timeless freedom of open intelligence is so easily accessible within the context of everything that's occurring right here and now, why add a lot of other things to try to make it occur? We breathe, and every single bit of that breath is filled with primordially pure open intelligence; that same open intelligence forms the essence of the plant or the meat we eat, so in that sense everything is equal. In the moment that we try to decide that things aren't equal or that some things are better than others, then that is a falling away from true wisdom.

The wisdom mind is the mind that knows everything as equal. Its wisdom comes from being all-encompassing—completely beyond all opposites and yet including all opposites—and not from categorizing phenomena. Wisdom itself is a ground of complete equality and evenness, which has never been bifurcated, divided or split. It's a big relief to not have to judge everything as good or bad! The undoable becomes doable in allowing everything to be *as it is*. This may go against everything we believe, yet when we begin to gain confidence in open intelligence, we see that it is the case.

Q: It seems to me that in all the ancient traditions the most sincere and serious seekers achieved their high state through practicing austerities, or if not austerities, then undergoing serious disciplines. Is practicing austerities or undergoing disciplines something that you also recommend?

A: Wisdom can't be shaped from austerities or anything else, because everything already *is* wisdom. If we say that through austerities we're going to arrive at wisdom, then we're stating that there is someone who's going somewhere. We have the subject headed towards the object of a destination. When we rely on open intelligence there is no subject or object from the beginningless beginning, and everything comes into a perfect balance.

We could look at a historical figure like the Buddha, who at some point in his life as a wandering seeker heard a teaching that told him he should be celibate and live in solitude. So he tried living in solitude and became celibate. Then he saw that this really wasn't enough, and he went to another teacher who gave him more instructions about how to control his thoughts and emotions, but that didn't lead anywhere either. Then he tried a practice of complete physical and mental austerity. He got completely away from everyone and everything, starved himself and put himself through all kinds of torture till he was nearly dead.

After he had tried everything else, he finally just sat down and relaxed, and the result was that everything fired up within him—his lust, his anger, his jealousy, his deep regret for having abandoned his wife, son and parents—everything he'd been trying to neutralize with those practices. When he relaxed and allowed all of that to be, he was able to sustain open intelligence, without trying to change or push away any of the data. He then realized the true nature of the reality within.

After his realization he didn't teach that everybody should just sit down and close their eyes, and that if they sat there long enough then something was going to happen. He taught that, no matter what afflictive states appear, one should not try to avoid them, replace them or change them in any way. Instead, one should just let them be as they are.

I know from my own experience and from the experience of others that this principle is true. No matter how bothered we feel by whatever's going on inside or outside, we need to relax completely, and in that relaxation the timeless freedom that is the unchanging basis of all data will be discovered. Relaxing the body and mind completely can take place anywhere, even when there are many thoughts stirring and there's a lot of physical activity.

Don't try to figure it out; don't try to hold to any of the ideas you have learned from reading books. It's all within your own experience; trust your own experience and the complete freedom that is the ground of every single perception.

Q: So many traditions from the East and West require that monks or priests be celibate. Is celibacy a prerequisite for the ultimate attainment in this life?

A: Well, if being celibate is what you want to do, that's fine, but it's not necessary. Nothing needs to be done to be who we are, because we already *are* who we are! If we say that something needs to be done, then we step aside from who we are. At the same time, nothing is excluded, so if a person feels naturally moved to celibacy, that's perfectly okay. However, if celibacy were taken to be like the golden key to the destination of who we are, then that would be a detour. If we choose celibacy because that is the way we want to live, that's another matter.

Celibacy is a very specific aspect of the much broader issue of sexuality that all people must deal with. Celibacy neutralizes sexual desire, but it doesn't completely resolve the phenomenon of sexual desire. Only by the power of open intelligence can the full scope of sexual desire be understood.

One of the big problems that adds significantly to all the other problems in the world is the increase in population. With that particular problem, the only hope of really containing the population of the human species is for more and more people to instinctively recognize open intelligence. Only by the power of open intelligence do we have a clear and beneficial perspective on sexual desire.

Q: Shouldn't one seek out solitude in order to avoid all the distractions of the world?

A: The more you relax, the subtler your perceptions become. Maybe your perceptions before had been involved in the world and being with everybody, but the more you relax the more you might have a whole new set of perceptions that will come up. One such perception could be wanting to be in solitude, but that's just another perception. When the true nature of phenomena is realized, then solitude becomes obsolete; there's no need for solitude or any other extreme. If you simply look at being in solitude as a choice you've made, rather than something that's leading somewhere, then that would be fine, but if you look at it as necessary for your freedom, then it's a prison.

There is another way of looking at this issue of personal solitude. One of the things that came up for me early in relying on open intelligence was the thought of living in solitude, but the context in which I held all such inclinations was: what's going to be most beneficial to the whole, and how are my gifts, strengths and talents going to be best used for the benefit of everyone? The human race is at such a critical juncture that we need as many people contributing as much as possible to the benefit of the whole in a marked way. This is so urgently important.

MEDITATION
CHAPTER TWELVE

"One moment of instantaneous open intelligence brings more open intelligence than a lifetime of contrived meditation. That one moment of instantaneous open intelligence introduces us to that about ourselves that will never change. In this sense, every moment would be the ultimate meditation, no matter what the moment may contain."

The goal of meditation is often defined as the mental stability that continues throughout day and night and complete equanimity no matter what is appearing in one's mind. The Balanced View Training is free of doctrinal views about all forms of meditation that require altering the mind to conform it to any creed. It's best to not continue trying to correct the mind in any way, but simply to relax in its changeless basis. People all over the world are finding that an underlying intelligence reveals itself through the power of leaving the mind in its natural state of open intelligence. There's no need to change or correct the flow of mental events. By altering the mind, this intelligence—open intelligence—remains hidden and outside one's experience. What we find in open intelligence is perfect mental stability, empathy and skillful activities and ideas that are of benefit to all. We are warmer, friendlier and more cooperative in a very natural way.

In simple terms, no one can proceed by means of meditative progress to their own open intelligence. It is a logical absurdity to look for something that is already present, and to do so distracts us from simple open intelligence. Within open intelligence, meditation appears as just another datum equal to all other data. It has no special right or privilege. Within open intelligence, all data are equal, and this is the understanding and recognition we must come to.

Relaxing the mind imperturbably throughout the day without altering its content in any way, guarantees very swift access to open intelligence. Relying on open intelligence for short moments is repeated many times until it becomes spontaneous and continuous.

In this way, wide-open open intelligence becomes predominant at all times. We don't need to contrive a special period when we rest our mind—as in a meditation session. If we set up a special period, then it may be that we're separating that time out as somehow different from other times, and this can create an obstacle to discovering the open intelligence that is present in every moment. We don't need to look for meditative absorption in a special time or location, because it can't be found by fixating on one point to the exclusion of others.

In what we could call "contrived" meditation, the concentration is directed to a particular point, whether it's a mantra that's being repeated, the breath, a candle flame or watching one's thoughts. It could be focusing on something or on nothing, but focusing on something and focusing on nothing are both focusing on something! When focused attention is used in meditation, it actually creates a new datum, which subtly strengthens both the personal identity and the subject/object dichotomy: there is a subject focusing on an object of meditative concentration.

Focusing on the breath or closing the eyes are attempts to do something special to alter the mind. Open intelligence has no underlying basis and doesn't depend on anything, so assuming specific postures is just an unnecessary contrivance. Without the confidence that comes from relying on the open intelligence that is naturally wide-open and spacious, we will be constrained by wishful thinking about the results of the meditation practice. If we follow such methods, we only blind ourselves to what's already here by believing that open intelligence is the effect of the cause of meditation. As open intelligence is already present and always accomplished, it is an error to expect it to be arrived at some time in the future.

In uncontrived open intelligence there's no need to have any special point of concentration, to have a special time-slot or special place, to put ourselves in a particular posture or to have any fixed reference points. All we need is to rely on the open intelligence that underlies all appearances. Open intelligence is a seamless expanse that is naturally present everywhere; it includes everything and is within everything. There is no "someone" observing "something else," because in open intelligence nothing has been made into anything. The seer, the seeing, and the seen all appear and disappear within open intelligence—the changeless nature of all that comes and goes.

The uncontrived moment of relying on open intelligence is all-inclusive and embraces all of life. All thoughts, including the thought of "I," appear and disappear within open intelligence; yet, open intelligence remains unaffected by their appearance and disappearance. Open intelligence is not a subject or an object. It has no reference points, so no specific focus of attention is needed. The simple approach is to maintain flawless open intelligence in all situations without needing to focus on any circumstance in particular or to correct mental events. To be non-distracted by thoughts is the key point; we maintain flawless open intelligence while allowing all perceptions to be completely unrestrained, unrestricted and unchanged. We don't try to neutralize anything in any way; we let the full force of the thoughts, emotions and experiences have free rein while empowering their underlying essence. We don't need a special kind of hiding place in which to put thoughts or emotions—we face everything and just relax.

We can create a new definition of meditation: "the freeing of all of the mind's constraints." This means that everything that appears is seen as a form of pure open intelligence, and therefore no problems are found and no constraints are necessary. Nothing is perceived as having ever been made into anything. The clear light of open intelligence has never been stuck anywhere. Within open intelligence—just like within stainless, flawless sky—there is nothing that's hold-able or keep-able. One moment of instantaneous open intelligence introduces us to that about ourselves that will never change. In this sense, every moment would be the ultimate meditation, no matter what the moment may contain.

Many of us are familiar with various types of meditation and may have been meditating for years. We've heard concepts that are associated with meditation like "extinction of mind" or "exhaustion of all phenomena," and we may interpret these concepts to mean that we would no longer have any thoughts or emotions. That is a profound misunderstanding. The important thing isn't in having no thoughts or emotions; it is instead in not being *distracted* by thoughts and emotions.

We can get into all kinds of sublime states in meditation, but they're not completely free. They're just states, and states are inherently temporary. Anything acquired through effort could eventually be lost, but our true nature is permanently with us and always will be. All the subtle refined states that are associated with spiritual practices—the non-conceptual state, bliss, emptiness, neutrality or whatever it might be—are just data. There's no need to take up a point of reference anywhere, including rarified meditative experiences. To do so would severely limit access to open intelligence.

Bliss and suffering are equal. This can be realized only from the perspective of open intelligence. Don't attempt to obtain bliss or to reject suffering; by simply maintaining open intelligence, all is accomplished. Being attached to bliss or other meditative experiences constitutes suffering. Please don't let yourself be infected by the disease of striving for meditative experiences!

The conventional mind and all scientific pronouncements about it are just data; there isn't something called "the mind" that is a warehouse for data and that has a nature independent of open intelligence. An easy way to deal with the mind is just to see it as a datum, and when thoughts about the mind come up, simply rely on open intelligence.

Even if there are the data of non-recognition of open intelligence, distraction by thoughts or extensive elaboration on thinking, increasingly it will be realized that all of it is due to open intelligence and nothing else. The only freedom there is, is the freedom in the immediacy of perception, and this is not something that we arrive at through thinking about it, philosophizing about it or meditating on it. All we need to do is rely on open intelligence, and all mental constraints will subside.

Even if someone has meditated for decades, the demonstration of the full evidence of open intelligence in everyday life doesn't come about through meditation. Open intelligence is already accomplished. What is already so doesn't need a cause to bring it about as an effect; it's simply a matter of noticing that open intelligence is present in each perception.

Many people who have practiced meditation have reached the point where they've said that there is ultimately no need for meditation, because nothing is needed to establish what already is. They eventually conclude that all the thinking about and meditating on the nature of the mind is unnecessary, because the ground of mind is the absolute ground of everything, and in that sense there is no separation. It is already here and already realized. Everything that appears within the ground of everything *is* the ground of everything.

I'm not suggesting that if you love meditation you should give it up. If meditation is one of the practices you choose to do, that doesn't need to change, but you should know that meditation is not a means of getting you to a destination. If you think it's a means to a goal, that will create the idea that the destination of freedom is always somewhere away from you to be attained in the distant future, rather than being right here in this moment and already attained.

Just look at it this way: every appearance in open intelligence is a meditation. Whatever it is—getting a massage, climbing a mountain, making love, defecating—it's all meditation and it's all equal. By the power of relying on open intelligence for short moments, repeated many times, every experience is like being on a meditation cushion. In this simple practice is a natural movement to be involved in everything in a completely organic way; a new connectedness with all of life springs up that is free flowing and truly happy.

Q: Where should the mind be focused during meditation?

A: Nowhere. Just rely on open intelligence.

Q: Can meditation with a mantra be combined with relying on open intelligence?

A: Let's put it this way: the ultimate mantra is complete reliance on open intelligence. One of the meanings of the word "mantra" is "that which soothes the mind." So, if we're looking for what ultimately soothes the mind, we will find that it's in relying on open intelligence. Once that's understood, then mantra repetition can just be an enjoyable activity like any other activity, rather than a practice leading to a destination, because through relying on open intelligence we will have found the destination to be right here.

Q: *I've been meditating for years, but I'm now trying to integrate that practice with relying on open intelligence. The problem is, when I meditate now, I feel like I'm forcing myself to rely on open intelligence, and this makes me doubt whether I should meditate at all.*

A: What every meditator is ultimately looking for is to have the meditative state all day long—in all circumstances—and not just in a special circumstance, such as when one is sitting on a cushion. We're talking about completely uncontrived meditation that will pervade waking, dreaming and sleeping. This can come about quickly or slowly through the introduction to open intelligence and the practice of short moments of open intelligence, repeated many times, until open intelligence is continuously obvious throughout day and night. The ultimate goal of meditation is to rely on open intelligence with complete equanimity no matter what is appearing.

Of course, most of us would want to arrive at that in the easiest way possible! Meditation should be an expression, in an easy and effortless way, of all-pervasive open intelligence. If we say we can only meditate when we're sitting on a cushion or if we're in a special place, then that's not necessarily true—it's just what we believe. In my own case, I didn't have a meditation practice where I would sit on a cushion each day, but I did meditate in my own way, which was to rely on open intelligence for short moments, repeated many times, in all circumstances and conditions. In that way meditation quickly became pervasive in waking, dreaming and sleeping.

I am not saying that you shouldn't meditate. You're welcome to do whatever you like, but when you are meditating, just allow everything to be *as it is*, as you would in any other moment. Don't force anything—just relax. Whatever the thoughts, emotions and sensations are, they're the unconfined capacity and creativity of open intelligence. They're inseparable from open intelligence, just as the brilliance of a diamond is inseparable from the diamond itself.

Initially, it may seem that there is open intelligence being aware of distracting data—similar to a cat watching a mouse. Yet, the more one empowers oneself in open intelligence, the more one sees that open intelligence and data are inseparable. Even if we say, "I am relying on open intelligence, and a thought is appearing in open intelligence," both are data that have open intelligence alone as their basis.

There is no need to do any kind of one-pointed meditation like following the breath, thinking of certain things, visualizing a deity, gazing at a candle flame or whatever it might be. Simply rely on open intelligence! Everything will then become more and more resolved, and it will become clearer that everything really is nondual by nature. If we say that certain conditions are necessary and open intelligence is dependent on conditions, it's going to be very difficult to realize that everything is a single nondual expanse, because we've placed conditions on it and said that open intelligence is dependent on something. Open intelligence is the basis of everything and depends on nothing.

Q: So, can we say that the goal of meditation is achieved when it makes itself useless?

A: Oh, I love it; that's music to my ears! What a profound expression of wisdom!

I'm not saying anything new about this subject. Throughout time the ultimate meditation of imperturbable rest has been handed down from generation to generation, stretching through time like a chain of golden mountains. The lineage of everyday open intelligence is so pure that it has no lines. Open intelligence is super-complete in itself. It doesn't need to adopt doctrines, traditions, methods, special costumes or locations, for it is the basis of all of these and everything else as well.

This practice is for all people. It is not dependent on conditions such as age, intellect, education, gender or location. We already are who we are, so why should we have to go through an ordeal of decades to be who we are? Relying on open intelligence is all that's needed. It is swift and sure!

Q: *In some traditions it is taught that deep sleep is similar to meditation, but it is my experience that sleep is sleep and meditation is meditation, and that sleep has no relation with meditation. Could you shed some light on this?*

A: Sleep and meditation are appearances that are equal to every other appearance, and all appearances have open intelligence as their root. It doesn't matter what it is—there is no "two." That's what nonduality means: there have never been two. Meditation means to rely on open intelligence, and when we just rest as that natural state, it becomes more and more familiar. As it becomes more familiar, we see that open intelligence is inseparable from everything. It's inseparable from dreams, waking and sleep, and inseparable from birth, life and death. By recognizing this, we go beyond all the labels we've used to describe ourselves.

If we've been meditating for many years and we get lost in a non-conceptual state of no-self, bliss or emptiness, then it's possible we could stay in that state for years if we wanted to. Some people have disciplined themselves to stay in all kinds of states, but if we realize that states are nothing other than open intelligence, then we pass beyond being bound up in states. Beyond being bound in a state is the clear light of wisdom that requires no state. It doesn't ever adopt any extremes and is of tremendous benefit.

When we're all wrapped up in states, it is very difficult to address the very real problems facing the world, because the state we're in is probably suggesting to us that there *is* no world. If we're in one of those states, we've actually found an obstacle to open intelligence, even though it may feel much better than our ordinary data. We've adopted an extreme position, whereas open intelligence has no extremes. From the vantage of open intelligence, there is no position-taking of "the world exists" or "the world doesn't exist." There is solely the total presence of open intelligence here and now. If we truly examine the nature of what's appearing and don't try to describe it, we'll see that this statement is very apt.

A state is just more illusion—another mirage or dream. Being in some sort of state may make us feel better, it may benefit us personally, and we may even be able to convince ourselves that it is of benefit to everybody. But how much benefit could it be to everybody when millions of the world's people don't have a balanced diet, clean water, or proper waste management? Beyond all these states is great wisdom that isn't tied to conceptual frameworks. This wisdom can say and do anything: it can move anywhere, it can be effortless and very fruitful in its benefit, and it doesn't have any ties or boundaries.

Q: I have been practicing a specific meditation for many years and have benefited from it very much, and I don't at all feel that I should give it up. Could you maybe explain to me what it is you are advocating in light of my practice?

A: Very often the minds and bodies of long-time meditators are already more at ease, so if they have the good fortune to be exposed to the training of relying on open intelligence, they can be fully present without needing to think over everything that's being said.

Some people may have been practicing different types of meditation for years—while someone else may have been dealing with being in prison for thirty years—but all these are practices. With most practices, we've trained ourselves to look at the contents of our mind and see some of it as good and some of it as bad. Whether we're an ardent spiritual practitioner or someone who's practiced persistent wrongdoing, there is a continuous engagement in basing our actions on our thoughts and emotions. When we look for a teaching, we often look for one that agrees with our predetermined data that some things are good and others bad. This isn't the best approach when our goal is to gain confidence in open intelligence, because open intelligence is beyond such conceptual frameworks.

Some of us get very involved with the data appearing within our minds, and we say, "Oh no, I need to get rid of these negative data. I need to be pure in order to achieve Buddha-nature!" Buddha-nature is nothing but a label for perfect open intelligence and extraordinary activities.

From the beginningless beginning of the great equalness of all, there's never been anything to change. There's never been any impurity anywhere. There's just complete openness, and in that spacious intelligence, everything is informed by the wisdom that is naturally present and primordially pure. Amazingly, it is by the power of relying on open intelligence without trying to correct mental events from bad to good that we find the wholly beneficial intelligence at the basis of everything.

If we're thinking that there is something impure or evil in us that can't be changed, then it's time to just relax as open intelligence and allow that data to resolve. This is the conclusion that Buddha himself came to. He had tried many practices, but finally he quit seeking and sat down under the Bodhi tree. And what happened? He let go of his previous practices and just relied on open intelligence. He didn't do that in any special way. Sometimes he stood up, sometimes he sat down and sometimes he took a little snooze, but no matter what appeared, he just let all of his thoughts and emotions have free rein, instead of trying to abandon, avoid or alter them through all kinds of intensive practices as he had previously done.

All the fears, doubts, regrets, sexual fantasies and everything else came up for him when he sat there. The ancient Buddhist scriptures refer to them as demons, but they weren't coming from outside; it was just his most intense stuff coming up. We all know what that's like, don't we? Have you ever sat in a meditation posture ready to have a great meditation, feeling so good about yourself, but then suddenly there it all is: *Playboy* magazine images, fantasies about beautiful movie stars or the person across the room and the raging desires that come with the fantasies. Next you'll be thinking about the diamond ring you want, or the car, or where you want to live, or the kind of job you want, or what you should have taken when you were in school, or signing up for the next meditation retreat!

Some form of this is what happened with Buddha under the Bodhi tree, but he just sat there and let it all happen, whatever it was. He didn't try to contain it or control it or change it. He stopped contriving completely, and then he just allowed everything to be as it was. He was empowered by the great equanimity that is the basis of all appearances. Then, relying on flawless open intelligence, he saw all *as* flawless open intelligence, until all *was* flawless open intelligence. When he had directly realized that the pure open intelligence that is the basis of all phenomena was his own true nature, he touched the ground and said, "This is it. I realize that all these things I've been trying to accumulate, change or avoid are all just wisdom appearances and inseparable from the ground of all being."

The simplest of all practices is just to rely on open intelligence in an uncontrived way, because it integrates everything from the beginning without separating anything out. You don't need to drastically change your lifestyle. Just begin relying on open intelligence throughout the day, and swiftly you'll find that open intelligence will be increasingly evident in your life. The ultimate approach is effortless and all-inclusive open intelligence—it takes in all of life. If you just rely on open intelligence again and again, conviction about that will dawn. You can count on this without fail.

TOTAL WELL-BEING
CHAPTER THIRTEEN

"Most of us have never known that every single moment throughout night and day we are actually resting in complete well-being. There is never a single moment when we are apart from it, no matter what we are thinking, feeling, or experiencing."

Even when I was quite young, I had the strong conviction that there was something about life that was totally precious. Though no one spoke about it, that preciousness was obvious to me. I intuitively felt that if I could fully discover that preciousness, life would be wondrous—I would realize I was enveloped by this preciousness, I would be able to live as that precious essence, and then there would just be a tender warmheartedness with everyone. My mind would always be peaceful, and my interactions with others would be powerful, sweet, easy and loving. Somehow I knew this was possible.

As an adult I discovered that what I'd thought to be true as a child *is* absolutely true! That way of living is possible, not only for me, but for every single person in the world. We all long for that perfect love and peace. We want that to be true, no matter how many other belief systems we may have taken on during our life. We long for every moment of our life to have the magical heartbeat of warmheartedness and well-being.

Well, that's not only possible, it's already present within us. Regardless of how things may appear—whether positive or negative, spiritual or nonspiritual, afflictive or exalted—every appearance has the same well-being as its essence.

To have well-being doesn't mean that we'll only have pleasant thoughts and sensations. Throughout our lives we'll continue to have a wide range of thoughts, emotions and sensations, but true well-being comes from the fact that we are no longer ruled by them. They no longer define us or affect us, for we know them to appear in open intelligence, which has never been entangled in anything. When we are established in the practice of relying on open intelligence, it remains obvious to us no matter what's going on. We no longer have the need to try to sustain it. Instead of being caught up in ordinary thinking all the time, our heart and mind open up, and we realize that everything is included within open intelligence, which remains unchanged and ever-free no matter what appears.

When we just relax into the wide-open spaciousness that is the essence of our being, then we see something about ourselves that we may have never known before. Most of us have never known that every single moment throughout night and day we're actually resting in complete well-being. There is never a single moment when we're apart from it, no matter what we're thinking, feeling or experiencing. However, to the degree that we believe that our thoughts and emotions have power over us, to that degree we won't be aware of the well-being that is always present. So, if we take ourselves to be apart from well-being and affected by every thought and emotion that comes along, then that will be our experience.

The well-being of wisdom is not like the state of happiness sought by ordinary thinking. Following after thoughts, emotions and experiences in order to find happiness isn't well-being at all. Following after thoughts is what we do when we *hope* for well-being, but this is a painful state to be in, because the hope is unending and ultimately unfulfillable. What's needed is to discover the well-being that's already present, rather than hoping for it to arrive in the future. The hoped-for future never comes—but what is timeless and eternal is here right now.

Hoping for well-being comes from the simple fact that we want to feel good. Wanting to feel good may take many forms, such as wanting to be acknowledged, wanting to rectify a wrong, wanting to be healthy, wanting to find balance in life and so on, but it all boils down to the same basic thing—wanting a life of well-being. Even people who are very egotistical, angry, abusive and self-righteous just want to feel good. Everyone is just like us; they're no different: they want to feel good, and they don't want to feel crummy!

We search throughout our entire life for how to feel good. From the beginning, when we first learn from other people to rely on ordinary thinking, a lot of what we learn is to manipulate our thoughts and emotions in order to feel good. For example, as a child we may exhibit anger and hit another child, and someone will say, "That's bad! You shouldn't be angry and hit other people!" So, we think, "Ah ha, being angry and hitting others is something that will get me in trouble. It's wrong and I must correct it." Another example would be that our parents usually teach us that we should avoid anger and replace it with good behavior: "Don't be angry; be nice to so and so."

The implication is that we need to contrive nice-ness even when we don't feel nice so that we can get along with others and feel good ourselves. But even the nicest people on Earth will not find total well-being merely in being nice. There will always be something stirring in the background that isn't so nice—like death or critical illness or some unpredictable emotion or event. "Nice" is just a label, and we can never find well-being in a label.

The manipulations of behavior we're taught in childhood never get to the essence of how to feel good, because they're just antidotes. They're like putting a band-aid on a deep wound. Although we might gain a bit of understanding in a practical way about how to live life, using antidotes to thoughts, emotions and other experiences isn't enough for real happiness. Strategies of manipulating thoughts and emotions will never make us permanently happy, no matter how much headway we might make with the thought-management programs that we institute. No matter how excellent we might believe these self-improvement programs are, we still don't feel good all the time, and having well-being all the time is what we want. Constantly sorting through our thoughts and trying to come up with good thoughts to replace the bad thoughts doesn't lead to happiness; it leads to a machine-like existence. We become 24-hour-a-day thought-sorters. That's not freedom—it's a life fit for a robot.

Trying to replace bad thoughts and emotions with good thoughts and emotions is merely switching from one datum to another, and that ceaseless agitation will never let us discover the non-agitated rest of total well-being. Within ordinary thinking there's no recognition of the indestructible reality of open intelligence, even though that reality permeates all data. When we're identified with our thoughts and believe we are the thinker, there will be no experience of wide-open intelligence, which is the basic space in which both the thoughts and thinker appear and disappear. That primordial basic space is what we are, but through constant identification with ordinary thinking, we've forgotten the space of open intelligence. Clinging to the temporary parts, we've altogether forgotten the timeless whole.

It is impossible to bring about a permanent state of well-being from ordinary knowledge. Even if we knew everything there is to know in the realm of facts and science, that accomplishment would never bring about a permanent state of satisfaction or well-being, because it's made only of temporary data. True wisdom lies in the capacity to not stray from open intelligence and is gained only by the commitment to relying on open intelligence. Rather than following after appearances, we continue relying on open intelligence for short moments, repeated many times, until the ease of being becomes continuous. In this way we gradually become fully familiar with open intelligence as the basis of perceptions. We become less and less identified with ourselves as being a separate entity stuck in a body, and discover our fundamental condition to be ever-free open intelligence that pervades and transcends all data.

As long as we're identified only with this soft animal body, it really seems kind of threatening, because it feels like we're trapped in it. There are always lots of people who will tell us that we came into existence only when we were born, and once we've believed that, we'll be afraid of this event coming up called death. If we think we're only the body, death may be a terrifying prospect.

Maybe we think scientific knowledge will help, so we immerse ourselves in facts of various kinds. But even if we could find out everything there is to know according to current knowledge about this vulnerable animal body and its psychology, are these conventional descriptions going to protect us from death? No matter what we've learned about ourselves, none of it has ever given us the total well-being that we want, because conventional knowledge overlooks open intelligence as the self-knowing aspect that is inseparable from the fundamental condition. It is open intelligence by which we know our own body and everything else; open intelligence is the primal root of all knowledge, existing prior to all thoughts, including the thought "I." Only in open intelligence can the well-being we're seeking be found, for that alone is permanent, and that alone is our fundamental reality. This is the only true knowledge.

There's only one thing that will bring us complete well-being, and that is to know our fundamental condition—and this must be a lived experience. When we return to open intelligence again and again, we gradually gain familiarity with our fundamental nature. Then our thinking loses its fearful edges and blooms into joyful well-being. In a totally uncontrived way we feel greater intimacy and connection with others. Our thoughts, when we notice them at all, are no longer so much about our own self-centered concerns; they gradually become more dynamic, more filled with energy and more concerned with the life of everyone.

We instinctively realize that everything truly is indivisible and that no one is a stranger. We feel a natural intimacy with everyone.

We come to care very greatly about our planet and all the beings on it, and a very dynamic expression of compassion and wisdom comes alive in us and naturally flows into the service of all. We see wonderful solutions not only to our own problems, but to everyone's, and we naturally find the strength and courage to bring those solutions into manifestation.

This is what we really need to know about ourselves at this point in human history—more so than at any other time. We have always had people among us who have known the true nature of reality, but today is the first time in human history when many people are open-minded enough and also have the available information to fully realize our fundamental nature. In this truth lies the ability to solve our own problems as individuals and also the problems of our world.

How can that be accomplished? We need to get familiar with the essence that is at the basis of each of us as human beings. All solutions spring from that essence.

The well-being that we're always looking for can't really be found—because it's never been lost. We try to find it in a thought, but we can't find it there, because thoughts come and go, and we can't hold on to them, no matter how hard we try. If we say, "I'm only going to have happy thoughts and that's how I am going to find well-being," well, no one has ever been able to do that. The truth is that well-being already exists in everything. It exists in happy loving thoughts, but it also exists in negative thoughts, experiences and emotions. All of these are comprised of the basic space of open intelligence, which is the nature of happiness itself.

Primordial open intelligence is synonymous with peace; it is love itself. We tend to label our thoughts as good, bad, happy or sad and try to cling to the ones we like. However, the label is not the ultimate definition of anything. All things share the same essence, and that essence of love and wisdom that is all-knowing and all-aware has never been trapped by any designation whatsoever. The essence of who we are has never been stuck anywhere and has never been made into anything. It is freedom itself and always will be.

Q: This theme of well-being is really important to me, because it seems that I have so little of it! I have wild mood swings. One minute I'll be feeling okay, and the next I'll be in a really bad mood. This is made worse by the relationship I have with my partner who's also subject to fluctuating moods. I don't think I can find well-being as long as I have these wild mood swings or as long as I remain with this particular partner.

A: Let me give an example that may help you get a perspective on the moods you experience. I got a phone call this morning from someone who was telling me about all the troubles she'd had in the last few days. These were really significant things, so I just listened to her with love, and this is what she needed. I knew her pain was just an expression of open intelligence, and although I didn't say much, my ability to remain at ease with her story helped her to see her situation in a new light.

Prior to my shift in perception I would have been very affected by having to deal with someone who had a lot of complaints. I would have thought, "Why do I have to listen to this?" My mood depended on outer circumstances and what other people were doing and saying, so it was constantly fluctuating. I would get up in the morning and think, "Oh no, not another day!" because I felt so victimized by my many moods and emotions. We've learned to give meaning to our moods, and this gives them more power. We'll say, "I'm in a mood today—watch out!" Or, if we've had enough of treating people badly, we might say, "Even though I feel awful, I'm going to act compassionately," but that's just adding an extra level of contrivance.

Twenty-seven years ago I had a profound experience that led me to see that everything is completely equal and that there's no need to describe things in a particular way. Whatever is, *is*. It's all made of the same intelligent ground or condition. I saw that I didn't need to be ruled by moods. There's so much freedom and relief in that realization! Moods mean absolutely nothing; they're just like weather patterns that come through, and they have absolutely no effect whatsoever on our innate well-being.

It's much easier to just rely on open intelligence and let everything be *as it is*. No matter what appears, it's like a mirage. Like a line drawn in water, it is its own undoing and will vanish naturally. There isn't a single thing that needs to be done about anything that appears. We don't need anything to make the clouds go away; they disappear in and of themselves. They come from space, they are space during their duration, and they disappear into space. The space remains unaffected, and that's what we really are: aware pure space. The coming, staying and going are all space as well.

So, what can we say? There's nothing going on. There's nothing to react to. When we just let go in evenness, then life becomes a lot easier, and we don't need so much for anything to change. In letting everything be *as it is*, we open up to the space of profound insight and the ability to act skillfully. If we don't let everything be *as it is* by the power of relying on open intelligence, then we'll never be in touch with this level of insight and skill.

If we're in a contentious relationship with a partner, we can be like little video game warriors doing battle with each other based on our conflicting data. Every conversation is a new battleground! But if one person in the relationship starts relying on open intelligence, then that person will know decisively that they don't need to get entangled or upset in their own data or the data of the other person. They no longer feel the need to defend or attack. Words that once seemed like bullets and bombs are now seen as harmless clouds passing overhead. Someone who is relying on open intelligence can remain in equanimity no matter what's being said and can skillfully relate to the other person in the most compassionate and loving way possible. I'm not just talking about being nice. Compassion isn't necessarily nice, but it always has the result of love and benefit.

When I use the word "love" here, I'm not talking about love that depends on the mood of love. That isn't real love—it's what I would call ordinary love. If you need to have other people act a certain way in order for you to feel love for them, that's ordinary love. If you feel you need to get love from somebody else, that's ordinary love. I'm not talking about an ordinary kind of emotion. Real love, or perfect love, which is what I'm talking about, is equal to unwavering open intelligence. I'm talking about empowering the love that is the essence of everything. The basic space of everything that appears is immutable love, and whatever is appearing is its dynamic display.

But we won't know that if we continue to describe everything with labels like "good" and "bad." The only way we can know the omnipresence of perfect love is to allow all the descriptions to appear and disappear as they will. By knowing all of them to be equal they're all transmuted into love and wisdom. It's like the process of refining gold. We heat the unrefined gold, and the dross melts away and only pure gold remains. If we were to continue the refining process until even the gold melted away, then there would be nothing but pure space, and that space is equal to love. The decisive experience of the love at the basis of every appearance is true well-being.

Q: There has never been a person, circumstance, spiritual practice or anything else that has ever truly given me well-being, and I despair of ever reaching the ideal you're speaking about. Why should I think that what you are offering here will be any different from what I've tried before?

A: From the beginning of our lives we look everywhere for well-being. We begin by looking for it in the home we were born into, but most of our homes and caregivers were not really able to provide well-being that we could count on. Pretty soon we began to look to things, such as toys and to all those make-believe worlds that we build in our imagination. But we can't really find complete well-being there either, so we continue seeking. As we get older we look for it in involvements outside the family: school, friendships, relationships, higher education, the workplace, institutions, romance, food or wherever it may be, but well-being somehow always escapes our grasp when we look for it outside ourselves. We're determined to find it, but most people have no idea how. Many people try various spiritual paths and practices, but for the most part they come up empty there too. Many go on looking for it until they eventually become too old and bitter to continue looking.

On a daily basis we are faced with all kinds of suffering, both in our personal lives and in the world around us. Suffering is everywhere and is now more obvious and undeniable than ever, because we have instant forms of communication for blaring out the news about the incredible suffering all around the globe. Nonetheless, it *is* possible to discover real well-being. The way to that well-being is to easefully rely on open intelligence for short moments, repeated many times, until it becomes continuous. That's all that's needed.

This is what makes the Balanced View Training distinctive. While most paths involve an attempt to purify or rearrange the contents of the mind in the hope of reaching a distant goal, Balanced View teaches that you are already whole and all that's needed is to identify with stable open intelligence rather than ordinary thinking. When open intelligence becomes obvious, a well-being is discovered that is beyond anything you could have previously imagined.

All of us have this precious opportunity in human life to enjoy the stability of open intelligence, but most of us don't even know that it's possible. Open intelligence is the basis of all perceptions, and in that basis there is absolute safety, absolute love and total well-being. It is our true nature.

More and more we see that not only are our personal data included within open intelligence, but *all* data are included. There is nothing to be rejected or excluded. It's only through seeing how much our attachment to certain data has caused our own suffering that we are motivated to maintain open intelligence; otherwise, we really can't. We've all been taught that clinging to data will give us strength and happiness, but the truth is it only makes us weak and miserable. Only when we see this clearly can we be free of clinging to ordinary thinking and take real delight in stable open intelligence.

When we understand how clinging to our own data has created the suffering in our lives, then we can immediately see that this is also true for everyone else. We see, wow, everyone else is just like me! Not only does this lead to natural care, concern and compassion for everyone, it enables us to really help others—perhaps for the first time—and to cheer up! We see that human suffering all comes from the same root: attachment to data.

Our true identity is found in naturally stable open intelligence and is found in gaining confidence in open intelligence as the basis of all perceptions. Open intelligence doesn't have any conditions at all, and it doesn't depend on your happiness or sadness or on whether or not you are seeking. In fact, in open intelligence, happiness and sadness are equal. To know this is to find the true caring that embraces all.

If that isn't your own experience, it can be, and if you rely on open intelligence for short moments, repeated many times, until it becomes continuous, it will be. At one time in my life I was torn apart by the same things you've been describing, because I'd just never learned anything different. I did not know how to attain stability in the complete relief I instinctively knew existed. Most of us have never had anyone say, "You don't have to suffer in this way." Once we begin to grow confident in open intelligence, we'll naturally know how to love ourselves and others. We begin by relying on open intelligence; that's the only way we can truly love ourselves. That's it; just relax. The efficacy of this simple instruction is profound beyond measure.

Only in this way can we really come to understand everything about ourselves and the world. When we rely on open intelligence, then we understand the true nature of ourselves and the world. We know what well-being is and where it's found, and we know what's real and permanent and what's temporary and fleeting. We also know all about our body and how to take care of it, and how to take care of our emotions too. We know about our thinking and about everybody else's thinking and emotions, too. When we get familiar with ourselves as open intelligence, then we see clearly. We're able for the first time to really be with people in a natural way that's based entirely on true caring and concern.

There's never any reason for anything other than care and concern to appear, because in the final analysis love is all there is. Everything is saturated with the essence of well-being, and when we empower that well-being, it flows through all of our actions. Care and concern in action always bring forth more care and concern. In this way, our own well-being can spread around the world, and reach everyone. We can be an example to others of the power of open intelligence.

THE PERSONAL IDENTITY
CHAPTER FOURTEEN

"We have a very easy choice. It's the choice of continuing to describe and perpetuate stories based on an inaccurate perception of our identity or getting to know the open intelligence that's the sole source and basis of all these descriptions."

Nature's open intelligence never takes form in a permanent way. It remains pure space, no matter what appearances may come and go within it. The limitless expanse of open intelligence is the only "you" that has ever really existed, so know it to be yourself. No individual intelligence has ever existed. The personal identity is just a datum within the all-encompassing pure view of open intelligence. It takes itself to be something that is born, that goes through a life of waking, dreaming and sleeping, and then dies. But the limitless intelligence that is your true identity remains unaffected by any of that.

Once the personal identity has been taken to exist, all subsequent data that appear will then relate back to that personal identity, rather than to their authentic source—all-encompassing open intelligence When we take ourselves to be an individual with a self-generated existence due to biological factors, we separate ourselves out from the single nondual expanse of nature. We think, "I exist as a separate entity, I'm substantial in and of myself, and everyone else is substantial too."

Each datum we cling to substantializes our personal identity further. Most of us take our personal identity to be the conglomeration of all our past data. Unfortunately, those personal histories can end up being the stories of endless conflict. We're automatically in conflict within ourselves and with others, because we are constantly involved in the grind of proving ourselves to be independently existent. We substantialize ourselves with data that we relate back to our personal identity, and then we compete with others and try to affirm our specialness and superiority. Separation is constantly being asserted, because we're fixed on an identity that's built on separation and split apart from the identity of others.

However, no one is anything other than a phenomenal manifestation of open intelligence itself. Infants don't have a sense of "I," no matter what the conventional beliefs may be. At birth we have no sense of being anybody in particular, and we have no sense of anyone else being an independent entity either. Our way of seeing is completely wide-open. It takes years to develop a strong sense of "I." Have you noticed how young children will first refer to themselves by their name rather than saying "I"? I noticed this with my own children and grandchildren. My grandson Jack was two or three years old before he ever used the word "I." He heard people referring to him as "Jack," so he would say, "Jack wants a piece of candy." He wouldn't say, "*I* want a piece of candy." Only later as he learned the "I am the body" idea would he use the word "I."

If we hear over and over again from the time we're little that we are somebody, then that's simply what we get used to, and we come to believe it. After years and years of being told that we are a person, we conclude, "Yes, I have an individual identity; this body and mind is who I am." We learn object-oriented seeing through repetition of seeing things as separate objects and then defining and labeling them. This further substantializes our personal identity, making it the subject of all those objects, and reinforcing our idea of all things as separate. This way of seeing comes about gradually rather than all at once. But just because we're told something over and over again doesn't make it true! It's just like someone saying, "The Earth is flat," over and over again. People believed it for centuries, but that never made the Earth flat.

The substantialization of a personal identity occurs thought-by-thought. This fixed personal identity is just made up—it's a complete fiction! The ultimate definition of the individual identity, like every description, is nature's intelligent ground. To get caught up in descriptions and what they mean is just endless folly.

Our real identity is open intelligence, as it is the fundamental nature of all our perceptions and cannot be destroyed or affected in any way. This is very important to understand. Open intelligence is not generated by a human being. A human being is dependent on open intelligence for his or her own intelligence and has no independent nature that is separate or apart from this nature. By the power of open intelligence, it becomes more and more obvious that it is the only basis of the personal identity and that open intelligence alone is what we need to identify with, rather than ordinary thinking that tries to prove the independent existence of the phenomenal world.

If we truly recognize that the personal identity is insubstantial and does not have an existence of its own, then it's much easier for us to identify with open intelligence and not hold on to the illusion of a personal identity. When, thought-by-thought, we make the most important choice to maintain open intelligence, rather than identifying with descriptions of a fragmented world of subjects and objects, then the reality of our true nature becomes obvious.

When we're living our life based on our data, all we will see are those data. We'll see ourselves as being the manager and controller of our identity, and we'll think it's up to us to defend and take care of it. The activities of our life are then all focused on defending and building up that identity, and this is a very exhausting and frustrating way to live. We're always trying to protect and guard ourselves against any kind of intrusion from anyone or anything and ceaselessly attempting to change the nature of what appears in our mind. We feel we need to substantialize ourselves and then compete with others to show that our independent nature is better than theirs.

Once we are convinced that we have a personal identity, we'll have all sorts of fearful consequences associated with trying to protect and enhance it. We get lost in a lifestyle of hope and fear: hoping that certain things will happen and fearing that they won't, and fearing that other things will happen and hoping that they won't.

If we've included the idea of a spiritual or religious path as part of our personal identity and are trying to purify ourselves to be a better person, then it's likely we'll be spending a lot of time doing that. Trying to get rid of an ego or other fictionalized identity is a lot of work—just like trying to flatten the Earth would be a lot of work! In fact, it's impossible to get rid of the ego or personality, because it has no independent nature and cannot be found to exist as any kind of changeable thing! In order to realize our nature, we will have to come to the conclusion that we've never had an ego. Once we can do so we will say, "Where is that individual I was working so hard to improve? I can't seem to locate the ego that I thought was at the control panel. There's nothing here but open intelligence!"

If we try to do something to perfect ourselves or try to get rid of the ego, then we'll always fall short of our goal, for there's no way to get rid of something that isn't there. You can't get inside the mind and erase an ego that you think is there; the attempt to do so will give the fiction of an ego more power. As there has never been a personal identity that can be altered, all this involvement with fixing, improving or eliminating it only leads to more belief in a personal identity! So, if we're examining our thoughts, emotions and experiences and are trying to make them better, then all that involvement serves only to reinforce the conviction that we have a personal identity—and the fact is, we don't.

Our only true nature is infinite and unborn and belongs to open intelligence itself. It is completely free of notions of causality, time and space. By the power of open intelligence we identify with the stable, underlying essence of all the biographical data that we have assumed ourselves to be. By the power of relying on open intelligence, we will increasingly experience our essential nature. The seemingly solid personal identity gradually begins to be less substantial. For short moments repeated many times, we simply acknowledge our essential nature, and as we do so that essential nature becomes more and more obvious.

We have a very easy choice. It's the choice of continuing to describe and perpetuate stories based on an inaccurate perception of our identity or getting to know the open intelligence that is the sole source and basis of all these descriptions. By the power of open intelligence everything is allowed to be *as it is*. We will come to understand the true nature of existence. The clear light of wisdom begins to dawn in us, and we can start to laugh for having taken ourselves so seriously! If you think you are your mind, just relax. In that complete relaxation is revealed the naturally present open intelligence that is the mind's basic space.

If you remain convinced that you have a personal identity, it might be helpful to look into where that identity might be found. Scientists have considered the question of where the sense of "I" might be located, but no one has ever come up with a definitive conclusion. Is it located in the brain? No, we can't really say it's in the brain. Is it located in the heart or in any of the other parts of the body? No, we can't definitively find it in any of those places either. If we look into the cellular level of the body, or if we look through an electron microscope at the particles that make up our body, would we find the "I" there? If we brought in your parents and showed them those particles, would they say, "Oh, look, there's our little girl!"? No. They would only see infinitely tiny subatomic particles moving at incredible speeds, emerging from space and then receding back into space.

Ultimately then, our personal identity is comprised only of space, and our "I" emerges from aware pure space. Everything, no matter what it is, is comprised of this aware space, which is equal to the timeless intelligence that is the ultimate nature of everything.

When we look into ourselves in this way, it leads to the joy of certainty that there has never been anyone here who is separate from open intelligence. This understanding debunks the whole idea of an individual subject who is separate from the whole. Soon we begin to see that there is nothing but an indivisible expanse of open intelligence itself, revealing itself moment by moment in a continuous flow of whatever appears. Everything is a natural expression of nature, spontaneously appearing as its vast, amazing display. Open intelligence is the basis of the ability to know and comprehend all appearances. We gradually gain confidence that open intelligence is our own basic nature.

Q: *I feel that I'm really caught up in judging myself and others all the time. For instance, when people walk into the hall, immediately my mind will go into overdrive with all these judgments about them. I see that this is a very negative trait, and I really want to give it up, but the habit is so ingrained. Can you help me with this?*

A: When we see people, we tend to identify them by their characteristics: black skin, white skin, blue eyes, brown eyes, attractive or unattractive, and we get all caught up in these descriptions about everything. We then make those descriptions into reasons to see everyone as separate from us. "This one is nice, that one is not nice, and these people I'm not even going to acknowledge, because they're everything I don't like!"

We strengthen our identity when we engage in subtle competition with everyone else. We want to prove that we're somehow better, or we end up envying others for the ways they seem to be superior. Through this process we develop disharmony and disunity within ourselves, and then naturally we develop disharmony and disunity with others.

Let's say a woman walks into the room, and you start to have thoughts about her. "Oh look, she has her hair in a ponytail. That's not very flattering, is it? I wonder where she got *those* clothes. And she doesn't have very nice skin, either!" Or, "She's so much prettier than I am. I'm so jealous!" The more identified we are with our personal identity, the more thoughts like this will arise. This is all part of the process by which we've created a false identity out of our data: our gender, name, hairdo, the clothes we wear, our age or whatever it might be. We've come to believe that these things define who we are. If we haven't recognized open intelligence as the basis for all those perceptions about ourselves, we'll begin to substantialize ourselves in this way. Then we automatically do the same thing with others. We judge and label whoever we see, and try to substantialize them by describing them and setting them up as either opposed to us or aligned with us. By this process we further affirm and solidify what we believe is our own independent nature.

However, none of us was born with a lot of opinions about ourselves and others. We weren't born knowing our name, gender identity, skin color or nationality. We were born as we are: a phenomenal expression of open intelligence, with innate wisdom that never needs to hold to any description. We are all born and live with instinctive knowledge of our identity. Fixed ideas about what we take ourselves and others to be in terms of gender, age, outward appearance, politics, philosophies and so on are completely unnecessary to our well-being and ability to skillfully function as a human. Indeed, the freer our perception is, the better.

As we relax more and more in our true nature, which is the pure open intelligence at the root of all our knowledge about everything, we look out at the world and we don't even know how it happened, but everybody and everything starts looking a lot better! All these ideas we had about how solid and stable our personal identity is and how solid and stable other people's identities are start to fade. Our need to show our abilities and compete with everyone else just naturally slips away, without doing anything but relying on open intelligence for short moments until it becomes continuous.

When we identify with open intelligence, we become caring, concerned and compassionate in an uncontrived way, and this compassion naturally spills over on to everyone. More and more we see everyone through the eyes of wisdom. Wisdom is our natural way of seeing. It is open intelligence that is seeing, so the more we rely on open intelligence, the more we see as open intelligence, and that pure seeing is synonymous with love, wisdom and energy. More and more we find that we are cheering up!

As we begin to rely on the stability of open intelligence more and more, our ordinary way of thinking about things gradually shifts. Instead of all the obsessive thinking about "me," "my stuff," and "how am I going to live," it all loosens up. We still love those who are close to us, but we don't desperately need our sympathetic attachments to people in order to identify ourselves or to be happy. Our thinking and emotions become involved in a very natural way in what will be of benefit to all. Rather than just thinking about ourselves and what will benefit us, through the ultimate self-benefit of identifying with open intelligence we automatically want to be of benefit to others.

We see how suffering is caused by clinging to a personal identity and taking it to be real. When we realize that we have fooled ourselves in this way, we feel such a deep connection with everyone and so much compassion and true caring. When people are lost in themselves they don't usually think about the suffering of others, because they're too busy with their own issues. But when we have understood the single root of the suffering we all share, then we can't help but respond to all the things that have caused suffering in the world.

The greatest power that any human being can have lies in the wisdom of complete open intelligence. When we find ourselves thinking with compassion about the well-being of everyone, well, that is just a very wonderful way to be. It's a very beautiful development! This isn't a compassion that can be cultivated or gained; it's already contained within open intelligence. Nothing special is needed; it is already accomplished. All we need do is gain confidence in open intelligence by relying on open intelligence repeatedly for short moments many times until it becomes spontaneous. This one simple change is the solution in all problems.

If we try to contrive special circumstances in order to familiarize ourselves with open intelligence, then we won't realize that our present situation, whatever it is, is the constant spontaneous flow of open intelligence.

Q: I find it very difficult to believe that we shouldn't try to improve the faults we find in ourselves. I feel that people need to put forth effort to improve; otherwise, they'll never become any better.

A: If we take ourselves to be a personal identity, and the desire arises to find out about the true nature of our being, very often our starting point is the assumption that there's something wrong with our personal identity. "I need to improve my flawed personality and purify my mind." But as open intelligence is flawless from the beginningless beginning, there is nothing within open intelligence that has ever been flawed. To try to analyze and transform a personal identity that doesn't exist only perpetuates the idea of a personal identity.

When we repeatedly return to open intelligence, wisdom naturally dawns within, and it requires no contrived activity, conduct, thinking or emoting. Wisdom is inseparable from the basic space of open intelligence that pervades everything. Everything you're trying to change is an appearance of that wisdom! Only in realizing this to be the case are faults exhausted and qualities perfected in timeless wisdom. The perfection of qualities cannot be contrived. Our own wisdom is innate and already accomplished; we don't need to do anything to get it—it already is! By the power of open intelligence, the clear light of wisdom becomes more and more obvious. We can count on this without fail!

It doesn't matter what kind of life you've lived. You can be the worst person on Earth and have done horrible things, or you can be the greatest person who's ever lived—or somewhere in between—it really doesn't matter. You don't have to be smart or educated or spiritual or anything at all. Open intelligence is naturally present in everyone. It is that by which we know we exist. We wouldn't know of our own existence or of the existence of the world without it. It's the root of all knowledge. By sustaining open intelligence for short moments until it becomes continuous, you realize that the perfection of qualities is inherent in wisdom and not in contrived actions to try to change thoughts, emotions, conduct and experiences. The exhaustion of faults and perfection of qualities is automatic in increasing identification with open intelligence.

Most of us have never heard anything other than that we must rely on our personal identity, and for want of better information we've believed it. We might have received an introduction to the possibility of something beyond the personal identity, but very rarely are we in a circumstance where the key points and pivotal instructions are present that can unerringly direct us to the complete certainty of open intelligence.

Q: Being put down by other people is quite difficult for me, but in my office there's a lot of backbiting, gossip and criticism by the people I work with. I don't want to change my job, but I find the environment there intolerable at times.

A: Many of us have a belief system that holds that no one should put us down and that our self-esteem will be wounded if someone does so. We're convinced that we'll be affected negatively if someone puts us down, so we aren't going to allow anyone to do that. We want to maintain our self-esteem and sense of importance, and we feel threatened by criticism.

But let's say one day it happens: somebody puts us down, and we get all fired up about it. It's like we had put out a big sign that said: "No Trespassing! No Putting Down Allowed!" But behold, we find a trespasser has ignored the sign and insulted us! We may hear that someone has said something really negative about us behind our back, and not only that, what he said wasn't true! All of a sudden we're enraged. "How dare he? I'm going to call him up and let him know what's going on, and then I'm never going to speak to him again!" Maybe we'll even think about punching him or hurting him in some other way. No matter what we end up doing, we'll be completely distracted, because we're following after each angry thought. This kind of ordinary thinking presents alternatives for action based on pride and self-importance, and the actions come from a very limited way of looking at things. And if we follow through on any of our plans, the result will be easily predictable: we'll have a small war on our hands!

Of course, there may be times when we need to speak to someone about what he or she has done, but if we rely on the power of open intelligence rather than jumping up to defend ourselves, we may start to see that there are other ways of viewing the situation. Many options become obvious other than feeling hurt and then retaliating. This is very important, because only in this way can we see that thoughts and emotions need not have power over us. Only then do we begin to have a broader vantage, and the only way we can possibly have this balanced view is through the decisive experience of open intelligence as the basis of every one of those thoughts and emotions. They are the vivid appearances of open intelligence and nothing more. If we give them a substantial existence in their own right, we can't possibly have the wide-open and spacious vantage that's necessary for true problem solving.

Instead of going into this spiral of hurt feelings and vengeful responses, we can simply rely on open intelligence and enjoy the complete equalness of everything, without any need to hold on to the descriptions flashing through our minds. What can the descriptions give us? They give nothing but pain and agony. What does open intelligence give us? Complete relief and the ability to act skillfully.

So, the choice is very simple!

By the power of open intelligence, we'll soon find that we're much more interested in the peace and wisdom of open intelligence than we are in defending ourselves from put-downs. We'll come to see that our true identity needs no defending and cannot be hurt by anything. Instead of perceiving the person's action as an attack, perhaps we'll be able to see it as a harmless appearance within open intelligence, and respond with skillful wisdom instead of retaliating. We may even find gratitude in our heart for the person's action, which has been an invitation to sustain open intelligence and a precious reminder to not identify with our ordinary thinking.

For you it may be difficult to deal with being put down, for another person it may be dealing with jealousy, for someone else it may be facing anger, desire, pride or fear. But whatever it is, just rely on open intelligence without wavering, and allow primordial wisdom to flower. When we rely on open intelligence in the direct encounter with any of these perceptions, incredible wisdom blossoms on its own. In this self-liberation from pride, jealousy, anger, desire and fear, wisdom-intelligence reigns—and in that pure mirror we can finally see our true face.

THE MIND IS GIFTED
CHAPTER FIFTEEN

> *"One term we could apply to the ability to access the full capacity of the mind is "giftedness." However, it is my feeling that giftedness is something that is inherent in every mind, rather than being a quality limited to certain individuals and determined solely by genetic or environmental factors."*

At some point we've all probably read an article on science or psychology that claimed that people generally use only ten percent of the capacity of their brains. It may be ten percent or one percent, we can't say for sure, because a percentage of an unknown quantity can't be determined. Regardless of the percentage, studies on this question have all similarly shown that the brain is underutilized.

One possible explanation for the brain's underutilized capacity is that we've simply been clinging to the small percentage of the mind that we're familiar with, unaware of our innate ability to explore the vast potential within ourselves. Maintaining open intelligence for short moments repeated many times is the means whereby a person can access the capacity of the brain that has gone unused. When a person chooses to sustain open intelligence in an uncontrived way, they are actually choosing to access the unused capacity of their brain.

The truth is that we are accustomed to using our minds in a certain way, which for many of us might be a very repetitive and limiting way. We think that this is the only way to use our mind, but when we familiarize ourselves with open intelligence as the basis of the mind's ability to perceive—that aspect of our mind which has no outside or inside, no dimension and no characteristics which can be found to exist in their own right—

we then discover a whole new capacity of the mind. Once we know this is possible, we can make a conscious choice. Do we choose to be limited by a mind ruled by habitual thought patterns, or do we choose to gain confidence in open intelligence and thereby discover what has hitherto gone undiscovered?

To facilitate this discovery, we should ask ourselves: "Where do the appearances within my mind come from, where are they now and where do they go?"

The truth is that all phases of the appearance of thoughts—the appearing, the staying and the going—occur only within open intelligence. However, in stable open intelligence itself, which is what the mind *is* in its ultimate sense, there is never any transition or change. The more deeply we examine our minds, the more we will see that just as mist arises in the sky and dissolves back into the sky, appearances arise in the mind and vanish back into it. The perceptions are the dynamic capacity of open intelligence—that and nothing more. Whatever appears within the mind is a form of open intelligence; the forms come and go, inseparable from open intelligence, but open intelligence itself remains unchanged. Mind and open intelligence are completely synonymous.

One term we could apply to the ability to access the full capacity of the mind is "giftedness." However, it is my feeling that giftedness is something that is inherent in every mind, rather than being a quality limited to certain individuals and determined solely by genetic or environmental factors. I was convinced from early in life that we all have incredible capacities, and if we could find a way to tap into those capacities, then they would become more and more obvious in us—and I was sure this was true of everyone. I grew up as a gifted child, but I never saw myself as different from anyone else, only as someone who had access to a capacity that everyone else also had as well. The only difference was that some people didn't know they had it.

Why is it that some people seem lethargic and unhappy, while others are so filled with vitality and brilliance? It is because the people who are exhibiting power and exceptional qualities like compassion are fully alive and have tapped into the essence of open intelligence. It doesn't have only to do with being unique or special or gifted; it has to do with the ability to access the true nature of the mind.

This wider range is actually the province of everyone. Even though we typically look at things in terms of differences—saying that this person is intelligent and that one is less so—in fact it is more of a matter of one person being better able to access what is available to all.

One thing I've noticed among people who are gaining familiarity with open intelligence is that they develop an extraordinary speed in processing information and that they're able to have a rapid and thorough comprehension of an idea or concept. There is a dramatic increase in the ability to perceive essential elements and underlying structures and patterns in relationship to ideas. Such people find that they have an increased ability to see models and systems that previously weren't perceived.

There is also an increased ability to perceive many sides of an issue, in other words, to have a balanced view. When only using a limited capacity of the mind, there might be the tendency to take one-sided positions. By the power of open intelligence the ability is developed to let go of fixed reference points and to look at an issue from all angles. One no longer gets so emotionally inflamed because of the need to substantialize oneself through identification with certain rigid opinions.

As people become more familiar with open intelligence, an attentiveness to detail develops that didn't exist before. As their practice deepens, even people who have considered themselves scattered and unable to focus on anything will naturally develop this attentiveness. It is not as though they are trying to be more organized or have brought in an organizational coach—the skill just comes about naturally. There is greater and greater awareness of detail and the ability to master one's internal and external environments.

Other characteristics that I see are the development of an unusual capacity for memory as well as a long concentration span, an increased interest in ideas and words, coupled with a more extensive vocabulary.

There is an increased precision in thinking and expression, as well as an ability to relate to a broad range of ideas and synthesize commonalities among them. One develops a greater ability to think abstractly, to deal skillfully with complex issues and to find myriad possible meanings in even the most apparently ordinary issues or problems.

One also demonstrates a higher degree of emotional sensitivity. This stems from a real caring for the feelings of others that comes when people no longer need to protect and guard themselves from other people and from the world. Instead of being so guarded and focused on attachments to oneself and one's immediate family, those attachments are loosened up and released to include everyone—the whole world and all beings in it. These are really beautiful intrinsic aspects of the mind.

When there is complete confidence in open intelligence, unusual intensity and depth of feeling come about. The intensity and depth of feeling that have been kept at bay come up in full force, and in that is great physical, mental and emotional energy. When we move beyond the limited scope of the mind into the infinite expanse of open intelligence, then tremendous energy is released. All of the capabilities I have described are the byproducts that come along with this release of energy. Extraordinary energy and zest for living are coupled with an irrepressible desire to contribute and be of benefit, not just on a small scale, but on a broad scale.

Lastly, in terms of morals and ethics, morality and ethical behavior are ingrained and inherent in open intelligence and are much more profound than when they are contrived. Through gaining familiarity with open intelligence, those qualities are discovered to be our own essential nature. People might have previously needed to have someone tell them what to do and what not to do and felt that they had no self-authority in questions of morality. However, through open intelligence people become more autonomous and self-reliant in terms of making decisive ethical decisions. They have profound insight into social and moral issues in a way that they didn't before.

These are all things usually thought to be characteristics of extremely bright people who are at the upper echelons of the IQ scale. But we find that people who become familiar with open intelligence have an ability to learn in an integrated, intuitive and nonlinear manner that helps facilitate these abilities. When we see these characteristics beginning to appear in numerous people through the simple practice of gaining confidence in open intelligence, the implication is that high IQ is simply the ability to access the unused capacity of the mind.

The next great frontier of human endeavor will be in the discovery of the full and complete capacity of the mind. Pioneers of the mind will come to the fore in the next ten years who aren't even known now, and due to their work the greater advances that will be made in science and other technologies in the coming decades will occur via this new frontier of the mind. The means to discover this new frontier will become the most valued knowledge on the planet. Whether it's in relation to business or to everyday life, it will become something that everyone wants. When people find out what the capacity of the mind is, that will be what they want and they will be willing to go to any lengths to know more about it and experience it themselves.

This is a very important time in history, and it's essential to know that we're on the brink of a new frontier and that there are people who are or will become expert guides into the new territory. We desperately need people with wise and helpful minds to be at the forefront of all fields, and we need people who know that the purpose of the mind is to benefit themselves and others. These are the people who need to be in the forefront of human life and who should be trusted as our leaders, and more and more they will be. They are going to radically influence human culture and the evolution of humankind, for the simple reason that they will know the connection between the part of the mind that is used habitually and the part that isn't usually used at all.

This application of the wise and helpful mind will be especially important in terms of guiding the future direction of scientific research. The current scientific model sees nature as a kind of encoded intelligence that is being decoded by human beings, and that now we are recoding that intelligence to some degree in order to cure disease or improve life in general. Of course, this is an interesting pursuit; however, the decoding, encoding and recoding implied in this belief system is only being done with a fraction of the brain's capacity and within a limited context of the nature of existence. Although there have been many incredible advances in science, many of these advances are not occurring in harmony with the greater capacity of the mind, and they do not necessarily provide the greatest benefit to the planet and its inhabitants.

We are now at a similar point in the understanding of the mind and its capacities as we were about two decades ago with the understanding of computer interfaces. In 1990 there was almost no easily accessible interface between computers and human beings, so computer technology was really at a primitive level compared to what we have now. In the meantime of course, we've seen incredible advances in this area. Similarly, in the near future we will experience great leaps in the understanding of the tremendous capacities of the human mind and the interface between its used and unused capacities.

To get to the root of these capacities, we have to ask ourselves what the most important function of the mind is. I have looked up the words "mind" and "brain" in different dictionaries, encyclopedias and literature on neuroscience and found many very erudite definitions there; however, I couldn't find anything in these sources that pointed to a definition of the mind as something which would contribute to greater human happiness or the immediate benefit of the planet. I thought to myself, "How are all of these scientific definitions of the mind and brain useful in terms of filling the world with wise and compassionate people who use the full capacity of their mind?"

We as human beings need to maintain sovereignty and self-authority over our minds and should not blindly turn over the definitions of what the mind is to those who specialize in only a partial understanding of it. We need to go beyond tired definitions and discover for ourselves, in a new way, the true nature and the real purpose of our own mind. More and more we are seeing people who are expressing that self-authority, who are going beyond what is ordinarily thought to be possible, and who are tapping into an extraordinarily beneficial nature that exists inherently within every human being. For people whose purpose in life is inherent human goodness that is wise and helpful, the question becomes: "Who am I really? What is my role on Earth, and what am I meant to be doing? How can I be of benefit to myself and others? What is my real potential?" These are crucial questions that human beings need to ask.

It really doesn't matter what kind of philosophical theories we have; it all boils down to what is going to make people happy, fulfilled, and beneficial, and what won't. What will show us the innate dignity and confidence that are expressions of open intelligence? The world is seeing some very important advances that will enhance humankind's ability to innovate and progress technologically and scientifically. Yet, it is even more crucial to apply these advances in ways that allow the Earth to be taken care of properly and in ways that move people towards being happier, wiser and more caring. Not only does everyone want this in their heart of hearts, but this is within our actual capacity as a species.

We need to be willing as individuals and as a species to go beyond what we know about ourselves and find out what we don't yet know. We really have to have the humility and the courage to do that. That means leaving behind all conventional frameworks that we might have had about our mind and body, and gaining confidence in what has until now been unknown. When we rely on open intelligence, we approach everything in a relaxed way, and then we don't need to be so wrapped up in conventionality or our usual ways of doing things. We can just let things be as they are, and that stance immediately broadens our outlook. We discover the balanced view that is already present. To the degree that we are committed to the goal, to that degree, we will be able to use our minds to achieve it.

Q: I was interested to hear you say that you were a gifted child, as I had also been given that label at a young age, and I've always been interested to know what gifted means exactly. Did you notice anything in your development as a gifted child that might have been a factor in your later life or which might have influenced your outlook and teachings?

A: Yes, I did indeed. I can speak to one particular incident that really had a formative affect on me. When I was a young girl I was exposed to the thinking of Albert Einstein, and I read a quote from him that really stuck in my mind: "The thinking that created a problem can't solve the problem." I was completely intrigued by that statement, because I could see that a lot of problems—whether they were personal problems or the problems of the world—came about due to people's habitual thought patterns. This idea that there could be a different way of thinking that could solve problems became very interesting to me.

Sometime later on I was given a homework assignment that entailed writing about how it was that everything in the world was in motion. The answer that the teacher expected was that the Earth is rotating on its axis and that its movement sets everything else into motion, but that wasn't the answer that I had. I wrote in my assignment that everything was moving because all the molecules and subatomic particles are moving, and that they are moving within space. In the process of writing my assignment I had another insight that really stopped me in my tracks. I recognized that the particles that are in such constant motion are never anything other than limitless, intelligent space and that they are comprised of space. I could see that somehow it was impossible for anything to ever come to an end, just as it was impossible for anything to ever begin.

I turned in my homework assignment, and I didn't know what to expect. In class the teacher started talking about the rotation of the Earth and how everything was moving due to that, and I thought, "Oh well, he has a different idea about things," but I was still totally convinced about the insight I had.

After the teacher read my paper, he mentioned to me that he really liked it, and that even though he had a different answer my insight was actually an excellent one. He told me I was very smart, and he had an interesting opinion about being smart. He felt that one of the great things about being intelligent is that a person could be of benefit to other people. He said that being intelligent did not have to be something that was only self-focused, but that using that gift in the proper way could be of great benefit to everyone. He also told me that by helping others I would also help myself. So, in one fell swoop he oriented my thinking towards wanting to be of service, and this was one of the most important things I learned in my early life.

My school eventually recommended that I be placed in a gifted program, and I went to another school where this program was offered. I began studying Latin, the Yale New Algebra and many other things that my peers didn't have access to. However, I felt very strongly that whatever this intelligence was that I and the other gifted children had, everyone else also had a similar intelligence, but somehow they hadn't yet tapped into it. I could see how one could tap into innate intelligence and see things in a different way by going beyond conventional thinking.

I could also see that this intelligence was naturally occurring and that it wasn't something that needed to be invented or discovered. If one could go beyond conventional thought, one would then be able to begin to see things in a more profound and balanced way. I was interested in how this natural intelligence could be of immediate benefit in one's personal life and also help solve big problems in the world. I really didn't know how to apply these intellectual insights to my personal life in other than very limited ways, but over time this focus on finding ways to be of immediate benefit became extremely important in my life and eventually became its focus.

However, it became clear to me that, although sometimes the way people tried to solve problems resulted in improvement, the overall thought processes being used were generally leading to quite painful or even catastrophic conditions. As I moved into my young adult years there were issues like the Vietnam War, political and corporate corruption and environmental degradation that were very much on people's minds, and I wanted to know how the desire to be of immediate benefit could be utilized so that things like that would be remedied and reversed. It seemed to me that even though there was some headway made in solving these big problems, there was never enough momentum generated to reverse the negative trends. In fact, the trend was that the environment became more degraded, and more and more conflicts popped up around the world.

In my late twenties and early thirties I reached a very critical point in my own thinking, because I saw that all the conventional knowledge that was available to me provided very little in terms of my immediate betterment and well-being, particularly in light of what I felt was possible for human beings. When I realized that I reached a crisis in my life, and I knew definitively that I needed something within myself that would be of greater support. I could tell that I needed to go beyond everything I knew at that time, even though I'd already had quite a few deep insights. I entered into a period of what could be called despair and bewilderment, because my intellectual, psychological and spiritual attempts at solving problems provided no real and lasting solutions.

It was when I was in this state of despair and bewilderment about my own lot in life and the lot of all of humankind that I suddenly realized that all of these mental processes had the same origin. I saw that their source condition was an intelligence or space that is entirely conscious and aware. I realized that all of the activities of the mind are in a certain sense entirely equal, because they had as their source this intelligence that is innately perfect and pure. Everything is a manifestation of that intelligence, and everything that appears within it has never been anything other than that intelligence. That insight brought an incredible sense of relief, because I was able to relax my mind into that aware intelligence and draw on the power of its balanced view.

It was clear to me that not only are my thoughts, emotions and experiences appearances of this intelligence, but also that all phenomena whatsoever are appearances of that intelligence. I could see, just like I did when I was a young girl, that this intelligence or space—even though it is experienced as an individual intelligence or space in a human being—isn't located only within one's body. It doesn't have any kind of perimeter, boundary or location to which it is limited. It simply *is*. I came to the insight that there is an aware intelligence that is unchanging, indestructible and all-pervasive.

I could see that any knowledge that I had was already naturally present within this intelligence, but that the intelligence would likely not be recognized in one's experience unless one allowed oneself to do so by relaxing the mind for short moments repeated many times. The primary characteristic of the open intelligence that pervades all is that it is of immediate benefit. The benefit is first recognized in realizing that open intelligence has complete mastery over all thoughts and emotions, including those that we experience as troublesome. By discovering conclusively that open intelligence is already a ground of complete benefit, it becomes possible for human beings to have complete psychological well-being, compassion and skillful qualities and activities that benefit all. This was the eventual fruition of the insight I had when I was a young girl.

Exhausting Faults and Perfecting Qualities

CHAPTER SIXTEEN

"When we simply acknowledge it, open intelligence becomes more and more obvious. Since the nature of our being is entirely free, it is completely uncontrived, so we don't have to do anything to be our natural and genuine being. We already are that genuine being, and in it the perfection of all qualities is ever present."

Conventional standards are such that behaviors are often labeled as either good or bad. Having accepted and adopted these values, we scrutinize our own behavior and compare it with this conventional standard. We then strive within ourselves to exhaust our faults and perfect our qualities. Though humankind has been going about this very effortful process for millennia, at this point it should be obvious that all of this striving hasn't worked. If it had, we'd not only have a much better sense about how to handle situations in our individual lives, collectively we'd have a much better understanding of how to deal with the grave problems that face us as a species.

There are four methods that are generally used in handling what are considered to be faults. The first method is to indulge the fault. Let's say an emotion like anger comes up, which is something that's traditionally been labeled a fault. With the indulgence method we just give in to the anger and act from that angered state. We feel angry, so we blow up and say or do angry things.

The second way of dealing with faults is to avoid them. In this case, we hope that through avoiding the thoughts, emotions and situations that tend to bring the anger to the surface, the anger will go away. In doing so, we may steer clear of our anger for a while and in some ways neutralize it, but its true nature is never seen or transformed, and it remains lingering in the background ready to spring forth at any moment.

The third way of handling afflictive states such as anger or fear is to try to replace what we think of as our negative impulses with something positive. For instance, we may attempt to replace negative thinking with positive thinking or negative emotions with positive emotions. We might replace criticizing and gossiping about other people with thinking and speaking well of them, or instead of being angry with people we might try doing charitable work to assist them.

The fourth way of handling afflictive emotions is to rely on open intelligence, seeing all *as* flawless open intelligence, until all is seen to *be* flawless open intelligence. This is the only approach of the four that actually works to exhaust faults and perfect qualities. As we rest when a fault arises, what was once seen as a fault is discovered to actually be nothing but a form of flawless, primordially pure open intelligence, and in that pure seeing the fault is transformed into a positive quality. When we're able to see faults as evanescent forms of pure open intelligence, we discover their inherent nature, and this is the only way that faults can be permanently exhausted. Only when we see a fault's underlying essence will we know its true nature. In the direct encounter with a fault or afflictive state as it appears, one maintains flawless open intelligence until all appearances are seen as flawless.

In that pure seeing, what was once perceived as threatening and harmful is now discovered to be inseparable from the primordial purity of all-encompassing open intelligence. The discovery is made that the faults themselves are actually pure, in that they are the natural appearances of the basic space of pure open intelligence. Whatever is perceived is in fact timeless open intelligence and has the qualities of timeless open intelligence. When a fault is perceived, that too is timeless open intelligence.

This is a major pivotal instruction: all mental and sensory appearances are free in their own place as open intelligence, even as they are directly encountered.

This is what it means to rely on open intelligence: to be at ease in a completely uncontrived way with whatever appears, maintaining flawless open intelligence for short moments, repeated many times until all appearances are seen to *be* flawless open intelligence. There is no division at all between open intelligence and its appearances; they are a single indivisible expanse. Rather than taking the appearance to be something in and of itself, we recognize and transform it by empowering ourselves in open intelligence. In this way, we realize everything to be of the nature of open intelligence. When afflictive states come up, it's absolutely essential to rely on the open intelligence that is the source of that afflictive state, without indulging it, avoiding it or trying to replace it with something else. The key is simply to continue relying on open intelligence.

When we live our lives in conventional ways, we won't really know what to do about our faults. We'll just keep trying to avoid them or replace them, and despite that we often find ourselves indulging them. We don't know any other way. We don't know that it's possible to relax our mind and not elaborate on thoughts and emotions or get caught up in impulsive action. Many people today are looking for an answer; they know that there's a better way to be. They know that as human beings we need to take essential steps to save the planet we live on, and many people now understand that the first step has to be taken within.

By resting the mind imperturbably and maintaining complete perceptual openness, we realize the natural state of open intelligence. In that, all qualities are perfected. The naked state of open intelligence brings about perfection of all qualities, not only in a philosophical sense, but in a very practical sense as well. As we go about our lives with relaxed ease, we know what to do and how to act, and we don't need to obsess about decisions and choices anymore. We find that the true nature of faults is unchanging and utterly stable and their domain is open intelligence's own naturally free manifestation. Whatever appears within open intelligence is by nature inherently pure. All faults are like this; all afflictive states are inherently pure. When seen clearly, all faults are found to be pristine open intelligence, and we rely on that open intelligence in the immediacy of perceptions.

We find that what once seemed to be a deficiency is seen more and more as an appearance of true wisdom—the sun of open intelligence shining as that fault. Data, including faults of whatever kind, are the dynamic energy of pure open intelligence, and are inseparable from open intelligence. There's no way to separate out the sunlight from the sky; similarly, faults cannot be separated from the basic space of open intelligence. When we take the faults to be something in and of themselves—as having an independent nature—then we feel preoccupied or even compulsively driven to either indulge them, avoid them or replace them. On the other hand, when we rely on open intelligence and see the faults as inseparable from open intelligence, then they are seen as the primordial purity that has always been their underlying essence.

When relying on open intelligence becomes predominant in our lives, all qualities are naturally perfected without anything needing to be done. All we've been attempting to do through indulging, avoiding and replacing is found in open intelligence. Open intelligence isn't something that can be cultivated or developed; it is inherently present within us and is naturally occurring without any effort. As we are only the dynamic energy of timeless open intelligence and nothing else, we are by nature primordially pure. Thus, if effort is made to perfect ourselves, then we are off course, because the truth is we are *already* perfect; what is perfectly pure needs no efforting. Understanding this is crucial to our own well-being and to our capacity to act in the world in an easeful, powerful, contented and beneficial manner.

As we empower ourselves in open intelligence, things fade without anything needing to be done about them. There is complete freedom in perceptual openness and immediate perception. This freedom is completely beyond time, beyond doing and effort, and beyond trying to achieve something. When we simply acknowledge it, open intelligence becomes more and more obvious. Since the nature of our being is entirely free, it is completely uncontrived, so we don't have to do anything to be our natural and genuine being. We already are that genuine being, and in it the perfection of all qualities is ever present.

What does all this mean exactly? It means that when we rely on open intelligence we find mental and emotional stability. The faults that we've associated with the activity of the mind are exhausted, and the qualities that are inherent in the basic space of our mind are enhanced. Instead of being obsessively preoccupied with self-centered fears, we're occupied with being of benefit to others and ourselves. It's not a matter of trying to be of benefit in order to prove that we're somebody. Rather, it's a natural desire to be of benefit that's inherent in the mind. It's not a need to feel better about ourselves, but rather the natural outpouring of a human life in compassionate service to all.

It's very simple: as long as the mind is all wrapped up in "I, me, and mine," we can know for certain that this is the conventional activity of the conceptual mind. When the mind is no longer wrapped up in the activity of "I, me, and mine," we can be sure that the activity of the mind is rooted in open intelligence.

Since whatever appears is actually just a form of open intelligence, resting as whatever appears *is* resting as open intelligence. When we rest as faults, we discover they are actually self-appearances of open intelligence and are therefore timelessly free and primordially pure. In this way they gradually cease to appear as faults and cease to create problems for us. When it comes right down to it, resting *as* faults or afflictive states is the path of true wisdom. The only way we can make the transition from the conventional way of using our body, speech and mind to the speech, mind, qualities and activities of wisdom is by relying on open intelligence. The qualities of wisdom do not show themselves anywhere other than in the instinctive recognition of open intelligence. They can't be learned, and they can't be perfected through avoiding, indulging or replacing faults.

It's absolutely crucial that we hold ourselves to account for maintaining open intelligence, no matter what is happening. Even though the habit of indulging, avoiding or replacing seems so ingrained, that habit is also a mirage-like appearance in open intelligence. There is no fault that can be perfected through indulgence, avoidance or replacement, and no fault that cannot be exhausted through relying on open intelligence. This is an essential key; there are no exceptions.

Q: I sometimes feel a desire to overindulge in things like food, specifically sweets, and I feel that I need to use some discipline to overcome this. How does discipline fit in with what you are saying here?

A: Well, a couple of things about that. Let's say the desire for sweets comes up. You can indulge the desire and rush in and eat all the sweets you want, or you can avoid the sweets somehow by going to a place where they're not available or you can replace the thought of getting the sweets for yourself with going to get someone else a sweet. Now, that's all fine; you can live that way all of your life, and in that way you can neutralize those troublesome data. But neutralizing the data does not fully resolve them in a satisfactory way. The question is, do you want to live your life neutralizing your conduct, or do you want to live your life as flawless wisdom?

If we choose to live a life of neutralizing our conduct, then we'll be paying attention to all the appearances, and we'll try to either accept or reject them in some way. Let's give another example: one day you want to eat your sweets and you start thinking it over. "Oh, that pie looks so good! I don't just want one piece; I want the whole pie! But I don't want anybody to see me eat the whole thing, so I'll eat one piece here and then take the remainder home and tell them that it's for someone else!"

So, then you eat the whole pie and it makes you feel sick; you have a sugar hangover, and you think about all the weight you've gained. Then you feel bad about yourself; you feel remorse for eating the whole pie, and out of that remorse you resolve to not do it again. You decide to be disciplined, but you doubt whether you'll be able to—and on and on and on. You'll just go on connecting the dots, one thought to another, one emotion to another, and your whole life could be based on that. That's one way of going about it.

The other way is to maintain open intelligence, which is the sole source of all appearances, when these data come up. As you continue relying on open intelligence you gradually become more and more familiar with it, and in the process you find that appearances have less power to distract you from open intelligence. Whatever the appearance may be, whether it's the desire for sweets or the desire to be disciplined, both are seen equally to be forms of open intelligence, arising and passing away within open intelligence. You're no longer only paying attention to the thought, but more and more your attention is focused on the ever-present open intelligence that is the basis of that thought. You recognize fully evident, flawless open intelligence as the source of the thought, and in that you have great freedom and liberty, whereas with the other way you only had the thoughts!

If you continue to rely on ever-steady open intelligence, you'll gradually gain more familiarity with it. Remember, it's very important that you do so in a totally uncontrived way. "Uncontrived" means that you don't put in any sort of artificial structure, like relying on open intelligence only for a certain time each day or in a certain posture. Instead of it being for only a certain time of the day, like a fixed meditation session, it should be throughout the day, for short moments, repeated many times. Whenever anything afflictive comes up, you maintain open intelligence. Instead of relying on a stream of thoughts and emotions, you rely on open intelligence as the source of your decision-making. In that, you gain familiarity with open intelligence in a very natural way—one in which there is no falling back.

It's as simple as this: in relying on open intelligence, all the same things can go on, but you're not distracted by them any longer; you see whatever appears as open intelligence. More and more it is seen that everything that appears *is* open intelligence. Only in that relaxed ease can we conclusively establish in our own being that everything is a single, nondual expanse. As long as we believe that some things are different from open intelligence, then we are saying that it is not a single, nondual expanse.

This is not merely an intellectual process; it's not just saying, "I am open intelligence" all the time and then indulging whatever comes up. Nowadays, many people say, "Oh, I am open intelligence; everything is open intelligence, so I can do whatever I want." That is a grave misunderstanding and the root of many errors. Statements like that are completely distinct from actually abiding as open intelligence. The real challenge is to live in complete perceptual openness in all experience to the degree of arriving at perfect mental stability, clarity, wisdom, skillful activities and profound insight. That's very different from just repeating an affirmation.

Q: *I have been completely incapacitated by a lifelong depression that has kept me from fully engaging in life, and I really feel guilty and sad about all that I've missed. Could you please help me with this?*

A: It may not seem this way, but your true identity has never been enslaved by depression. Whenever the depression comes up, you may feel like you need to do something about it. Either you try to avoid it somehow or you replace it with something to get you out of the depression. Instead of using any antidotes when the depression comes up, I would advise you to empower yourself in open intelligence without seeking anything and without describing anything about the state that appears.

There are many fields of knowledge that describe all kinds of things, and when it comes to depression, it can be described in many ways as well. Today we have many books on psychology, and using these models we can try to figure out why we are depressed. We may assert that our depression is situational and related to certain events in our life, or we may say our depression is physiological in origin. These are examples of the conventional ways we have for explaining things, but these ideas never say anything definitive about the nature of who we really are. When we relax into the wide-open spaciousness that is the essence of our being, then we see something about ourselves that we've never known before.

When a strong point of view like depression comes up, the wisest thing we can do is to choose to rely on open intelligence and to not indulge, avoid or replace the point of view. We simply come to a complete stop and maintain open intelligence without elaborating on the perception of depression. When we do so, we may gradually be able to experience that perception as appearing within a vast expanse of freedom and peace and have a whole new openness towards it. It's through complete perceptual openness to the thoughts, emotions and experiences that open intelligence is realized. Once this realization dawns, we begin to experience a warmth and directness within ourselves, and we have a much greater sense of ease, joy and wisdom, as well as compassion for ourselves and others.

The commitment must be to relying on open intelligence instead of elaborating on the story. Many of the things you've described may continue to come up for a while, but just continue to empower yourself. If you find that you are acting out of old data, please don't be hard on yourself. Instead, say, "Oh, I fell down, but now I'm going to get back up. I forgot about relying on open intelligence, and I tried some of my old data, but so what. I am now going to return to my commitment to relying on open intelligence." There's always the opportunity right here and now to rely on open intelligence. No matter what course the depression takes, when we rely on open intelligence, rather than being overwhelmed by the depression, we're able to make clear decisions about it.

THE NATURAL WISDOM OF OPEN INTELLIGENCE
CHAPTER SEVENTEEN

"No matter how much we may have already contributed to the world around us, in gaining familiarity with our wisdom nature, we unleash a power of benefit that is truly extraordinary, which will allow us to exceed anything we have ever accomplished before."

When we think about who we are, we usually think in terms of a combination of our body and mind as comprising our identity. We think that we are this biological mechanism contained within a skin line that has a conscious mind. When people speak of their mind, they are usually referring to the conscious entity that has all the thoughts and emotions related to the experiences of their individual biological mechanism. Then there is speech, which is considered an expression of who we are. The speech of that individual biological mechanism is understood to be the means whereby the things that are needed to feel comfortable and fulfilled are acquired.

Most people believe themselves to be nothing more than a person—a mortal body and individual mind—separate and distinct from all others. The thoughts and activities that stem from that identification with the body and mind are for the most part very self-centered: how I am going to get my needs filled, how I am going to get food I like to eat, how I am going to get work I like, how I am going to get the relationships that I want and how I am going to get money for me and those close to me. Virtually all of the thoughts that stem from that core identification with the body and mind will be about this supposed self that imagines it needs all of these things. We grow to believe that we are indeed dependent on those things for our well-being.

Conventional speech, and the mental constructs that are its basis, is always focused on the division of subject and object. It alternates between happiness and sadness, fame and defamation, exaltation and punishment. All that appears is seen in terms of opposites—right and wrong, good and bad, positive and negative, hope and fear, benefit and harm, indulgence and renunciation, acceptance and rejection. The conventional activities of the body, speech and mind all reference back to an intangible individual identity, which is attempting to improve its self-esteem and self-respect, both by seeing faults in others and by eliminating faults and developing positive qualities in itself.

If we believe ourselves to be a person—an independent agent and the only source of all of our thoughts—then we're going to be lost in those thoughts all of our lives. Within ordinary thinking, rooted in the "I am a person" idea, there will be no insight into the indestructible reality and timeless freedom of our fundamental condition.

However, we have a choice: we can either continue to live a very ordinary life locked inside a box of conventional perceptions, or we can get to know ourselves as an expression of open intelligence. We can either continue to have conventional beliefs about the body, speech and mind with all the limitations brought on by that choice, or we can discover our fundamental condition, which is open intelligence itself. We can then manifest the powerful speech and mind that are inherent in that intelligence.

Open intelligence is an inconceivably sublime reality that is pure like infinite space. Within it everything is perfect all at once. This is the true intelligence of everyone, and that is what we must gain familiarity with. This intelligence is unimaginably beautiful. It can never be defined, because it has no limitations, parts or segments. It has never been divided into any kind of thing, whether small or large, gross or subtle. Suffice it to say that it is the one timeless and changeless reality in which all phenomena appear and disappear. It is our fundamental condition, and whatever appears is made only of that.

No thought, emotion or experience has ever been anything other than an expression of nature's pure intelligence. When we discover open intelligence as our direct connection with this wisdom, it gradually reveals itself to be the true nature of all phenomena. When pure perception dawns, the absolute simplicity and spaciousness of mind becomes more and more obvious. It intensifies in and of itself through our simple acknowledgement of the carefree ease within our own being. This is our own natural intelligence, which has nothing to guard or defend against, for it is timeless and indestructible. Supercomplete wisdom is at ease, stable, insightful and compassionate beyond words and concepts. It includes thinking but does not rely on thinking. It relies only on the spontaneity of its own intelligence and effortlessly sees its own intelligence in all.

Wisdom speech is courageous eloquence that doesn't need any conventional thinking to inform it. In other words, it tells it like it is with no need to argue or debate! It has nothing to prove and nothing to compete with. It can never be judged, because its quality is so profound. True wisdom speech is inconceivably beautiful. The mind is restored to peace and wisdom just through hearing it. It places us in the irreversible state where we never again return to the impermanence and suffering of belief in the independent nature of data. This is the power of the indestructible melodious sound of wisdom speech.

There has never been any possibility of wisdom speech being destroyed. It can never be snuffed out, altered, owned or changed in any way. It is the original, continual emanation of the supreme reality and a direct doorway into that reality. As all forms are forms of formless open intelligence, so are all sounds the self-sounds of the basic space of open intelligence.

The activities of the wisdom-body, wisdom-speech and wisdom-mind all stem from resting as the expanse of equalness and evenness that pervades all appearances. This wisdom expanse is the one naturally occurring reality, the primordial unity that has never known any split or division. It sees everything as perfect all at once and all phenomena as indivisible and mutually interpenetrating. The speech, qualities and activities that emanate from someone established in that infinite expanse of wisdom are the ultimate expression of great benefit for all beings. No matter how much we may have already contributed to the world around us, in gaining familiarity with our wisdom nature, we unleash a power of benefit that is truly extraordinary, which will allow us to exceed anything we have ever accomplished before.

The golden key to discovering this inherent wisdom is to establish ourselves in fully relaxed perceptual openness throughout the day and in all experiences, no matter what may be happening. This means experiencing everything totally, allowing that wide-open spacious intelligence to be the one context in which everything occurs. This releases a tremendous energy that is usually constricted by the preoccupation with data, of trying to label, sort and control everything that appears. If we've been constantly depending on the fixed reference points of our personal identity, then in a sense we have been retreating from a direct experience of life. The more we let go of those limited ideas which have made up our personal identity, the more our wide-open intelligence can release the tremendous energy inherent in our true nature. This energy automatically cuts through barriers created by habitual emotional patterns, empowering confidence in open intelligence.

No matter what our habitual emotional patterns have been, they will be completely dissolved in naturally restful open intelligence. Relying on open intelligence in the face of all experience is a treasure trove of benefit for our individual lives, our families and all the communities and nations of our world. To talk about it in a simple human way, when we maintain open intelligence, life gets better and better! Instead of being all wrapped up in ourselves, we become more and more devoted to benefiting other people and our planet, and we become empowered to do so with extraordinary potency.

This primordial wisdom is not achieved by effort involving cause and effect. The qualities of wisdom body, speech and mind show themselves by relying on open intelligence; they cannot be learned by studying, and they cannot be perfected through avoiding, indulging or replacing faults with positive actions and qualities. They don't come about through doing good works, developing meritorious activities or positive states of mind or avoiding negative states of mind. The wisdom of timeless open intelligence is naturally present, and it is not realized as a result of any circumstances. It is here now in its fullness.

As amazing as it may seem after years of trying to better ourselves or trying to keep a tight control on our thoughts, emotions and experiences, when we begin to rely on open intelligence, we come to see that the natural space of open intelligence is already perfect and therefore doesn't need any adjustments to make it perfect.

All human beings have the capacity for wisdom. Another term that has been used to describe this inherent wisdom is "basic human goodness." Open intelligence is the wisdom of great benefit, and it is that wisdom itself that emanates the speech, mind, qualities and activities of each of us. These are not traits that are endowed to some special beings who then pass them on to others. The wisdom I'm speaking about is the natural wisdom of all seven billion people on this planet and of everything altogether. When we rely on open intelligence for short moments repeated many times, we become effortlessly familiar with this wisdom identity, which is our ever-present fundamental condition, our own natural being.

In the ease of our own open intelligence, wisdom powers of great benefit are already naturally occurring. Just because we've never learned this about ourselves doesn't mean that it isn't the case. It *is* the case, and it has always been so throughout time for every human being. This is not something that can be cultivated, developed or learned; it naturally manifests as we gain confidence in open intelligence. We tap into this wisdom of great benefit by relying on open intelligence for short moments repeated many times.

Through the simple act of relying on open intelligence for short moments, we come to see that our essential nature is truly indestructible. Indeed, we are immortal—not immortal as an individual body, but immortal as the wisdom of open intelligence, which is timeless and already free.

Data are inherently fleeting, whether they are the data of birth, life, death or the process of dying, but the open intelligence in which all data appear is permanent and changeless. Only through stable open intelligence being the priority in all situations does one gain complete familiarity with its powers. It's as simple as that. It can't come about in any other way. It's absolutely impossible that one can have the decisive experience of open intelligence by thinking about it, or by trying to improve one's data, or trying to get into some sort of altered state.

Q: I have to admit to a fair amount of unease when I hear you, because you don't seem to be part of any tradition that I am familiar with. You're speaking only from your own experience without direct reference to any of the wisdom teachings or teachers from the past. How can you justify putting this out to people when it seems to be something that you just came up with on your own?

A: First of all, it's very difficult to understand through ordinary thinking how teachings like this occur. Ordinary thinking tries to make sense of an appearance by making it the result of a cause, but that can never explain the way teachings like this appear.

Throughout all of time teachers have communicated profound wisdom that has enriched the lives of hundreds of millions of people. It is very likely that many of these teachers were asked the same question you are asking me. The teaching may emerge from an individual living in a specific time period; yet, all phenomena have their source in open intelligence in its self-cognizing capacity. Even though various teachings have appeared in different forms throughout time, they always appear in, of, as and through open intelligence. They're not simply the accomplishment of an individual person. They speak to the needs of people living in different eras who will benefit from them. The true measure of any teaching is whether or not it benefits many people. If a teaching benefits many, many people and inspires them to be happy, caring people who contribute to human society, it is said to be of great benefit.

Such unconventional wisdom speech can directly convey the decisive experience of open intelligence to receptive listeners, but there is no way that this can be described adequately through conventional logic. Teaching people how to gain confidence in open intelligence is by far the most important of the powers of open intelligence.

Many different forms of relying on open intelligence have come forth throughout the ages. The Balanced View Training is one of those forms. It allows people in the current era to live authentically by drawing on the power of fundamental human goodness that is implicit in open intelligence. There is only one simple method to become familiar with open intelligence that all human beings can readily understand and implement: to rely on open intelligence, for short moments, repeated many times, without altering or indulging the thoughts, emotions, sensations or experiences that appear.

The introduction to open intelligence is crucial; it can come about in a number of ways. One way is that suddenly one's mind will spontaneously open up to the vast perspective of open intelligence. A second way is to be directly introduced to open intelligence by a teacher. A genuine teacher will have the power to convey the experience of pure open intelligence to others directly, using one means or another. When the teacher's skillful means and incisive insight are fully present, open intelligence can be unerringly shown in a way that is appropriate to many people living in a given era.

A third way is to hear teachings about open intelligence and to be liberated simply upon hearing them. A fourth way is to combine relying on open intelligence with the conviction that gradually dawns by listening to the teachings that are available face-to-face, online and in other media. The fifth way is for the person's mind to already be naturally restful, so when the person hears the teaching it makes perfect sense and conviction comes about spontaneously.

The ideal disposition of a person who wants to rely on open intelligence is simply to be open enough to listen to the teachings for a while. It's no big deal really. The teaching may not make sense to everyone immediately, and for many it will remain puzzling until it becomes part of their direct experience. For most people conviction dawns gradually.

This means you must be willing to consider the possibility that the conventional identity you have always taken yourself to be may not be altogether accurate, and that something far greater about you awaits discovery. Just by being open and continuing to rely on open intelligence, you come to see that there is a profound identity that is an alternative to conventional ways of identifying yourself.

Regarding the teachings of the past, it's important to understand something about the historical and cultural circumstances surrounding them. Those teachings all started out as something new! At one time human culture was quite fragmented and isolated into tribal or national cultures, because people couldn't readily travel long distances or communicate with each other easily across countries or continents. People were separated geographically, and it was difficult for them to come into contact with people outside their native areas. The teachers of that day could only directly teach people who were close to them, geographically and culturally, so the teachers would be speaking within a certain cultural context that was understandable to the people who were coming to them. Very beautiful traditions grew up within those cultures to serve the needs of the people, and many excellent methods and practices were developed that were culturally specific to that time and place.

Today, however, our planet is going through an amazing change, and all of a sudden we're all connected in a way that was impossible in the past. For the first time in history there is a global human culture with rapidly dissolving boundaries. Not only national boundaries are dissolving, but also the boundaries of the human body as the only means of relationship are dissolving. We can talk to each other very conveniently wherever we may be in the world with no contact other than an Internet connection. We don't need to be face-to-face to communicate any longer. Often, all we can verify about the identity of the people we are communicating with is that somebody, somewhere, is reading our words and sending a reply. When we correspond with someone via the Internet we may have no idea who they are on a personal level, and that's okay.

We have incredible means of acquiring and distributing information through the Internet and telecommunications. We can easily travel all over the world, and we have tremendous access to all kinds of information about philosophies and teachers that were not available even fifteen years ago. The teachings of the present day cannot be limited to the specific context of geographically isolated peoples any longer, as most of us no longer live that way. We are all, to one degree or another, participating as a global human family that has a shared responsibility for each member of that family and for the planet we live on as well.

Thus, the Balanced View Training is available to a much broader range of humanity than teachings in the past, because the communication obstacles I just described are no longer present. We've become a global human culture, and the primary need of this age is the unification of humankind. More and more we want to be able to communicate easily with everyone, and we now have the communication tools to do that.

Whether ancient or modern there are certain direct teachings that can be called pinnacle teachings, which are simply about the ultimate nature of being human. These are complete teachings with unerring instruction on how to completely realize basic human goodness and share the power of its balanced perspective for the benefit of all. There's no need to call them "spiritual teachings." We don't need to spiritualize, religionize, philosophize or psychologize this kind of teaching. They are first and foremost about being human—that's all. They're not owned by any person or any tradition.

Because the Balanced View Training is available to people throughout the world via the Internet and other means, we use language that is accessible to many, many people, and that helps develop a common understanding regarding the shared experience of what it means to gain confidence in open intelligence. Through our example of a powerful worldwide community, which includes trainings and trainers focused solely on communicating the profound choice of relying on open intelligence, we offer a way of life that is immediately beneficial to everyone.

If wisdom teachings are presented in a manner appropriate to the current circumstances and understanding of people in a given age, rather than cloaked in unfamiliar cultural traditions and practices, then many more people can benefit from them. There are many people worldwide who benefit from the Balanced View grassroots movement who might not otherwise have been served if the teachings were limited to a specific social, cultural or religious context.

Many people around the world are now opening up to basic human goodness and its expressions of tremendous benefit. This benefit comes about through powerful activities based on truly caring about each other in an uncontrived way. The shift to relying on open intelligence as an alternative way of life is not only an imperative for the individual; it is an evolutionary imperative as well. If our species is to survive, a broad-based group of people must arise from the grassroots, and they must be endowed with the instinctive wisdom that is implicit in stable open intelligence. That is the only way we can successfully solve the problems currently threatening our species and planet.

It's very interesting that at this critical juncture in the history of humankind the people who are most likely to realize the wisdom and skillful powers of open intelligence aren't necessarily the people trying to do so through timeworn traditional norms. The people most likely to recognize open intelligence are those who have a disposition of openness and caring, whatever their outer circumstances may appear to be, and the teachings that will bring about their recognition will increasingly be unlike the methods and practices of the past.

Often organizations fail to thrive because they don't completely meet the needs of the people who come to them. Most people today don't want to engage in practices that don't have a measurable outcome that's immediately beneficial to their life. This is the correct attitude for one wishing to recognize and rely on open intelligence; it shows the power of discernment. These days open-minded, discerning people are unlikely to participate in a method or practice that doesn't ensure results for themselves or others. They are far less likely to buy into a system where most people don't achieve what has been promised by the prescribed practices.

People today are also far less likely to allow themselves to be blamed for the failure of these practices to deliver what has been promised. More and more people simply will not tolerate hierarchies in which the leadership is idolized as being somehow greater than everyone else. We no longer live in the age of hero worship, where we turn our lives over to an authority who is supposed to take care of us and parcel out what they think we need.

We live in the age of collaboration. Like bees in a hive we collaborate to make honey! Each person is essential to the collaboration; everyone is important. The model of "servant leadership" is the model of the hive. The leadership serves for the benefit of all, and that is its only goal—not authority, status, fame or money. Such things may come along with servant leadership, but they are not at all the goal of the servant leader, who is motivated solely by the desire for benefit of all. Hierarchical organizations will fade from view as humankind continues to evolve in its ability to collaborate for the benefit of everyone.

No matter how strong our emotions may be in relation to the belief systems and practices we've learned, if we can rely on open intelligence, we will discover what we've been seeking in those other practices. We will gradually move into a space of wisdom beyond words and concepts—and there discover the living essence that is at the root of all faiths and of nature itself. This we will find in our own direct experience of reality.

As we gain confidence in open intelligence ourselves, it will be increasingly clear that there are others around the world who are doing the same. Through individuals like you and me and through organizations like Balanced View, humanity is developing a very strong instinctive wisdom that is demonstrating itself in the dignity, confidence and skillful activities of people everywhere. This is like a wisdom army of open intelligence, an army that has very powerful weapons, such as the balanced view of equalness, abundant equanimity, perfect mental stability and genuine passion for the service of humanity and the planet. This is true caring and true wisdom.

By the power of relying on open intelligence for short moments repeated many times, these wisdom qualities and activities of great benefit come about naturally and effortlessly.

NO EFFORT, NO SPECIAL CIRCUMSTANCES

CHAPTER EIGHTEEN

"This natural wisdom is truly magnificent and unparalleled. When most of us hear about something this grand, we think that it is going to require many years of education to become acquainted with it. However, this wisdom is not something that needs to be learned. It is the birthright of everyone and is already within everyone."

I have only one message, and that is: stop seeking! There is no search to be undertaken, and everything there is to be known or realized is *already* known and realized. What's already been given doesn't need to be sought. The super-complete, superbly helpful nature of everything lives as our own open intelligence. There's no destination to get to, and there's no one going there. All there is, is stainless, flawless, ever-present open intelligence.

If we can simply listen to the instructions that have been given—relax body and mind completely and rely on open intelligence for short moments, repeated many times, until it becomes continuous—it will become more and more obvious that everything is perfect all at once. There are no adjustments whatsoever to be made. The idea that adjustments need to be made is a fiction. What is super-complete and present everywhere has to be easy. What could possibly be required to obtain what you already have?

The relationship between super-complete open intelligence and the data that appear within it can be compared to the air through which a breeze blows. Both the breeze and the air are just air. It's impossible to say where the breeze began, where its middle is and where it ends, as the breeze is inseparable from the air. In the same way, no matter what appears within open intelligence, whether it's a thought, emotion, perception or experience, it's never been anything other than open intelligence.

The only way to realize this wisdom is to stop trying to control thoughts; in other words we just relax and allow the thinking to do whatever it will. As we let go of our habit of trying to change the contents of the mind and simply rely on the open intelligence in which all thoughts arise and pass away, that basis becomes more and more obvious. Just as the morning sun appears in the sky and outshines all the planets and stars, so too when we relax and allow all the thoughts and emotions to do whatever they will, the clear light of the wisdom mind begins to outshine all the thoughts and emotions that arise.

Wisdom is completely beyond thinking and doesn't need any opinions whatsoever to prove itself. We don't even have to do anything to realize this wisdom, because it is so natural to us. If we simply hear about it over and over again, it will become more and more obvious that wisdom really is the true nature of the mind. We come to see that the original purity of the mind has never been obscured by the thoughts and emotions that have come and gone. We also see that we've never really needed those thoughts to describe or define who we are and that all our attempts to define ourselves through thought are fleeting at best. Our true nature is beyond anything that thoughts can conjure up.

This natural wisdom is truly magnificent and unparalleled. When most of us hear about something this grand, we think that it's going to require many years of education to become acquainted with it. However, this wisdom is not something that needs to be learned. It's the birthright of everyone and is already within everyone. The only way to know it is to acknowledge it—to completely relax and allow the clear light of open intelligence to shine through everything. When we do that, it becomes very obvious that no education is necessary. All that is required is an open mind, and since everyone *already* has a completely open mind, everyone is qualified to realize it!

Whatever our IQ is, wherever we live or however many possessions we have, none of that matters. There is no hierarchy of any kind in open intelligence. Wisdom has never been owned by institutions, religions or authoritative historical figures. No one can claim ownership of wisdom, nor can anyone dole it out; it is not the possession of an elite part of the population. In wisdom there is no higher or lower, no this way or that way. It is all-pervading, all-encompassing, indivisible and fully present everywhere in each moment. When the certainty of it in our own being dawns, all the thoughts that were once so persistent no longer have a hold on us. The recognition of this turns everything upside down about who we thought we were, what we thought life is and what it means to be a human being. When we learn to tune into open intelligence and simply listen again and again to the melody of what is really true about ourselves, the result is that open intelligence becomes more and more obvious—with nothing to learn, nothing to effort for and nothing to achieve.

If we feel plagued by any kind of persistent thinking, when it comes up we only need to rely on open intelligence, rather than getting distracted by the thinking itself. All thoughts are temporary appearances that have no substance; they're nothing but the clear light of the wisdom mind. Whatever the phenomena or data are, they're all primordially pure. Birth, life, death, war, famine, young, old, up or down—they're all primordially pure. One thing that's guaranteed about all appearances is that they will vanish of their own accord like the flight path of a bird in the sky. Absolutely nothing needs to be done about them. The true nature of the mind is sky-like and always remains so; it has never gotten wrapped up in any thought or been affected by any thought.

Trying to change something about ourselves in order to have a greater likelihood of enjoying our true nature leads nowhere and just adds more confusion. It's just more of someone trying to get somewhere. Whether it's the appearance of an ego, an "I," a personality, or anything that's being enacted by that "I," it's all mirage-like. A mirage can't cause a problem unless we take it to be real. None of us would try to fix or improve a mirage or try to get something out of it. That would be a useless and frustrating endeavor leading nowhere. In the same way, trying to work on a non-existent ego or personality just leads to exhaustion, because it's futile to work on nothing! Rather than wasting our time trying to fix a mirage, why not empower the powers of great benefit and enjoy the natural glow of everything just *as it is*?

There is nothing to realize. Realization is simply resting as the stainless knower of all phenomena, and that's already right here. If we say, "I have to realize something," then we've taken up a position somewhere and adopted a data set. But if we give up all the positions of a realizer realizing something definitive, then we don't have to worry about any position-taking. We're just relaxed all the time. "I am seeking" is a datum, and "realization" is also just a datum. Beyond them both and untouched by either is open intelligence—timelessly free and fully present in every moment.

If we give unnecessary power to the appearances within our mind, then we are complicating our lives and we'll feel uncomfortable a lot of the time. When we give power to the appearances, we'll always be looking for the right thought, the right emotional state or the right experience to relieve the discomfort inherent in a personal identity. However, the wholesome goodness of our original being isn't dependent on or affected by the contents of our mind. It has never been touched by our judgments and has never been ensnared in a personal identity. True wisdom is found in knowing that everything is equal.

Seeking cannot bring us to freedom, because we're *already* free! We can't say that seeking will bring us to liberation, because we have never been bound. Our freedom is here and now! We don't have to live anywhere special to enjoy our true nature, neither do we have to have any special setting or be remote from other people or renounce the world. We can do that if we want to, but in itself it doesn't really lead anywhere or produce any cause for realizing our true nature. Our lifestyle has nothing whatsoever to do with the recognition of primordial purity. *All* lifestyles are primordially pure. We can be a monk in Tibet, a housewife in Texas, a programmer at Microsoft, a ditch digger, a cake baker or whatever it is, and it's the perfect circumstance for the realization of our true nature.

To live a life permeated with self-criticism will lead to criticism of others. That's just the way it is. To gain familiarity with the open intelligence that is at the basis of everything gently relieves us of that self-criticism. We come into the wholly positive goodness of our own being, and as we do so we begin to feel that same gentleness and kindness with other people too. Relying on open intelligence shows us that other people are just like us. This is true interconnectedness.

Q: I don't disagree with anything you are saying, and I would personally be troubled if everybody sort of looked inward and stopped doing things. How can society progress if people are only focused on themselves?

A: Thank you for bringing up that point; it's an important question. Relying on open intelligence doesn't mean getting into a state and then being cut off from the world. That is a misperception about what instinctively recognizing open intelligence means. Relying on open intelligence doesn't mean inaction; on the contrary, when we rely on open intelligence our compassion is empowered to flow into action in a whole new way. True open intelligence is a force of immense benefit for all.

Q: Okay, but doesn't concentrating on one's own open intelligence tend to make a person passive?

A: No! I mean, I am working around the clock; that's certainly not passive! Is a training that provides 24/7 support all over the world a passive event?

Before I had this shift twenty-seven years ago, I was focused on achievement, and I had accomplished many things, but I never felt like I could do enough, no matter how much I accomplished. I would often feel distraught: "Oh, I accomplished all this, but what next?" I had worked very hard to do the right things in my life in order to be a good adult, but when I got into a great crisis in my life, none of that helped at all. I was completely at a loss, not knowing how to go on. I tried everything, both positive and negative, to feel better. There was just no relief to be found in any of the belief systems I had previously relied on, and that is when this recognition of open intelligence appeared in my mind stream.

The distinction between my endeavors before the shift and after it is that my present activity is effortless and tireless and completely focused on the benefit of all. The purpose of our life, of anyone's life, is to be of tremendous benefit to ourselves and others. When we rely on the open intelligence that is the essence of all our perceptions, then we get familiar with wisdom that can't be learned. True open intelligence is potently beneficial and is not passive in any way.

Q: If people relax but they are not ready to fully rely on open intelligence, what they probably will do is to fall into laziness, and that is not really a good state to be in. So how can people not fall into laziness?

A: Laziness, like agitation or any other description, is just a datum. The most important thing is to relax as flawless open intelligence and see all as flawless open intelligence until it is clear that all is flawless open intelligence. In this is tremendous energy, for open intelligence is synonymous with tremendous energy. When the cage of labels has disappeared and the confines of all these data are seen through, then there is only open intelligence itself. If initially laziness is one of the data that you drift around in, just maintain open intelligence with full force. There's no need to judge anything that appears or change anything that appears. Everything you need to know about laziness or anything else is best known from open intelligence.

Let's say that you find yourself being lazy, and then there might be a story about the laziness: "If I'm lazy like this, I'll never get anything done. I should be doing this, and I should be doing that." Then the next thing is that you're thinking about the past. "I've always been lazy. When I was growing up my mom and dad said, 'You're lazy!' Maybe it's their fault that I'm lazy!" This is simply a proliferation of data coupled with a distraction by these data. However, when laziness appears, and in response there is just the relaxed ease of open intelligence—rather than the need to be lost in the story—then open intelligence will be obviously present, despite the perception of laziness. When we begin relying on open intelligence, we start to see with greater clarity how data proliferate and resolve, and then the tendency to be distracted by them starts to dissolve. Data and open intelligence are inseparable, but if we go off into the story and let the thoughts overtake us endlessly, then it will be impossible to see that.

Q: What does "realization" mean to you?

A: Realization is just a concept within the all-encompassing pure view of open intelligence. There's no one who's ever been anything, including "realized." On the other hand, by the power of understanding the nature of phenomena, there is the demonstrable power of beneficial qualities and activities that is evident in one's voice, mind and body. Nowadays, realization is often mistaken to be a liberated mind; however, the liberation of the mind is not the ultimate fruit.

All is pure presence, which is primordially aware. Without any conventional frameworks, such as the idea of a "liberated mind," there will be true spontaneity. We go beyond imitations of any kind. Making no distinction between self and others, there is a display of the powers of great benefit to all. Detached from whatever is said, speech is like a melodious echo. All is free from the beginning, in the same way that bright light is free in the sky. Effortless compassion, love and tremendous energy radiate impartially like sunlight blazing from the sun. Know that such a way of being represents the birthright and natural state of all beings.

Q: So, we're all realized now?

A: Yes. It's nothing more than enjoying the natural settledness of everything *as it is*. It's so amazing, because the more we relax, the more the naturally manifest joy that is the essence of everything becomes apparent. There's a kindness and a lightness of being that's absolutely evident. It's very likely you'll smile more and not be so hard on yourself or others.

The mystification of the reality of our being is something that's come about through the development of elaborate philosophical systems to describe what is actually totally simple. There's no great esoteric nature to anything; it is all just the pure presence of open intelligence. When understanding the nature of being becomes so marginalized through overcomplication or oversimplification that almost no one can understand it, then it's time to strip everything naked and get back to basics.

The beauty of everything *as it is*, is that it is so simple and benevolent. The entirely beneficial and wholly positive fundamental nature of being is the one and only reality, and it includes everything. That's very simple. There's no way to talk about anything or describe anything as finite and definitive in and of itself, because nothing is separate from this all-encompassing reality. Who we are is entirely indescribable, so the dissociated ways of talking about things that we sometimes hear are completely unnecessary. To say things like, "There is no experiencer, there is no doer, I am unborn, all is unborn"— this kind of speaking is what I call "the nondual shuffle." When you see clearly in to your own nature, these kinds of intellectual supports are unnecessary.

If you begin relying on open intelligence and you feel that you are "experiencing open intelligence" or "practicing open intelligence," that's perfectly okay in the beginning. The whole idea of someone practicing or experiencing open intelligence will naturally slip away without any need to think about it. There's no need to take up a position anywhere, no need to say this way is right and that way is wrong. Just relax into the essence of your own being, and all is revealed exactly *as it is*. There's no need to describe anything as fixed or definite, no need to put labels on your experience. Just relax. In the natural equalness of everything *as it is*, there's perfect wisdom.

Even the term "equalness" is just another label. The reality of what we are can be described as "equalness," "the nondual expanse" and so forth, but none of these terms are needed. No linguistic support is required; in fact, no support whatsoever is needed for that which is the basis of everything. When we look at everything *as it is* with simple human perception, we can see that there is a natural order to everything. Even in chaos and confusion, there is the pure presence of a natural order that is completely at ease. There's never been anything separate from that. There is no need to define it as a finite something or as an infinite nothing. No description about reality is either right or wrong. Reality is always beyond descriptions—yet the experience of it is always present within us as the ease of our own being. Short moments, repeated many times, become spontaneous!

DIRECT TEACHINGS
CHAPTER NINETEEN

"Direct teachings state in no uncertain terms that there is no destination and no one going there, because the innate reality of our being is unachieved and unachievable."

If we aspire to realize our true identity, it's important to take advantage of teachings that can bring about that realization in a very practical way. The easiest and most direct of all teachings instructs us to naturally rely on open intelligence in the ease of our own being and to return to that repeatedly. This is one of the most ancient of all practices, and throughout the centuries many people have realized their true nature through this practice because it is so easy and direct.

When I say that the fundamental nature is already present, absolutely accessible and available to everyone, I mean *everyone*. Anyone can rely on open intelligence! Realizing our fundamental nature through relying on open intelligence doesn't depend on any special circumstances. It doesn't depend on being a particular gender or nationality, living in one place or another, being spiritually inclined, able to understand deep philosophical concepts or even on being able to read! Maintaining open intelligence for brief moments until it becomes constant is all that's required, and that's an ability that comes with being human.

The words I'm using here to communicate are only a gateway to the recognition of open intelligence that happens within you. One could term what is being imparted here a "teaching," or it could be called a "training" as it is called in Balanced View. No matter what word is used, it points to the same thing: when we simply remain open to words of unerring open intelligence, they start to work in a wondrous way, and the essence of the training begins to be obvious in our own experience. There's something completely indescribable about how that happens. Let's say a person hears about relying on open intelligence and maybe experiences an overwhelming resonance with the training. Then something very profound happens and the person experiences a profound change, but no one can say exactly how that occurred. The person can't really say, "I learned this, then I did this and that, then I spent five years doing this other thing, and then *boom*, I got it!" What already *is* cannot be made to come about—and when it is revealed, we can't say exactly how or why. All we can say is that by basking in the truth of who we are in a very simple way, certainty dawns in us; the how and why of it are beyond words.

If we're only looking at things in terms of cause and effect, we'll think that achieving something as incredible as enlightenment or liberation—which simply mean the optimal way of being human—must involve incredible effort—in fact much more effort than the other things for which we've had to exert ourselves all our lives. Maybe we'll think, "With the kind of mind *I* have, I'll have to use superhuman effort all day long for decades!" These are just assumptions based on the belief that the body and mind have to be mastered in order to achieve some future goal. The truth is that enlightenment is nothing but the direct discovery of our own open intelligence, which is already fully present.

People meditate, do yoga and repeat mantras in order to become enlightened, but the crucial factor is not the activity itself, but maintaining open intelligence—the fundamental condition—while performing the activity. Repeating mantras or meditating need not be any different than writing computer software, cooking a meal or driving a car; they all provide an equal opportunity to rely on open intelligence. I always tell people that if they have a practice that they like, such as meditation or mantra repetition, they can feel free to continue with it, but they should do so without thinking that it's leading to any goal. They can just do it as something they enjoy. But thinking that methods and practices lead to the achievement of a goal just serves to strengthen the illusion of the personal identity and keeps the already present goal out of reach. This is a crucial point.

Open intelligence cannot be realized through striving, and pursuing data as though they lead somewhere will not serve us. As we continue to rely on open intelligence, coming to know the truth about ourselves happens in a very simple and straightforward way. Direct teachings don't assert that we must develop virtue and practice different meritorious activities in order to be pure enough to recognize our true nature. Direct teachings state in no uncertain terms that there is no destination and no one going there; the innate reality of our being is unachieved and unachievable.

If we want direct instruction, then that's the kind of teaching we should look for, rather than one that says, "Oh yes, your essential nature is nondual and free, but first let me tell you what you have to fix about yourself in order to be free! You've got to get rid of this and this and this, and you must cultivate this and that and the other thing!" Indirect teachings declare that the fundamental condition is already present but then turn around and add, "But you are flawed and need to be fixed." That's talking out of both sides of the mouth—and it's entirely misguided, because there is essentially no one to be fixed and no one to do the fixing! This becomes effortlessly clear as one gains more confidence in relying on open intelligence. There is no need to engage in the extremes of stiff language to describe or support ideas about the lack of a personal identity or a doer.

What we really need is unerring instruction. There are two types of speech: the first speaks *about* something, and that could be called ordinary speech. The second type directly transmits what's being spoken about, and that is called wisdom speech.

Ordinary speech is all wrapped up in conventional data, while wisdom speech emanates from the pure expanse of the basic space of open intelligence. When utilizing ordinary speaking or writing, one usually tries to understand the words intellectually, relate the words to all the data one has and give the words meaning and significance based upon what has been read or heard before. This is how we've been taught to learn from a very young age.

Wisdom speech is entirely different. It doesn't require any learning, because it is innate. Wisdom speech, whether it's spoken or written, introduces open intelligence in a very direct way, and it has the inherent power to expand that introduction into full confidence in open intelligence. The power of wisdom speech places the minds of listeners in an irreversible state of well-being. When a listener simply relaxes and is open to what is spoken or written, that openness evokes wisdom from within.

Most modern languages don't really have any term for the subject-less, object-less, wide-open expanse of radiant open intelligence, and even in languages like Tibetan or Sanskrit which are nondual language systems, no words can fully encompass it. We can use terms that point to it, but there's nothing that can fully describe it, and the experience of it is completely beyond words. And yet, words have their value. The words you're reading now have only one purpose: to evoke the direct experience of timeless open intelligence in you. So, don't try to comprehend these things merely with the critical intellect or understand them based on what you've learned or believed before. Just relax deeply into the powers of great benefit and discover directly that timeless open intelligence is already fully present.

Instructions relating to the realization of open intelligence have been handed down from one generation to another in many cultures around the world, but there have been relatively few direct teachings that give unerring instruction on how to realize open intelligence. These direct teachings have actually been available for many thousands of years; an unbroken lineage of those who have realized their true nature through relying on open intelligence stretches back like a range of golden mountains throughout time. And what do these teachings state? Exactly what is described here in the Balanced View Training: rely on open intelligence for short moments, repeated many times, until it becomes spontaneous and continuous at all times.

Nonetheless, for the most part, until now the single focus on relying on open intelligence has been available only to a relatively small number of people, and in the past it's been very difficult to find a way to be instructed. Those giving such teachings were often quite inaccessible; maybe they were teaching in a cave on a snow-covered mountain in the Himalayas or in Tibet in a distant monastery, and you'd have to walk for days under difficult conditions to find them. In this way, we can all be thankful that times have changed!

In the past most of the teachings for realizing open intelligence have been rooted in specific geographical, cultural and social circumstances and were therefore not readily accessible to someone outside of that culture. However, today we have a global culture with technologies such as the Internet and telecommunications that can instantly connect people all over the world. We have tremendous access to all kinds of information, as well as an increasingly common language and a similar cultural context. So now this ancient teaching has arisen in a new form—one that's easily accessible to just about everyone.

In the lineage of those who have realized timeless open intelligence, it has always been up to the people in any given generation to take the teachings and communicate them in a way that's directly understandable in that time period. For the first time this unerring instruction is being given freely and openly to all of humanity in a language that almost everyone can understand. These teachings are for the benefit of all beings. They come out of open intelligence, and they don't belong to any culture or person and are not owned by any sect or tradition.

Although studying ancient texts may have its value, to limit ourselves to antiquated texts and instructions that are difficult to comprehend isn't really helpful. It just makes a reality that is always fully present seem distant and inaccessible. In the Balanced View Training, if we had chosen to use words and concepts that were limited to a certain culture, then that specificity would have limited the number of people who would be able to understand the trainings on relying on open intelligence. For instance, if we used terms such as *dharmakaya, sunyata, Absolute, Atman* or *moksha*, a majority of modern listeners would either be completely baffled or incorrectly think they know exactly what we mean! Either way, it could be an obstacle. But if instead we use simple terms such as "open intelligence," and "data," then it's likely that more people will be able to relate to those ideas and come to a decisive experience of the essence of the Training.

It's very important to have instruction that is absolutely suited for the people living in the era in which it emerges, spoken in a manner that the people of that era can understand and offering a complete system of support for participants. Most importantly it has to be instruction that leads to the swift accomplishment of timeless open intelligence. Unerring instruction from a skilled teacher can transmit the decisive experience of our true nature to many people all at once. But for this to occur, the teaching has to be open, direct and accessible, and not hidden away on a dusty shelf.

Relying on open intelligence is a teaching for people who can move beyond concepts. The ones who are completely open are the ones who can say, "I'm done with everything else! I just want a simple and direct approach. If you teach me, I'll listen." If people are truly open to what they are seeking—one hundred percent open, with all of their heart—then they will eventually find themselves in a circumstance where they will hear a direct teaching, and there will be nothing that can keep them away from it. Yet, if they're more committed to their former practices and ideas of moving towards a future destination, then that will remain what they're committed to.

I don't try to convince anyone who isn't ready or interested; I just wait for those who are really ready to show up. I believe in attraction rather than promotion!

Now, what is a direct teacher? A teacher is really the ultimate friend. The relationship between the teacher and the people who come to participate with that teacher is one in which there is great intimacy, total well-being and love. A skilled teacher already has the decisive experience of fully evident open intelligence in her or his own life and is devoted to bringing that open intelligence to others in a loving and supportive way. Direct teachers are able to teach in an authoritative and convincing way because of their unfailing wisdom, insight and skill in all circumstances.

When teachers are manifesting the full capacity of their true nature, other people will naturally want to learn from them. Those who are fully familiar with their own true nature have a tremendous ability to attract others through that profound familiarity and confidence. Others see them and say, "I want what they have! They're a human being just like me, and if they can embody those qualities, then so can I!" So many people want to be at peace, accomplished, loving and wise, and a skilled and direct teacher can facilitate the recognition of these inherent gifts.

A direct teacher has the power to introduce people to open intelligence and can support people in becoming fully familiar with open intelligence through the use of clear language and supportive conditions. Furthermore, the teacher's power is evident in the written and oral teachings, which contain key points and pivotal instructions that directly benefit those who read or hear them. A direct teaching is also able to provide centers for study and practice that are relevant to the needs of those being served.

Of course, throughout time there have also been highly visible teachers whose teachings led nowhere or who took advantage of their students in harmful ways. The result is that many people all over the world don't trust gurus or spiritual teachers at all. Some people have had negative experiences with teachers, and as a result they no longer feel drawn to seek out a teacher, and this is quite easy to understand. Enlightenment teachings are one area of human endeavor where a certain kind of result is often promised but rarely delivered! If some kind of assurance is made or implied, and then no result is forthcoming, then obviously that can lead to diminished trust.

This is one aspect of the whole issue, but to contend that no teacher is needed under any circumstance would be to adopt an opposite—and extreme—stance. One might take the position, "Because so few of these promises have ever been fulfilled, no teacher is needed," but that would be a gross oversimplification. I am certainly not advocating that we do away with all the teachers! But it is important to be able to distinguish between what is helpful and what is not.

If we want to learn something new—plumbing, cooking, playing tennis or whatever it is—then it's always wise to seek the advice of someone who has more experience in that area than we have. If, for instance, we want to climb Mount Everest, we wouldn't try to do so without a guide. We'd want to learn from someone who's experientially familiar with Everest and who knows exactly how to reach the summit and what the conditions are going to be along the way. Without a guide or our own prior experience, we might end up taking the wrong direction, falling into an abyss, getting buried in an avalanche or succumbing to altitude illness.

With mountain climbing, as with teachers, we can find different kinds of guides, and some guides are more likely to get us to the summit. The unerring and clear approach of a direct teacher can take us to the summit. We can have confidence in the accomplishment of someone who has realized the fundamental condition and who has supported many others in doing the same.

Only we can decide which teaching is most suitable for us, but whatever it is, we must commit to it one hundred percent. The commitment isn't a small one where we say, "I will try it some days and not others." If we choose a practice like relying on open intelligence, but we make only a partial commitment, then some of the time we will be relying on open intelligence, and the rest of the time we will be engaging in the stories of ordinary thinking. If, on the other hand, we make a one hundred percent commitment, then indwelling confidence will develop, and with that confidence certainty will come about.

Sometimes, even if we've really made a firm commitment, the commitment may wane for a while. That's just how it is. If we feel our commitment waning a little, then we simply need to recommit to the decision we've made to rely on open intelligence and to continue to do that alone. It's as simple as that. The truth is that we're always committed either to our data or to relying on open intelligence, so the choice is very simple. A one hundred percent commitment is the easiest, because then there's never any thinking about it. First comes the introduction to relying on open intelligence, and once we fully recognize what that is, then we can easily make a wholehearted commitment to it.

Another word we could use for commitment is enthusiasm. We really have to have enthusiasm for the true nature of our being. The word "enthusiasm" has its root in the Greek words "in God," but another way of defining it is a lively interest in the inspiration of being at ease. To be enthusiastic means that we allow our naturally easeful condition to be *as it is*. Even if we're experiencing the intense emotions of rage, sadness and depression, we can nevertheless remain totally enthusiastic and committed to open intelligence as the root of these perceptions.

In this day and age we should be discerning consumers wherever we shop, and that includes being discerning about the teachings to which we intend to commit. We should ask ourselves, "What can I expect from the practice that I'm interested in?" Like any good consumer, before we make the purchase, we should find out if the promised results are actually being delivered. If we want to buy a TV set, an MP3 player or a car, we'll seek out a store that's provided that product to many satisfied customers. We wouldn't continue going to a store where they said again and again, "Yes, yes, we'll have it for you tomorrow," and then day after day the item wasn't there. Well, if we have that much discrimination when buying a TV, shouldn't we have at least that much discrimination when we're talking about the most important aspect of human life?

Discernment in seeking a practice is no different from acumen in the business world. We have lots of information today about almost everything, and we also have a lot of information about many different methods and practices. We should be very careful about choosing the teacher and teaching we want to follow. I mean, really, wouldn't we want to choose the approach that's most effective? Relying on open intelligence has worked for many millions of people throughout time, and no matter who you are or how you've lived, it can work for you also if you are committed to it. Of all practices, it's the simplest and most direct.

Q: How exactly would you describe enlightenment?

A: Enlightenment is described in many ways these days—and increasingly so now with the Internet and the growing number of books on the topic, but there are very few wisdom texts that actually speak directly about what enlightenment is and also provide the unerring instruction about its realization.

We don't use the "e-word" in the Balanced View Training, because it's been so tarnished by many years of misinterpretations, and using it would only create confusion. Once we call it "enlightenment," then that might mean that it belonged to a tradition, a religion, a historical figure or a country. There's simply too much misunderstanding about what the word means for it to be used with people from widely divergent backgrounds. So, we say "gaining complete confidence in open intelligence" or "realizing perfect mental and emotional stability."

What's been termed enlightenment is simply the full revelation of the seamless expanse of nondual open intelligence that includes and transcends all. To the degree that we rely on open intelligence, the qualities of potent benefit inherent in open intelligence will become obvious and our lives will be a source of great benefit to others. It's as simple as that.

Q: Aren't these teachings you're giving the same as ones from other teachers that deal with stillness, emptiness, living in the present or enlightenment?

A: Well, I'm not here to comment on any other teaching; I'm just saying that there are two kinds of teachings. One type of teaching occurs within cause and effect and focuses on getting into a certain state like stillness, emptiness or living in the present. These are some of the popular contemporary themes. The other type of teaching is beyond causality and does not involve adoption of descriptive frameworks. It is the teaching of relying on open intelligence, in which everything, moment-to-moment, is absolutely equal and seamless. The goal is already present and nothing needs to change. Everything, just *as it is*, unfolds in a continuous open flow of pure presence.

I see in many other approaches that people are able to have a preliminary experience of open intelligence, but it's an experience that is somewhat like a cat watching a mouse. The observer is identified with open intelligence and is engaged in observing what appears within open intelligence, as though it's something different from open intelligence. In other words, there's still a strong sense of duality between open intelligence and what appears within it.

Such experiences are vastly different from the complete resolution of all data in the basic space of open intelligence, which is what the Balanced View Training offers. I can only recommend that you give this Training a try. The benefit of relying on open intelligence is immediate and instantly verifiable. I don't ask that anyone take my word for it. I would suggest giving it a try and finding out for yourself by simply relying on open intelligence for short moments, repeated many times, and see what happens.

Maintaining Open Intelligence in Sleep and Dreams

CHAPTER TWENTY

> *"If we maintain open intelligence as we drift into sleep, then we will have directly introduced ourselves to open intelligence in a whole new way. When we accomplish undistracted open intelligence in sleep, then it will also be much easier for us to enjoy undistracted open intelligence at other times of the day."*

When we go to sleep at night, normally we just sort of conk out, and then some hours later we wake up. Most of us don't have any control over what happens during those hours. When we fall asleep, we're just asleep; we can't consciously do anything while in that state, and consequently we believe that we're at the complete whim of sleep and dreams. We don't know how it all happens, but something is happening to us, and we don't have any power over it.

When we don't recognize the open intelligence that is at the basis of sleep and dreams, we're just lost in those worlds. When we have a dream, anything can happen in it. It can be the craziest and most bizarre thing or the most sublime thing. All these phantasmagorical images appear, some of which we remember and some we don't. Generally speaking, while in the dream we have no idea that it's a dream and we take it to be real.

The same can be said for the waking state, which is truly just a dreamlike appearance within the changeless reality of open intelligence. If we take our bodies and the various events sandwiched between birth and death to be who we are—while ignoring the substratum of open intelligence that alone can truly be said to exist—the result will be alienation from the timeless freedom and perfect peace that constitute our true nature.

This is what non-recognition of open intelligence is: being lost in the belief that the thoughts, emotions and experiences define who we are and thinking that the states we pass through are real. For the whole of our lives we've been thinking that the everyday states of waking, dreaming and sleeping are who we are. Most of us are deeply convinced that our birth, life and death completely define who we are. We think that without them we would not be, and we depend on them for our sense of identity. However, when we rely on open intelligence, more and more we find that we're not dependent on any concept whatsoever. We're not dependent on the body or the mind, nor are we dependent on the waking, sleep and dream states. We don't even depend on air, the Earth, the sun or even the universe! It's very important to go beyond all the ordinary descriptions we've learned to identify with, and we do that simply by maintaining open intelligence.

I want to share with you a very powerful practice that can help you use the pivotal moment of falling asleep to discover the substratum of open intelligence. When we go to sleep at night, we can begin to maintain open intelligence as we're falling asleep. As we do this, we'll see that all the activity of the conceptual mind—the stirring and proliferation of thoughts and emotions—gradually merges into a non-conceptual state, which is the sleep state. This is still a state of mind. It's not real freedom; it's just another datum within open intelligence.

At that pivotal moment when we find that all the concepts have merged into a non-conceptual state, we can then pose a very important question to ourselves: "What is it that is *aware* of this non-conceptual mind?" This question leads directly into the substratum of pure open intelligence. By relying on the open intelligence that is revealed through this inquiry, we will be able to differentiate between the basic space of open intelligence, which is our true identity, and the non-conceptual sleep state, which is just another state of mind. When we have discovered the open intelligence that is the same in all states and conditions, it will become easier and easier to maintain open intelligence throughout the day and during the night as well.

We don't have to make a big deal out of it. It is as simple as relying on open intelligence for short moments, many times, while falling asleep. This is the single practice with all data, including falling asleep, dreaming and sleeping. If open intelligence comes easily when falling asleep, it'll come easily, and if it doesn't come easily, we don't try to force it. At some point it may just naturally appear, and we'll fall asleep totally aware and remain aware during our sleep. We don't have to try this every night, but if only once we can be aware in this way as we move into sleep, we will see that sleep and dreams are themselves data within open intelligence. If we maintain open intelligence as we drift into sleep, then we will have directly introduced ourselves to open intelligence in a new way. When we accomplish undistracted open intelligence in sleep, then it will also be much easier for us to enjoy undistracted open intelligence at other times of the day.

Some people practice remaining aware all night long, even in deep sleep. What's most important about this practice is to see through firsthand experience that dreaming and sleeping are appearances of open intelligence. Through relying on open intelligence the three categories we use to describe our 24-hour experience—waking, dreaming, and sleeping—are completely gone beyond. We see that all three of these are just data within the all-encompassing pure view of open intelligence.

When we maintain open intelligence in the dream state, we realize that all the component parts of the dream can be changed or manipulated just by deciding to do so. If we choose to do that, we will be able to actively participate in the dreams we have and change what goes on in them. We'll be able to be aware in our dreams and be a master of the illusion of dreaming.

When there is a feeling that we are at the whim of dreams, they seem totally beyond our control. But with the decisive experience of being able to change what is going on in a dream, it becomes possible to directly experience open intelligence as not only beyond all phenomena, but also as having mastery over all phenomena. However, rearranging the figures in the dream—whether it is the waking dream or the sleeping dream—is not really a pastime we need to get into. In and of itself it is not a goal worth striving for, but the ability to do so is a natural byproduct of the complete mental mastery that comes through the practice of relying on open intelligence.

What's most important is to decisively realize open intelligence as the pure space of all images that occur within it. There's no need at all to try to analyze any of the images, whether they are daytime images or nighttime images. Like all phenomena, the nighttime images in dreams are just self-appearances of open intelligence, as are the images during waking life. They're identical in that respect. When we acknowledge open intelligence as the ground of our being by relying on open intelligence in the direct encounter with all phenomena, then we realize in a very powerful way that all images that appear are due to open intelligence and nothing else. So, there's nothing that needs to be done about any of them.

By relying on open intelligence, more and more we know open intelligence as the benevolent reality of our being, and all phenomena are then seen as benevolent and perfect just the way they are. They don't need to be analyzed, improved or changed; in fact, nothing at all needs to be done about any appearance. If we've been accustomed to analyzing the images in our dreams, this is a perfect opportunity to bring that to a complete stop, for the ultimate substance and meaning of all images is the same. They are all just passing forms of open intelligence, and that's all we need to know about dreams.

Although most people believe that the waking state is reality and the dream state unreal, the "waking dream" and the "sleeping dream" are identical in that they're both data within the changeless reality of open intelligence. The wisdom benefit of flawless open intelligence is completely uncontained and has never been made into anything. Even though the various phenomena that appear in waking states and dream states may seem incredibly substantial, when we examine them we find that there is nothing hold-able or keep-able within any appearance. When we maintain open intelligence in the face of what appears, then we can relax and know that the appearances are nothing at all to be afraid of.

We can rest assured that whatever appears—whether it is an event during the day or an image in a dream during the night—it is nothing but an appearance of open intelligence. This understanding is a very powerful resource for working out our daytime data. The phantasmagorical content of our dream states at night can bring about a very powerful resolution of data within us, so that during the day it will be easier for us to rely on open intelligence. When we can be at ease with even our most frightening dream imagery, the images we face in our waking state become significantly easier to face.

When we awake in the morning, normally all the data of our waking state that were in abeyance during sleep immediately come flooding back in. If we rely on open intelligence in the moment when we wake up and the thoughts return, we find that we need not get caught up again in the torrent of thoughts and emotions. Giving in to the thoughts that appear when we wake up in the morning is just a habit we've sustained for a long time. It may have seemed that it's impossible to feel ourselves empowered because of the immediate onslaught of thoughts, but if we can maintain open intelligence we'll see that we don't have to be ruled by the thoughts or sensory impressions.

When we sustain open intelligence as we wake up in the morning, it will be easier for us to see the workings of the mind and not get caught in habitual patterns of identification with passing phenomena. Rest is best upon waking up in the morning; otherwise, we may be tempted to think, "Oh, after such a beautiful vacation in sleep, here's all this garbage again!"

Instead of getting into endless stories about thoughts, emotions or images—identifying with some thoughts and rejecting others—we can see all phenomena as equal and allow the relief of open intelligence to be our constant comfort. Thoughts and emotions never have an independent nature and will vanish of their own accord, so there's no need to do anything about them. What do we need to do about them when they're going to vanish anyway? If we don't see that thoughts are their own undoing and are free and perfect in their own place, then we'll think we have to do something about them. But when we practice seeing perfection in all appearances and relying on the open intelligence that is the substance and essence of all appearances, the illusion of a personal identity and its workings is recognized to be insubstantial and without conflict.

With continued practice we come to see that open intelligence pervades not only our waking life, but also sleep and everything that is contained within sleep. If we bring this presence of open intelligence to the process of falling asleep, we'll soon see that open intelligence is present in all that appears.

As we feel more and more empowered, we may eventually be emboldened enough to pose the question: "If open intelligence supersedes waking, dreaming and sleeping, then could open intelligence also supersede birth and death?" The question might not mean very much if it remains only a philosophical idea, but if there is a direct experience of open intelligence as the unchanging basis of *all* phenomena, then something quite extraordinary could occur. One would come to see that even birth and death are just passing data within changeless open intelligence, and the irrevocable realization of this truth can only come through getting fully acquainted with open intelligence; mere theoretical acknowledgement is not enough.

It's quite likely that no one has ever told us this very important truth about ourselves, namely, that dreams and sleep and birth and death are just data within changeless, timeless open intelligence. Each datum that appears is complete and identical and equal to every other datum that appears. There's never been any differentiation, inclusion or exclusion, because open intelligence is indivisible—and its own appearances can never affect that oneness. This is crucially important.

The practice of relying on open intelligence while falling asleep can help introduce us to the fundamental nature of open intelligence. Then, while maintaining open intelligence as we experience the states of sleep and dreams, we can know that it is open intelligence alone that encompasses and transcends all states of mind. When we've discovered all-encompassing, all-transcending open intelligence to be our fundamental nature, the treasure of perfect mental balance becomes our own, and it is a treasure we'll be happy to share with all.

COMPLETE PERCEPTUAL OPENNESS
CHAPTER TWENTY-ONE

> *"It isn't that there is "someone who is perceptually open" looking at a datum which is something apart. There is nothing but indivisible open intelligence manifesting equally as the seer, the seeing and the seen. The experiencer is indivisible from its experience and its experiencing, and all are mere appearances of open intelligence."*

When we completely relax our seeing without any need to focus on all of the descriptions that we've learned, then we find open intelligence already present in ourselves—something we may have never before recognized. We're not finding anything new; we're just finding our natural way of looking, sensing and experiencing the world. It isn't a destination we're going to get to; it has always been present from the very beginning of our life—and even before our conception.

To have complete perceptual openness means to relax our perception into wide-open spaciousness with no need to close in on any thought, emotion, object or experience to make sense of what's happening. When we completely relax our attention from its habitual pinpointed focus, we see everything *as it is*: a limitless, seamless expanse of changeless pure open intelligence in which myriad ephemeral forms of open intelligence appear and disappear. Most of us have learned to fix our attention on whatever is appearing and to describe it as if it had a separate existence, but when we do so we immediately disconnect from our natural openness and collapse into the idea of a separate self that relies on thought to describe what's going on. When we have this individualized thinking and the fear-based emotional field that thinking creates, then we're very restricted and limited to that emotional field. We live on the head of a pin when we do that, and that's a very cramped and uncomfortable space!

When we relax our perception from that narrow focus, then we discover the vast openness of what's right here, the ground of reality that is completely beyond any of the information contained within it. In that spaciousness there's no need to use any kind of limited information to describe what's going on. When we relax into our own wide-open seeing, then we enter the primordial space of wisdom and all-knowingness. There's complete perceptual openness in the immediacy of all experience, and in that is inherent benefit for all beings, including ourselves.

All the contrived notions of needing to describe a world and its beings in myriad ways are simply conventions and beliefs, and they're entirely made up. The supreme oneness that is our true identity is equally present everywhere and is the sole underlying reality of all forms and situations. If we describe ourselves as the thinking and emotions that we've accumulated over our lifetime, then we separate ourselves out from the enjoyment of what is immediately open, spacious, free and timeless. We may be doing something as simple as buying a shirt at a store, but if there is complete perceptual openness in that experience, then Wal-Mart becomes a temple, because *everything* is seen as a temple of nondual equalness.

Open intelligence—complete perceptual openness—is the sovereign ruler of all. It is the greatest of monarchs, and everything is united within it; in fact, everything within it, *is* it! There's never been any kind of separation. We don't need to figure out any pieces of the puzzle to understand the puzzle. To describe this in philosophical terms and come to an intellectual understanding is one thing, but to really know it fully we have to decisively experience it in our own being. To do so, we just relax in naturally present openness that is the natural presence of uncontrived love, wisdom and energy, for short moments, repeated many times. This is the easiest way and the most ancient of ways. What is being stated here is not new. Throughout human history there have always been people who have discovered their true nature through relying on open intelligence.

The uncontrived presence of love, wisdom and energy is always wide-open and completely relaxed; it is never tight, tense or restricted. It has never been made into anything or tied up into a thought, emotion or experience of any kind. Always and forever flawless, stainless and totally free, it has no need to depend on anything. It stands alone, which really means "all-one." It is the all-encompassing super-complete wholeness. To say that it depends on something would make it incomplete, and that can never be.

We shouldn't be satisfied with somebody's idea about what this perceptual openness is; we need to take it all the way in terms of our own experience. If we get locked into ideas about what different historical figures or contemporary figures have said about the ultimate reality, then it really limits our own familiarity with it. Complete perceptual openness is not anything that someone can give us or take away from us. If anyone is telling us that the nature of our being will be realized through their grace, we simply need to recognize that grace is synonymous with open intelligence and is not given by someone else.

It doesn't matter where we are, who we are, how we're feeling emotionally, what we're thinking, what our job is, what our gender is, what our skin color is, how old we are or anything else we can describe about our body or mind—we're always and forever beyond all those descriptions. In every era of humankind, the descriptions about the body and mind change radically. There was one way of describing the body and mind a hundred years ago, there is a way of describing them now and a hundred years from now there'll be something completely different. The good news is that our fundamental condition never changes and is beyond any description. Anything that we describe about our body and mind has nothing to say about our fundamental condition, and our fundamental condition doesn't depend on anything we can say about our body and mind.

The conventional understanding is that we are dependent on the organs of the body, the air coming in and out and the water and food we eat, drink, digest and excrete, but the truth is that we're not dependent on any of that to be aware. Open intelligence is permanent, limitless and forever free, and it requires nothing—not the breath, not a body, not even the existence of the universe. We are the primordial condition in which the entire universe appears and disappears. When we enjoy complete perceptual openness in the immediacy of every moment, then we come to decisively experience that in a way that is unarguable and unimaginable.

Luminous mind is the nature of everyone, and it doesn't matter what the previous thoughts, emotions and actions have been. The true nature of luminous mind is untouched by any of those things and is always completely available. Whether the actions or thoughts have been moral or immoral, social or antisocial, the mind which contains them is completely luminous, wide-open, and free. The wondrous display of data is just whatever it is, but whether it's a horror show or a charming fairy tale makes no difference to the open intelligence in which it all appears. To try to rearrange the perceptions or to think that it has to be this way or that way is to enter into more duality.

Of course, the ordinary thinking mind tends to balk at this. "How could moral and immoral perceptions be equal? How could antisocial and well-socialized activity be equal?" But the wisdom of luminous mind doesn't need to divide everything up into tight little categories that the thinking mind can grasp. The natural activity of luminous mind remains at ease regardless of what appears, and no matter what appears it is all like a burst of the infinite light of wisdom mind. Whatever descriptions are given to the appearances, they are all equally free and spacious. They are indivisible from open intelligence and do not have a beginning, middle or end.

This morning I was drying my hair, and I was noticing how the hairdryer takes air in from the back, warms it up and then directs it out from the front end. I saw that if the back end got blocked somehow and the air couldn't flow through easily, the whole thing would overheat and melt. That is kind of what happens when we train our perception to focus on data instead of relying on the spaciousness in which the data appear. When we focus on all the appearances and try to define them all, the life-giving flow of wide-open open intelligence and the continuous flow of tremendous energy of love and wisdom that is naturally present is blocked. This is how modern minds are trained to function. No effort is required to get acquainted with perceptual openness. If we repeatedly relax our body and mind, the perceptual openness that is our true nature will begin to flow naturally, and we'll discover basic goodness, warmth and compassion that are spontaneously present.

It isn't that there is "someone who is perceptually open" looking at a datum which is something apart. There is nothing but indivisible open intelligence manifesting equally as the seer, the seeing and the seen. The experiencer is indivisible from its experience and its experiencing, and all are mere appearances of open intelligence. We train ourselves in the belief that there is a separate perceiver, but when we maintain unwavering open intelligence and gain confidence in it, we don't have to worry about any of these philosophical concepts. We relax and allow open intelligence to be *as it is*, and in the wisdom of that, all questions are answered.

When we're relying on open intelligence, we're not *looking* for open intelligence; we simply are as we are. If what's looking is looking for itself and believes it will find it elsewhere, it's going to get very confusing! Rely on open intelligence alone, which is the source of the looking. This is naked open intelligence that's forever undistracted by whatever appears. Forever empty open intelligence is the source condition of all. All data that occur within forever empty open intelligence are already completely relaxed, as they are nothing but the pure sky of open intelligence. There is never any effort needed to rest as the essence of what's looking. If you rest as what's looking, pretty soon you'll see that what's looking is not limited to you. It's not trapped within the skin line of your body. It is open intelligence itself, and open intelligence is without boundaries. It is the raw intelligence of nature, the universe and all the universe contains.

Open intelligence is not an object to look for. It's always here as the looking itself. When we enjoy just that, without seeking anything or describing anything that appears, then that pure looking—unattached *as it is* to an individual looker or datum that is looked at—is discovered to be timelessly present, everywhere.

But if we continue to focus on data, we will always be involved in the labels and tangled up in dictionary definitions of appearances. We'll always be trying to convince ourselves that life makes sense by putting together an endless string of words. However, all the words in the dictionary point to a specific definition of something as existing in its own right—as something fixed, stable and solid that can be separated out from everything else and depended upon in some way. But if all those seemingly fixed and solid things were put into a linear particle accelerator, we would find they are all made of nothing but space. Space is the one underlying reality shared by all things. The partial definitions in the dictionary are therefore not only misleading, they have nothing to tell us about our fundamental condition or the condition of anything! As long as the fundamental aspect of the defined phenomena is missing, the definition is incomplete and inaccurate.

We can rectify this situation by adding an ultimate meaning to every word in the dictionary, and that is, "the pure presence of nature's indivisible and aware intelligence, dynamic and unconfined, devoid of an independent nature." If we add that phrase to all the definitions in the dictionary, then we can begin to know what everything really is. Every word in the dictionary has these two aspects: its aspect as a description or label, and its forever empty, always abiding and clear aspect that is the aware intelligence at the basis of everything. These two together inseparably comprise the forever empty open intelligence that manifests as all we see. In other words, there is no two!

Open intelligence is our natural being, and to experience that natural being in a definitive way moment-to-moment requires complete perceptual openness in all experience. By simply hearing about it over and over again, the certainty about it will dawn. Nothing else is required. As we relax we'll find that our perception naturally eases and becomes more and more open and free. Whatever appears will then be seen as inseparable from restful openness. After having lived with constant anxiety due to all the years of focusing on passing data, the ease will be a welcome discovery. Once complete mental relaxation has been tasted, even for one moment, the mind will naturally go to that relief again and again. Short moments, repeated many times, become continuous.

Q: All of us have the very real experience each day of the various aspects of happy and sad, good and bad, positive and negative, so it's really hard for me to get my head around this idea of the equalness of all appearances, because this is just not something that I've experienced in my own life. Could you maybe help me understand how things are ultimately equal?

A: All things are ultimately equal, because all things have the same changeless essence. The basic space of mind is always in complete equilibrium and evenness, and whatever appears within the mind is made only of that basic space. That open intelligence is the reality, whereas the inner and outer phenomena that come and go within it are like images seen in a mirage. Whether we label the images good or bad, painful or pleasurable, that doesn't change their mirage-like nature. The reality underlying all of them is the same.

All of us have observed as we age that over time the reflection in the mirror is changing as our physical appearance changes. But almost all of us have also had the experience of knowing that what is looking at that image in the mirror has never changed. The image I've seen in the mirror has varied, as I went from being 5 years old to 10 years to 20 to 40 and now to 60. The face of a young girl has now changed into someone who has wrinkles and gray hair, but *what's looking* is completely unaffected by all these physical changes. The face is different, but the essence of who I am has always remained the same.

If we recognize the equilibrium and immutability of what's looking, then we can let thoughts and appearances come and go without needing to label them or give them importance. We drain ourselves of our vitality when we persist in holding to the importance of something that is nothing other than an appearance of open intelligence. Whether we label an impression of the mind as anger or joy, it's of the same basic space. When we start to think that some things are good and other things are bad, we fall out of the total simplicity of the great equalness into a realm of division and endless complexity. When we give thoughts and emotions significance in their own right, we're ignoring the changeless basis of all the thoughts. We just don't notice that it's there.

When we discover spacious open intelligence, we see that all appearances are sourced in that. Then the equalness of all becomes self-evident. If you write the words "fear" and "happiness" in the air with your finger, is there really fear or happiness in either of them? They're both just space and are completely equal.

Relying on the basic space of open intelligence means complete perceptual openness in all experience. It means complete ease with no need to cling to anything or push anything away; it means not attempting to describe or define the indescribable. Open intelligence reveals itself everywhere as a single nondual expanse. There is no need to think about it, toy with it or write a philosophy book about it. It's just so simple; who we are couldn't be simpler! Open intelligence, by which we know we are, is timelessly free. We wouldn't even know that we are present without open intelligence. Where would we be looking for it and who would look, as both are data of open intelligence? If you say, "I am looking for open intelligence," then you are stepping away from it, because open intelligence is what's looking.

If we're worried about the depletion of natural resources on planet Earth, it is important to recognize the ultimate natural resource—open intelligence—and rely on that, and then by the power of its wisdom, insight and skillful activities, we can begin to solve the many problems that have come about from having exhausted the Earth's natural resources. When we rely on wisdom, then we are naturally of benefit to ourselves and all beings, and we enact this in a very immediate way.

The personal stories we had about things that once bothered us and really got us upset—stories about fear, anger, jealousy, pride or desire—we see that somehow these things do not affect us anymore or affect us less and less. We may have told stories based on cause and effect: "I am angry because…" or "I am jealous because…" but now we see that there is something about us that is beyond causation. Now that there is just the relaxed open intelligence of what's looking, where are all those causes and effects? Where we used to have a story, there isn't a story any longer.

For most people this comes about gradually. As we continue to rely on open intelligence in the face of whatever appears, disturbing states that once would have upset us now gradually begin to vanish in and of their own accord like the flight path of a bird in the sky. We remain like the sky, ever free.

Q: I have a lot of doubts about my being able to have the perceptual openness that you describe. I have a very stressful job that has a lot of pressure and high-level responsibility, and I am in some way or another working at this job almost all the waking hours of each day. If I just relax in the way that you are talking about, I could never get my job done.

A: Your own circumstances, whatever they may be, are always the perfect opportunity for relying on open intelligence. Whether you're in a high-stress job or doing nothing, whatever your data are, they're the perfect opportunity to rely on open intelligence. I know this without any doubt, but you must be willing to make relying on open intelligence a priority in your life and find a few moments here and there throughout the day to practice it. Anyone can do that, no matter what the job is. You just have to make the choice. In the long run those few moments of open intelligence will make you much more efficient and productive in your job and more successful in every aspect of your life.

If you continue to practice relying on open intelligence for short moments, repeated many times, soon you'll be relying on open intelligence without trying to do so. For most people progress is made gradually. No matter how doubting or skeptical you might be right now, if you keep relying on open intelligence every day as is being suggested here, I can guarantee you that you'll eventually be able to say, "I didn't think it would ever happen to me, but it has!" Relying on open intelligence is the swift and sure approach. Don't be fooled by thinking you need to do anything else.

Even if your day is filled with stressful activities, remember that your entire life is a free-flowing appearance of open intelligence. That fundamental condition is always present and always aware of whatever stressful activities are occurring. Wide-open spaciousness is the true nature of your mind, and it is never anything other than that. It is urgently important to know that about yourself and to never collapse into mundane ideas about who you are.

Who we are as human beings is extraordinarily simple, and today there are many, many people who can realize this. It may not have been so easy for people to understand a message like this at other times in history, but today it is.

Open intelligence is total love, total splendor and extraordinary energy with no possibility whatsoever of being disconnected from anyone or anything. We are limitless and beyond all fear by virtue of our fundamental condition. There is no need to defend or protect negative or positive states of mind, because nothing can ever happen to the open intelligence that is the source of their appearance. Even your own life does not need to be guarded, because what you are does not depend on a life. You are the timeless essence of life itself.

Simply develop great enthusiasm for relying on open intelligence and persevere in a cheerful, caring and relaxed way. Short moments, repeated many times will carry you through.

DECISIONS WITHOUT DECISION-MAKING
CHAPTER TWENTY-TWO

"If you're struggling to make a decision, you might want to ask yourself, "Which choice will be of the greatest benefit to me and to the greatest number of people?" That's a simple and straightforward guideline for making decisions."

Many people struggle long and hard in making decisions, trying to think out every possible angle. They may even torture themselves emotionally by imagining all the possible ways things could go wrong and then they blame themselves for their indecisiveness. The good news is that thoughts and emotions aren't necessary for decision-making! Thoughts and emotions are a limited basis for good decision-making and are only a small part of our capabilities.

If we had a recipe for a great cake but used only a few of the required ingredients, no one would want to eat our cake! Similarly, relying solely on our thoughts and emotions is like using only part of the ingredients required to make good decisions.

Haven't we noticed how our obsessive thinking and emotions work? "Oh, I have to make a decision. Is this going to be the right decision, or should I have chosen the other option?" Then after making the decision there is more thinking and emotion. "Is this what I should be doing? Is this going to work out all right for me?" This idea that we have to think continuously about everything in order to arrive at any conclusion is simply a habit.

Within the perfect ease discovered by maintaining open intelligence lies wisdom that is entirely non-conceptual, beneficial and super-complete in itself. The more we rely on open intelligence, the more we really know that we don't have to micro-manage all of our thoughts and emotions.

We can't plan what is going to happen. In fact, the only thing we can count on is that we *don't know* what's going to happen! So, why come up with all these ideas about what should happen? When we rely on open intelligence and start to trust the natural order of everything, then we have insights that are truly worth having. They aren't like the kind of ideas we've had before; they are wisdom insights. The more we rely on open intelligence, the more we trust this wisdom. Our decisions then flow with the natural order of everything, and everything is effortlessly the way it is. I used to toy with decisions, but now I never do.

Q: I'm dealing with an illness that involves making a lot of decisions about health care, and quite frankly, I feel very unsure about the proper decisions to make. How could I use what you're saying in a practical way to make these very crucial decisions?

A: As we become more adept at relying on open intelligence, we find that we can be at ease in all situations, and we know how to respond whatever the situations are.

Nowadays we have a lot of very different lifestyle choices and a wide variety of healthcare options as well. When a decision has to be made about what care is needed, one person might choose to go to a medical doctor, another might go see an Ayurvedic practitioner, while another might try a nutritionist. In other countries someone might go to a shaman or village healer. In an emergency, one person may use as many telephones as they can to call 911, while another person may decide to not call for assistance at all. Whatever occurs is appearing in, of, as and through the same unalterable, unchangeable open intelligence.

When dealing with illness, one choice might be to not have any intervention at all. I've seen a number of examples where people have received a very frightening diagnosis but have chosen to not have any kind of invasive treatment. I know of one woman in particular who had been diagnosed with cancer, and she decided to not have any medical intervention at all. She was able to understand that she had choices. Those choices came from being profoundly at ease with her human nature and knowing herself so well that she saw exactly what the right course of action was for her. It has to be entirely up to us; no one can tell us what the right course of action is.

If we are relying profoundly on open intelligence, then we will have a cornucopia of choices, because rather than just seeing one option, we are able to see all options. When we deeply acknowledge who we are in a very simple way, then it becomes easy for us to act as nature does. After all, we are nature—human nature—and we are profound participants in open intelligence, which is completely at ease. Even chaos, confusion and war all appear in the natural order and then resolve into it as well. When the mind is completely at ease in all situations, we act as nature does and we are in harmony with the natural order of everything. The open intelligence that is looking, touching, tasting and sensing through us is always completely at ease, no matter what the emotional or physical states are. Whatever we decide to do with our life, it is perfect, and we do it with complete ease.

Now, whenever I talk about rest or ease, often people think that I'm talking about being a couch potato, but that's not my meaning. The ease of our own open intelligence will guide us in how to act most skillfully. For people who are relying on open intelligence without trying to do so, there is only immense energy, love and wisdom that shower benefit everywhere. Our minds and bodies have one single purpose, and that is to benefit ourselves and others. That means that we treat ourselves and others in a natural and friendly way that comes from being at ease in our being.

So, if you're struggling to make a decision, you might want to ask yourself, "Which choice will be of the greatest benefit to me and to the greatest number of people?" That's a simple and straightforward guideline for making decisions.

Q: Do we begin to make different choices as we rely more on open intelligence?

A: I'll share an experience from my own life in that regard. I am married and I have children and grandchildren, so I have lived the life of a householder for at least part of my life. But then ten years ago, I decided to go live by myself in a house in a small town in California. That just came about naturally, because my life became more and more committed to the benefit of all and my primary focus had become the Balanced View Training. I have complete, loving, wonderful relationships with all members of my family, including my husband, and the relationships are better than they've ever been. It just naturally came about that I would be living in another way. So, this is just the way it is, and there is nothing to think or worry about—it just naturally occurs.

Q: I have a lot of trouble making decisions, and I find that the period while I am trying to decide can be very stressful. The same sort of stressful circumstance is at work when I have to prepare for something where my performance will be judged, like say, giving a speech in front of people. Do you have suggestions to help with that?

A: Our natural way of speaking is completely uncontrived and doesn't require any studying or preparation. Everything happens in a completely relaxed way, and we know this through simply relying on open intelligence no matter what's going on. When we're caught up in a personal identity, we might work on a speech for days, read through several books and spend hours on the Internet looking up things to make sure that everything will be included. We'll be so nervous that the night before the presentation we won't sleep much, because we'll be thinking about everything else that should go into the speech!

There is no need to dive into a scenario where your identity is based on your accumulation of thoughts, emotions, experiences and conceptual frameworks. If you are able to just be at ease, you are greatly fortunate, because that means you've experienced a decisive openness that allows you to relax with no need to rely on conceptual frameworks. In that openness there is the ability to understand the underlying implications of what I'm saying in a broader scope. There is then no need to get upset and worried about all those speeches you may need to give.

In the conventional way of thinking about things, intellectual prowess is valued very much, and if we show that our intellectual prowess is better than everybody else's, then we're really at the top of the heap! However, when it comes to getting acquainted with who we really are, intellectual prowess is a small reward when compared to the vital knowledge of pristine open intelligence. The constant efforting of intellectual prowess is evidence of an inability to relax. But when there is total confidence in open intelligence, clear speech and action occur without reliance on thinking. The melodious song and dance of open intelligence appears naturally without ever needing to twist thoughts into a certain shape or language, and from that the most sublime words will flow. The intellectual prowess that is so highly prized nowadays is gone beyond in pristine wisdom.

Relax completely. Even if you have a propensity to intellectually scrutinize, examine and speculate about everything, relax as the essence of all the intellectual speculation. Whatever your circumstantial thoughts, emotions and experiences are, they are all okay. Whether you are an intellectual analyzer or subject to effusive displays of emotion—all is the magical display of open intelligence.

Q: So, do you prepare for your talks or do you just wing it?

A: To begin with, no, I don't prepare what I'm going to say. Whatever is said is just an expression of dynamic benefit and of complete responsiveness to whatever is occurring right here. There isn't any need to memorize, study, learn, make an outline, get nervous, wonder what everyone is going to think or if it will be liked; none of that is going on.

We learn in the course of our lives that in order to be smart or to speak well we have to learn a lot and gain knowledge from outside ourselves and get it inside ourselves. All this activity is associated with the idea that there is a personal identity doing all these things. The personal identity is just a conventional belief, and when it is looked into, the personal identity can't really be shown to exist in its own right. That's a huge relief, because when we no longer have this personal identity to feed, then we can just relax and feel total relief. Everything we need is already present. The thoughts we need to be thinking, the wisdom we need to have, what we need to know, and the ability to speak about it—all these things are already present.

Q: I really resonate with what you said before about thinking too much about things. I'm one of those people who always has to figure it out with their intellect.

A: If you're a big thinker, then just relax! We as a species have seen that our thinking has led to many problems. We've created so many problems, and no matter how many thoughtful solutions we've put into solving them, many problems still seem insurmountable. Does that mean that we can't solve them and that we're doomed to extinction? No, it doesn't. It means that we need to make a shift from our primitive mind into the mind that has complete familiarity with open intelligence—which is inclusive of conceptual frameworks of cause and effect, but which remains always beyond causality.

Open intelligence is the sole cause and the sole effect and all causes are uncaused. If you're playing around with all the ideas about cause and effect and you don't know that the causes are uncaused, your efforts are going to go essentially nowhere. This is the calamity that we face today as human beings. It is a calamity within ourselves, and it is a calamity for us as a species.

There are a lot of people who are thinking, "Okay, wisdom, yeah, I gotta think my way into that. I've got to go to at least three universities and keep attaching letters to the end of my name: M.A., Ph.D., M.D., and maybe a B.S." Well, you know, B.S. actually has another meaning as well! We continue going after wisdom in that way, because we don't know any other approach.

What will be achieved through this type of thinking could be called "conventional knowledge." It is knowledge based on data but it is not true wisdom at all. So, do we want to identify with that kind of intellectual achievement, or do we want to rely on the wisdom that's at the root of nature itself and which is tapped into through uncontrived easefulness? There are a lot of people wrapped up in thinking, thinking, thinking—and then thinking more about what they've been thinking! That type of process is really a barrier.

When one is completely at ease, there are no big decisions anymore. You know what big decisions are? They are ones that involve a lot of thought, emotional activity, mood swings and doubts about the decision. But when there's complete responsive ease in relationship to everything that's appearing, the unnecessary thinking and emotional activity just kind of slip out of life and become unnecessary.

In relying on open intelligence there is tremendous power, energy, force and creativity. Just on a simple human level there is immense brainpower that wasn't there before. When the brain is in the suboptimal condition of trying to sort everything and make sense out of it, then the brain is completely de-energized, because its natural state isn't acknowledged. In sustained open intelligence there is tremendous intellectual and emotional power, and with it the energy to be of benefit to others and oneself. This comes about naturally from relying on open intelligence for short moments, repeated many times.

THE QUALITIES OF OPEN INTELLIGENCE
CHAPTER TWENTY-THREE

> *"Open intelligence is shared by everyone and doesn't belong to any kind of category, institution, philosophy or religion. It has never been owned by any country or any person; it is the great treasure equally owned by all. We can either become familiar with it or continue living in the poverty of data."*

The natural state of the human mind is completely clear and relaxed at all times. It is inherently open and infused with open intelligence that is present in every moment. This clear mind registers different impressions that are called thoughts. Many of us learn that our mind is comprised of these thoughts, and we learn to pay attention only to them; we never learn anything about the completely relaxed, clear, stable, insightful and skillful nature of the mind itself. Most of us do not even know that this clear basis of the mind is there. Even if we hear something about open intelligence, we're so convinced that we're flawed that we can't bring ourselves to believe it. And even if we *are* able to believe in it theoretically, we think it couldn't possibly apply to us!

This is because we've trained ourselves to pay attention to each and every thought and to believe those thoughts define who we are. Although we continue to try, we just can't get rid of negative thoughts completely. We take our identity to be the history of all the thoughts and experiences we've had throughout our life, and for most of us that paints a rather mixed picture. If we think we are an accumulation of all of our thoughts and data, then we will feel batted around like a ping-pong ball as we are knocked back and forth from one thought to another, constantly seeking better thoughts and trying to avoid the unpleasant ones.

that the labels we have put on everything are merely descriptions pasted onto indivisible perfection. After discovering open intelligence we see the essence of open intelligence in all, and this means that we can be fearless, even in situations that involve great fear!

Beyond all the labeling of thoughts as good and bad is the natural wisdom that is completely spontaneous and always present. Our natural state is completely at ease with whatever is occurring. It is wisdom on the fly, which means that it is without any forethought or afterthought. When we are established in that wisdom, we don't need to think for long periods of time in order to come to a decision, nor will we regret our decisions or feel the need to justify them. Universal wisdom will be flowing through us, and we'll know it because that the expression of that wisdom will be so clear.

Of course, I can sit here and talk about this all day, but unless each person gets familiar with it in their own experience, there will be no real knowledge of what I am talking about. We can't think ourselves into this. We can of course gain some superficial understanding of it through thinking about it, but that's not enough. We need to decisively experience the basis of everything in order to allow that wisdom to become totally alive within us. This is within the scope of everyone—anyone can do it. It's like a dimmer switch: the light becomes gradually brighter the more you turn up the switch. The more we rely on open intelligence, the brighter its light grows. The only reason we haven't known this about ourselves is because we were never exposed to it. If we have only taken ourselves to be the descriptions that have been handed down to us by others, then we won't have the view of open intelligence; we'll be mired in data. We will only see what we've been taught, and generally speaking, that's a long way from wisdom.

The only way to fully realize true wisdom is to relax and allow the thinking to do whatever it will. As you rely on open intelligence, which is the basis of all thoughts, the wisdom that has all along been ignored becomes more and more obvious. When we relax and just allow all the thoughts and emotions to do whatever they will, our mind opens up and the clear light of wisdom dawns quite naturally. To see the background of ordinary thinking even once is very self-affirming, because we are able to glimpse the open intelligence which is changeless, permanent and forever free from suffering. Even though we may have searched for all kinds of ways to bring an end to our inner disharmony, in one instant of the light of open intelligence we find within ourselves the key to the relief from all suffering.

During the night the lights of the stars and planets can easily be seen because of the darkness, but during the day the radiant light of the sun outshines everything, and none of the stars or planets are visible. The dim light of the stars and planets is still there, but it is completely outshone by the sun. Similarly, stable open intelligence is like a clear sky filled with pure, bright daylight. Although thoughts and impressions may still appear, they are now fully outshone by the radiant light of open intelligence.

When the true nature of the mind is evident, the impressions continue to exist, but they are no longer the interpretative context that gives meaning to life. The clear light of open intelligence is now seen to be the one reality underlying all appearances, and that fundamental truth provides life's true meaning in all circumstances. Only with this revelation of the true nature of our mind can we find real happiness. When we give this to ourselves by the power of relying on open intelligence in a totally uncontrived way, for short moments, repeated many times until it becomes spontaneous and continuous, then we give ourselves the greatest and most precious gift human life can offer.

No matter who you are, what I'm saying applies to you. The pure light of open intelligence shines through all eyes, no matter whose eyes they are. It's not a mysterious or esoteric matter. The best way to describe it is to say that, when we get familiar with open intelligence, we just feel better all the time.

When we enjoy the ease of our own being, we become wise beyond compare. What exactly does it mean to be wise? It means that we know which mountain to climb. Others may choose their own mountains as they see fit, but many of those mountains are not ones that we would want to climb. If we are committed to relying on open intelligence, a very powerful source of wisdom will open up within us, and we will have a completely balanced view that will guide us in taking only the wisest actions. Tremendous energy will spontaneously arise that will bring forth greater levels of wisdom and knowledge which are devoted to activities that are of service to all.

All-encompassing open intelligence contains all knowledge—not just things we have personally learned, but *all* knowledge: past, present and future. It may seem inconceivable to us that the mind that seems to be concentrated here in our own body actually contains all knowledge, but the more familiar we get with open intelligence as the basis of all thoughts the more we'll discover that it's true. Instinctive knowledge begins appearing within us that gives us all we need to know in every situation we face. In addition, we find we have more skill in virtually everything we do, and are able to use those skills in a way that is far more powerful than anything we had ever known before.

Now, since we're talking about the wisdom inherent in open intelligence, it's important to have a very clear idea of what open intelligence actually is. Open intelligence is that by which we know we exist. It is the fundamental essence or pure intelligence by which everything is known. We would not have any knowledge of our own existence without indestructible open intelligence. It is the timeless ground of open intelligence in which all phenomena arise and pass away and it is unaffected by changes such as birth and death.

Open intelligence has four primary qualities. The first is rich and vital *openness*. To say that intelligence is "open" means that although it contains within itself all phenomena, in the final analysis it is unobstructed and phenomena-less. It has never been made into anything or entangled in anything and is completely wide-open and free. Everything that appears within it *is* it. Open intelligence has never had any taint, flaw or stain anywhere within it. When we fully rely on open intelligence, we are able to see the complete openness of everything. That openness is not a void—it is the central vigor of intelligence itself. It can also be called the primordial basic space that contains and transcends all. Nothing that appears within open intelligence has an independent nature, substance or identity in its own right. Open intelligence is the one reality of all.

No matter how much power we thought any appearance had in the past, when we rest with that appearance, we find that its true nature is stainless space. Again, we don't know that by merely thinking about it. We know that through relaxing in the natural ease of open intelligence that is the essence of our own being.

The second quality of open intelligence is *indescribability*. This means that open intelligence cannot be characterized in any way or expressed in words, and so we no longer make the attempt. Seeing the folly in using concepts to try to define open intelligence in order to grasp it, we let go of concepts altogether. Open intelligence is beyond any descriptions, and the attempt to describe it just creates more data. Rather than relying on descriptions, we rely on this great emptiness that cannot be described and does not need to be described. In that is found true freedom. There is no contradiction in expressing the fact that open intelligence is inexpressible; what I am speaking about here is in the context of nothing needing to be said or described ultimately.

The third essential quality of open intelligence is that it is *spontaneously present*. It is already fully present within us and therefore is not a goal. In stainless space there is no destination or goal anywhere. Open intelligence is timeless and locationless; it doesn't have a periphery and its center is everywhere! It is complete and identical in every single moment. There is no need for thoughts such as, "Am I there yet?" or "When am I going to be there?" or "I was there, but then I fell out of it." All those thoughts only appear and disappear in open intelligence; there is never any leaving it. To have no goal is freedom itself, for when we drop the idea of a goal we discover that what we've been seeking is already here. There is no need to think about it, write about it or speak about it. Just rest! Rest is best.

Where there is no goal, there's no need for effort. No effort is needed to pour light into light or space into space. If we draw a circle around a little section of sky, that wouldn't mean that portion of the sky has actually been separated from the rest of the sky; the sky is indivisible. In the same way, there is no way to separate anything out from flawless open intelligence. Since all is seen as equal and completely pure, to rely on open intelligence means the complete perceptual openness of the here-and-now—spacious and free—with nothing needing to be done.

The fourth essential quality of open intelligence is *indivisibility*. The sun of open intelligence shines, illuminating the entirety of data. All data are embraced as a single self-knowing open intelligence. All positive, neutral and negative data arise from the basic space of open intelligence and are automatically resolved as they appear. Therefore, all data are a single, nondual expanse of open intelligence that is vital, dynamic, unchangeable, unalterable and unfabricated in any way.

These are the four primary qualities of open intelligence: openness, indescribability, spontaneous presence and indivisibility. When we these qualities become obvious to us, we find that they are ever-open doorways into our open intelligence—doorways that are gently opened by relying on open intelligence for short moments, repeated many times. We then discover open intelligence to be an unending fount of love, wisdom, energy and potently beneficial compassion.

Q: On the one hand I find what you're saying very inspiring, but on the other hand to hear these things really depresses me. Given the life situation and outer circumstances that I have, I don't think it will ever be possible for me to realize what you're speaking about.

A: First of all I want to tell you that there is absolutely no obstacle whatsoever to your realizing this wisdom. Just keep coming back and keep listening to the teachings, and if you continue to rely on open intelligence, confidence and certainty will dawn within you. Experiment a little with relying on open intelligence, just for short moments. Don't push for anything; relax the body and mind completely and see what happens. That's very easy. Test it to see if this is of benefit to you. Keep listening, and the teaching will definitely have its effect.

The circumstances of your life are never an obstacle to relying on open intelligence; they're actually the perfect situation for becoming aware. Anything that can be described between the bookends of birth and death is nothing other than an appearance that is due to open intelligence itself. Whether it seems to be located inside or out, it's all due to the same open intelligence. We may have descriptions about our life situation, our outer circumstances and about where we are and where we need to get to, and there are many ways of describing everything that is occurring, but what can be counted on totally is the restful essence of open intelligence. Just relax in that.

I also want to encourage you to reach out for the support the Balanced View organization offers. There are many wonderful trainers available twenty-four hours a day to give support by telephone or email. We have meetings and trainings face-to-face and via teleconference or the Web. In Balanced View we have the Four Mainstays: relying on open intelligence, the trainer, the Training and the community. They are always here for you as a refuge and resort.

Just move forward very gently one day at a time. I'll compare my painful stories with yours any day; I can guarantee you, mine are worse! If I can rely on open intelligence continuously, so can you. Give the Training the benefit of the doubt, and it won't be long before it works its magic.

Q: How did you get this wisdom?

A: From nowhere and everywhere! You see, it's not in a location, and there is no one going to a location. Forever stainless open intelligence has never been located anywhere, and we don't have to travel somewhere to get it. We're in California right now, but let's say that we went to somebody on the street and asked them to tell us where California is, and they said, "Sure, just travel 26,000 miles that way and you'll end up in California." Well, it would be best not to follow that advice. Or we might meet someone who said, "Well, if you go sit on that rock for four years put your body into certain postures and think intently about California, then you might be able to get there," but of course we wouldn't want to do that either. So, then, if we're fortunate, we might meet someone else. We ask them, "Can you tell me how to get to California?" and they say, "Hey, you're already in California!" That's the person we want to listen to!

BEYOND CAUSE AND EFFECT

CHAPTER TWENTY-FOUR

"Our true being is timeless, uncaused and uncreated. In actuality the fundamental condition of everyone has never been limited by time and space or cause and effect. This is simply the way it is. Everything, no matter what it is, is a perfect expression of love, wisdom and energy that is beyond any concept or reference point."

Open intelligence is that by which everything is known. We wouldn't even be aware of our own being without open intelligence. Our own open intelligence is our direct connection to the ground of being and is completely inseparable from it; it is inherently free, already present and fully attained. Trying to attain it is like trying to attain the color of your eyes. You already have it! All you need to do is relax and see that the color of your eyes already is as it is.

Similarly, trying to employ methods to reach the ground of being is like polishing wood hoping to obtain a diamond; doing one doesn't lead to the other! More to the point, when the diamond is already present as our own true nature, what is the use of polishing wood? When we attempt to follow causes in order to get to the uncaused, we get lost in fruitless and unnecessary effort.

From the moment we're born we are told that we are flawed and that we need to be fixed. We're told that we live in space and time. We're told that everything has a cause and every cause has an effect, and that life is about effort and achievement. Taking these concepts to be real, we then attempt to try to fix ourselves so we will not be flawed. Yet, when we start trying to fix ourselves by using a variety of methods, all we end up doing is piling data on top of data and rearranging our symptoms of imperfection. With each attempt at self-repair we actually move a step away from the perfection that is here and now.

Thinking that we are making progress, we're really just running on a hamster wheel in pursuit of an imagined goal that will always remain out of reach. Adding data to other data will never lead to that which has no parts. Our true being is already perfect, does not need to be fixed and is untouched by any appearance.

Many of the human belief systems that have to do with a personal identity are completely intertwined with the ideas of time and space and cause and effect. However, what we really are is beyond time and space and untouched by cause and effect. Our true being is timeless, uncaused and uncreated. In actuality, the fundamental condition of everyone has never been limited by time and space or cause and effect. This is simply the way it is. Everything, no matter what it is, is a perfect expression of love, wisdom and energy that is beyond any concept or reference point.

The only possible way to realize this truth is to do nothing, because that which is, is already present and need not be acquired anew. Unless we know that our personal identity exists only as an expression of primordially pure open intelligence, doesn't have an independent nature and doesn't need to be altered, we will remain frustrated and confused.

Open intelligence is already accomplished and to return to it repeatedly for short moments, many times until it becomes continuous is absolutely all that is required. In this way, as we gently maintain open intelligence in the face of our various thoughts, emotions and experiences, open intelligence is gradually revealed to be the one reality. We then evolve beyond primitive thinking that is bound by time and space and cause and effect into an altogether new way of seeing. We're not really evolving into something new; we're just opening up into our true nature—the pristine intelligence by which everything is known. Discover that in yourself which is timeless, unborn and uncaused. This isn't found through thinking, but by simply relying on open intelligence.

The true nature of our being is already super-complete in itself and is an expression of superb helpfulness and benefit. This benefit is naturally present, and we can gradually gain more familiarity with it. In this way our inherent power to be of benefit to ourselves and others naturally becomes manifest in our lives.

By not being distracted by fixed ideas like cause and effect or time and space and simply relying on open intelligence, we gradually go beyond the limitations of descriptive frameworks. We go beyond words and concepts and the need to think about everything; we gradually find ourselves freed from the tendency to cling to data and to proliferate them endlessly. It's much easier to see everything as inseparable from open intelligence than to cling to any kind of conceptual framework like time and space or cause and effect. These concepts become less necessary as we become more confident in open intelligence.

As each thought appears, we simply rely on open intelligence that is completely free from thought, and in this way we find that the thought and open intelligence are one. No-thought and thought are not two; this is what nondual means; they are completely inseparable. The basis of every thought is always completely at ease. If we are only familiar with the dynamic expression of thought, then we don't know anything about its fundamental condition, which is the open intelligence that is always completely at ease and which has never been made into anything.

Let's consider for a moment the concept of "space," which usually refers to the expanse of the three-dimensional field of everyday life. We all have some understanding of that concept, but we can also use the term in a different way to point to something that is completely beyond the conventional model. The term "basic space" points to an unspeakable pure presence that is everywhere but doesn't have a residence or location. It can also be called "meta-space," the prefix "meta-" meaning "beyond." It includes three-dimensional space but is not limited to it. Meta-space includes all of time but is itself completely beyond time. Similarly, meta-space is beyond causality, yet includes cause and effect. There is no way to pin it down through ideas or theories, because it is itself the origin and basis of all ideas and theories, and yet it remains untouched by any movement of mind.

We cannot say that one part of that space is the cause that led to the effect of another part of that space. It is an indivisible seamless expanse of open intelligence that includes all and transcends all; absolutely nothing is excluded. Being the source and substance of all phenomena it has complete control over all phenomena. What is entirely uncaused has no causes within it. It has never been made into forms or thoughts—or into anything else for that matter! The only way to get familiar with the natural ease of this basic space is to simply allow it to *be* by the power of maintaining open intelligence. We relax the mind completely for short moments, repeated many times, until that relaxation becomes continuous.

If we examine with elementary discernment any of the "cause and effect programs" that are supposed to lead us to the fundamental nature of our being, we see that very seldom do people realize the fundamental condition through such methods and programs. It is very important to understand this, because most of us have been accustomed to employing methods and practices in the hope that they will lead to an ultimate destination. Timeless freedom is not a destination; it is here now. No method or practice can attain what is already present.

Most people create a cause and effect relationship between everything that occurs: we have a thought, then we have an emotion, then we have an experience, and we think they are a direct cause and effect chain. Using that same kind of reasoning, we say, "Wow, I've got the solution to my problems. If I just do this and that, things will be better. If I do such and such a practice, I'll gain true happiness!" If we consider ourselves to be cause-based human beings located within time and space, we are denying our true identity and obscuring our inherent happiness.

We attribute our unhappiness to various causes and effects; we blame people and events or ourselves. Attributing everything to causes leads to confusion, suffering and judging of ourselves and others. When we attribute every thought and emotion to a cause, we're actually taking our own power, which is limitless, and giving it away to an imaginary cause, saying that the cause is something in and of itself which has the power to affect us. The truth is that what we really are can never be affected by anything.

To live a life based on attributing individual causes to everything is really very primitive, and it doesn't give us any real ease of being. We are choosing to be a victim of our data, and as long as we do that we'll continue to suffer. That's what's most important to understand about this way of thinking: it never gives us any real ease or relief. Why? Because it isn't based on the true nature of phenomena. The fundamental condition can never be hurt by anything; it is the sole cause and the sole effect of all appearances and yet remains unaffected by any appearance. Open intelligence is inseparable from the clear light of wisdom, which is completely beyond thinking.

What does it mean that open intelligence is beyond thinking? It means that it doesn't have to use words or concepts to arrive at conclusions about anything. Open intelligence is the flawless knower, the clear light of wisdom that effortlessly knows everything about everything. It knows every appearance *as it is*, which means it completely understands its description, but it knows that description to be lacking an independent nature. Simply put, it knows the essence of all things to be itself. When we choose to rely on open intelligence and to allow the immediate relief of complete mental relaxation to be present in each identical moment, then we realize a wisdom that is beyond discriminative thinking. Then, if we ever use discriminative thinking at all, it's seen only as a practical tool rather than as an end in itself. We become so confident in this wisdom that eventually we won't feel compelled to rely on thinking. Instead, we rely on the profound insights and ensuing skillful activities that are implicit in genuine wisdom.

In the same way that we can find no satisfaction in the images of a mirage or hologram, we can find no satisfaction in the various phenomena of the world without understanding their underlying essence. If we try to continually find satisfaction or fulfillment in something that doesn't have an independent nature, then we will always feel frustrated and confused.

How can we get beyond our enslavement to these long-held tendencies? When we acknowledge the open intelligence that is at the basis of every thought, emotion and experience and get familiar with that open intelligence by which we know we are, we discover that we're already completely free and have never been enslaved by anything. We then find that we don't need to use conventional beliefs to describe the world or ourselves, because conventional beliefs simply don't apply when we have confidence in open intelligence. All thoughts, emotions and experiences are the dynamic energy of pure open intelligence and nothing else. What further description could be needed? They cannot be separated out from reality and accurately described, for they have no independent nature. They have a label, but that label refers back to something that cannot be found—and that label too is nothing but open intelligence.

The whole idea we have about needing to decide whether things are good or bad in order to establish moral and ethical order within ourselves as individuals is just a belief system—and a profoundly limiting one at that. First of all, this belief system says that we exist as something in and of ourselves, separated from everything else by a personal identity. It also says that all things exist in and of themselves, separate from each other and from the ground of being, and are held within an overall system of time and space and cause and effect. Most of us live our entire lives trusting in this belief system—and being limited by it. Due to this, it is very hard for us to cheer up!

Just as in stainless sky there is no flaw anywhere, our own open intelligence is flawless and forever pure and free. It is the source and essence of all phenomena, and nothing can be said to exist separate from it—including cause and effect and time and space. When we only know descriptive frameworks, then we're living on the surface of life, unaware of the underlying unity that pervades all diversity. The flawless knower that is beyond causation knows everything about cause and effect and time and space and knows itself to be the sole source of all appearances. This is the vantage that is all-pervasive, that understands everything and that is completely beyond all the descriptions of causes and their results.

We are the all-encompassing vast expanse of open intelligence that includes and transcends all data. It's as simple as that. All data are contained therein, and whatever they may be, they are all originally pure, in that they are all only open intelligence. No matter what we call an appearance—positive or negative, good or bad, beneficial or harmful, cause and effect, time and space—it is really nothing other than open intelligence. In that balanced view lies complete freedom.

Q: I have periods of really intense sadness and depression, and I can see very clearly that the causes of this sadness come from the neglect, abuse and mistreatment I experienced in my past. But you seem to be saying that those things have no power to affect me. How could that be?

A: I totally understand your question and want to explain this in a way that will be helpful to you. Let's say that this sadness comes up, it washes over you and you get completely lost in it. The feeling comes, "I'm sad again." There is "I," and then there is "I'm sad," and then there is "again." First there is the idea of a personal identity, and then the idea that the personal identity has a certain appearance within it, namely the sadness, then with "again" you're hauling in all the past data and saying, "I'm sad because such and such happened in the past, and the sadness comes again and again because of those causes."

What you're doing is describing and labeling what is appearing. Rather than going that route, you could look at the data of sadness and say, "This only has as much reality as I give it." When the thought of sadness is indulged, it means that it's accepted as having an independent nature and then it's elaborated upon. In your elaboration you go into all the stories about your sadness and where it came from and what it means.

But instead, if you rely on open intelligence, which is unaffected by any story, and allow the ease of being to be apparent, then you show yourself in that moment that you have mastery over the appearance of sadness. You see that the nature of the sadness is actually easeful open intelligence. The sadness and open intelligence are not two. Moreover, *any* thought or emotion can be mastered by open intelligence in this way. This means complete freedom in the immediacy of all experience, no matter what the experience is. You thought that sadness was controlled by the laws of cause and effect and that you were at the mercy of those laws, but that which is completely beyond causality is sitting right there in your chair! We have to know that there is more to us than what we have taken ourselves to be according to conventional ideas.

To set ourselves free, we've got to keep it very simple, and we can do that with two straightforward terms: "the all-encompassing pure view of open intelligence" and "data." If we take the individual data to exist in their own right and define and label them, then it seems there are a whole bunch of things that have to be dealt with. First you have a person, and then that person has to figure out how they feel, and then they'll have to look back at their lives and dredge up all their experiences to figure out why they feel what they feel, and then they'll have to start looking at all the other people—mommy, daddy, wife, husband—and figure out what they did wrong. What a mess!

It is much easier to just relax, and it's more effective, too. In relying on open intelligence, open intelligence and data come together for us, as they have always been together. Data are inseparable from open intelligence and are made only of that primordially pure nondual expanse. If we rest imperturbably for short moments, repeated many times, it's guaranteed that no appearance can pose a threat or be an obstacle to maintaining open intelligence. We find that open intelligence is self-maintained. When you just relax in perceptual openness, who you take yourself to be loosens up. Instead of taking yourself to be only this finite body or a person with a certain name, the spaciousness of your being becomes much more obvious. Your identity isn't defined so much anymore by the person who's sitting here, and your identity is no longer limited by somebody who's born or who will die.

Now, some people don't like it when I talk about perceptual openness or the ease of being or appearances as being originally pure, wholly positive and beneficial. It's possible that they don't like to hear it because it brings up feelings of being impure, bad or negative and brings into doubt all their judgments about themselves and others. It isn't so much that they necessarily dislike the terms I'm using, but the words stir up intense resistance within them. They feel, "Oh no way—*I'm* not pure,

I'm not beneficial; I'm not wise! I couldn't possibly be happy in life, considering my past!" I call this the "Big No."

When I use the words "pure," "pure space" or the "wholly positive ground of being," what I'm referring to is the infinitely expansive ground of being that is stainless and flawless, and which has never been made into anything other than what it is. Even though there may be all kinds of labels that describe all kinds of things, everything is originally pure and flawless, and we realize this through relying on open intelligence imperturbably in the face of all appearances.

Q: I want to ask a question about cause and effect. I drank some bad water the other day that upset my stomach, so I took a particular medicine, and that helped sort out the problem. In theory cause and effect isn't real, but in real life it has meaning.

A: Here is what is going on. We get so accustomed to dualistic thinking and sorting everything out into opposite terms that when we hear something like what I have been saying, we respond, "It is either cause and effect, or it is beyond causality— one of the two." What I am saying though is that "causation" and "being beyond causality" are *not two*. The realm of causation appears *within* that which is beyond causality and is truly made only of that and is inseparable from that. It is only in relying on open intelligence that this can be understood and realized. By the single power of relying on open intelligence for short moments, repeated many times, its pure presence will become obvious as pervasive of all experience.

You are making some assumptions about your situation that you might want to re-examine. You think the bad water was the cause of your stomachache, and the stomachache was the cause of your taking the medicine, and taking the medicine was the cause of your feeling better. You see it all as a direct cause and effect chain, but there are other ways of seeing the situation which might be equally valid, or perhaps more valid.

One way of seeing things is that all events are actually uncaused, unrelated appearances that arise and pass away unpredictably as the dynamic energy of open intelligence. Since all events in time and space are merely ephemeral data within open intelligence, they are dream-like, similar to an appearance within a mirage or a hologram. To assume that one event causes another is to give events more reality than they actually have.

Can a dreamlike image have the power to cause anything? Can a wave in a mirage be said to be the cause of another wave? Can it even be said to exist? When we realize the mirage-like nature of all phenomena, we no longer imbue events with the power to create other events; we are empowered by open intelligence, which is the sole reality underlying all appearances. We know that primordial basic space to be the only true power, the only true cause and the only true existence.

Everything that appears, including the appearance of cause and effect, is a circumstantial wisdom appearance of timeless open intelligence. When we rely on open intelligence, we find that we have complete freedom in the direct encounter with all data. The more powerful that becomes in us, the more we have complete mastery over mental, emotional and physical phenomena.

Why not keep relying on open intelligence and see what happens? In relying on open intelligence *as* that illness, you will discover that the experience of illness can be of tremendous benefit to you and to all beings. You might find it to be an open doorway into your limitless, timeless nature. But you can never know that if you continue to look only at causes and effects and conditions. When you discover that illness and pain can never affect who you truly are, then any condition of the body and mind will be an invitation to rely on open intelligence and an entrance into deeper abidance in the pure open intelligence that is your true nature.

By the power of confidence in open intelligence you find within yourself the tremendous energy of love and wisdom. This is the supreme healer. By maintaining open intelligence you will have the profound insight to know how to respond to mental and physical data. Moreover, you will no longer be bound to limited ways of thinking about them.

COMPASSIONATE BENEFIT
CHAPTER TWENTY-FIVE

"In open intelligence, all the beautiful dreams we dream become possible: people can have a good standard of living, and the world can become a place where human beings are of profound benefit to each other and to their habitat."

When we have complete ease and perceptual openness in all our experiences—especially the negative ones—then we find a superb helpfulness already present within us, which like the sun is always shining. There's a natural ease of being in which no one is a stranger. Compassion never needs to be cultivated or developed—it is always naturally present in open intelligence. In fact, compassion is equal to open intelligence and can only be found in open intelligence. The compassion that can be cultivated and developed is limited compared to the unstoppable compassion that shows no bias. True compassion is totally innocent and totally free. We can become acquainted with this compassion only by seeing that open intelligence has complete mastery over everything that appears in our thoughts, emotions and experiences.

Just as the lotus arises out of the mud but is completely unaffected by the mud, the beautiful flower of compassion appears out of our deepest, darkest emotions, thoughts and experiences. How is this possible? When we remain in open intelligence without correcting the flow of thoughts, then—sometimes quickly, sometimes slowly—we begin to see how these thoughts that have troubled us so much are free in their own place and are their own undoing. We don't have to think about these troubling data to make sense of them. Like a line drawn in water they vanish in and of themselves; this is absolutely guaranteed. When we are at ease with these muddy places within, we find something incredible about ourselves: a space of complete peace and freedom that is the fundamental condition of the mud.

We have caused so much suffering by constantly interrogating ourselves about all our data and interrogating others about their data. When we find the equanimous nature within ourselves, wherein everything that appears is equal, then we have compassion for ourselves. When we see this compassion in such a super-complete way, we see that this not only applies to us, it applies to everyone. We go through a dramatic shift, where instead of our data being only about us, we start to think, "Wow, everyone has these problems. These intense emotions and deep, dark thoughts are there in others also. It isn't just me. Since I've found healing for myself, maybe I can help others, too."

This is the true birth of compassion. We see that the good, bad, beautiful and ugly about ourselves are all equal, and then from that clear vantage, when we look at ourselves and at everyone else, we all just start to look fantastic! No matter what other people are doing, we understand completely and we understand how to help. If we need to act, we act spontaneously and skillfully. What's more, there are no buttons in us to be pushed anymore. One person can say to us, "You're the greatest person who ever lived on earth," and another can say, "You're a total creep," and we are not moved either way, because we completely understand the total context. We know that what we really are is beyond either of these judgments. This is not passivity; it's radical freedom that has not been tied up anywhere. It has no conventional constructs. From the perspective of that perfect freedom, conventional descriptive frameworks are no longer necessary.

We experience a tremendous depth of compassion that appears with the release of energy that comes from no longer believing that thoughts and emotions have an independent nature. With the arising of the profound self-compassion that is the only true self-respect, we instantaneously have compassion for everyone, because we know we are all in the same boat. No longer are we in this partisan position where we are saying, "My ideas are the right ones and yours aren't!"

When we let go of all our fixed data sets, a tremendous amount of energy appears. This is the wisdom energy of superb helpfulness, and its intent is entirely beneficial. We become naturally compassionate. Even if we've had a long habit of growling at people, the more we rely on open intelligence, the more the growl will just dissolve in and of itself without our having to do anything to make it happen! When we find that the fundamental ground of our own being is unalterable and flawless wisdom energy, then we can love completely without conditions. We love ourselves in an ultimate way, and we are able to love others in the same way.

Life is a precious human opportunity to benefit ourselves and others. This self-benefit and benefit of others is already present within us and is not something we get from somewhere else. Getting in touch with that is very straightforward and simple. When we rely on open intelligence repeatedly for short moments, many times, we get familiar with the self-benefit that really allows us to be of profound benefit to others. It's in that self-benefit that the love, wisdom and energy arise that allow us to go completely beyond anything we ever thought we could do or contribute. No matter how accomplished we may be now, when we rely on open intelligence and get in touch with the self-benefit that is natural to us, a whole new way of seeing comes about—including seeing our own capacity to be of benefit in a new way.

We can know that we are relying on open intelligence through the benefit that is displayed in our lives. It could be beneficial activity in terms of our own individual life or for the sake of the people or causes we care about. It is urgently important for each of us as individuals and for all of us together all over the world to tap into that natural resource of benefit. When we rely on open intelligence for short moments, repeated many times, the insight and skillful means needed to take care of everything in life naturally come about. This includes the ability to truly love and be intimate without ever thinking about it—not only with a few people, but with everyone. There is total and complete intimacy with no fear anywhere. From the very beginning we are longing for this love that has no name, in which everything is of a unified and single nature. This is not a cut-off or passive state. It is the reality that is naturally present as the fundamental condition.

When we become familiar with the natural order of everything, we see that it is at ease, ordered and beneficial in its own way and that everything is already resolved. When we're at ease in our being, then we recognize that natural order. We know what it means to be human. Relaxing our mind and body completely in all situations, we start to feel a part of the natural order of things. For every single one of us, no matter how hideous or how saintly our actions have been, the nature of our mind is to benefit ourselves and benefit others, and only the person who has learned this is truly able to be of benefit. Who we've been in the past is not what we should take ourselves to be now. We are not our history— we are timeless.

Everything is sweet and good, even the things that don't appear to be sweet and good! To recognize this is true bliss. True joy doesn't come from trying to get into a state of joy; rather, it arises from seeing the lack of separation between joy and sorrow—without trying to change anything. True bliss is the eradication of a mood-based life. Does that mean that there are no longer moods? No. It just means that there is no separation between bliss and whatever mood happens to be appearing. One moment we might have an incredibly ecstatic experience, and the next moment we may be experiencing great suffering, but we recognize that all appearances are inherently equal. Each experience, whether positive or negative, is like a shooting star in the vast expanse of space that leaves no trace. It appears from space and resolves in space.

Great benefit can never come from seeing appearances as unequal. Seeing appearances as unequal is a sub-optimal strategy for living. It is taking a system and reducing it to its lowest level of operation, which is only one of the ways we can choose to live. However, when we choose to rest as the basis of all appearances, then we are living optimally, and we are what we are meant to be. In this way we become truly intelligent—just as nature is. There is nothing to fix anywhere, and when we realize this, the self-benefit is enormous.

We can be with ourselves in a way that is totally free—free from the content of our thoughts and emotions. We don't need to change any of it or make it any different. Non-difference means nothing needs to be made different! That is real freedom. The sense of non-separation is so obvious that benefit to the whole is just naturally flowing, and we become a fount of that benefit for all.

Q: I'm interested in reaching my full potential in life, relationships and in my ability to be successful in my work. I've read a lot of books about accessing one's inherent energy and power, and I would be interested in your take on that.

A: Inseparable from open intelligence is the sheer force and power of everything exactly *as it is*. If you are looking for power or force or whatever it might be called, it has never been anywhere else but in your own open intelligence. Power or force is completely relaxed. The greatest power you'll ever encounter is the power of the openness of your own open intelligence. All displays of whatever kind are projections of that alone. Open intelligence and its powers of benefit will continue to intensify once they are recognized.

It's only in open intelligence that we will find a wisdom that is unparalleled. How do we know it's unparalleled? Because there are things that people who are confident in open intelligence can do that nobody else can do. They can do great things that benefit many, many beings: feeding hungry people, providing health care, education and shelter and introducing people to open intelligence and helping them gain confidence in it. Most importantly, when one is confident in open intelligence, one has perfect mental stability at all times and is able to act skillfully and insightfully. Wherever people abide as this sublime nature of open intelligence, there are incredible powers present that are completely beyond causality.

The truth is that everyone has those powers that I just mentioned, and many more that I didn't mention, but they may remain dormant within us until the discovery of our own open intelligence. They're not in any individual—they're inherent in the self-perfected fundamental condition of everything. We as humankind need to get acquainted with these powers.

Q: I am very eager to help save the world from disaster, but I doubt my own ability to make a real difference. I also fear the insecurity that comes from living a life of service in which my own personal needs might not be directly provided for. Can you offer some advice in this?

A: Only through relying on open intelligence can we access the potency of pure wisdom, and in that potency the thoughts, emotions and everything else are always related to the benefit of all. The solution to all problems is timelessly available within the fundamental nature of reality.

Regarding the problems for which we may be seeking solutions—within ourselves, our families, communities and the world—the solutions are all within the potent, beneficial powers of timeless wisdom that are inseparable from our own open intelligence. When we simply rely on open intelligence repeatedly, then eventually we see the full evidence of open intelligence that is the spontaneous ground of everything that appears. When we rest naturally in that spontaneous ground, we increasingly know how to act in a very powerful way in every situation.

When we hear that nothing need be done about appearances, this does not suggest that we become a couch potato or that we have a license to go around doing whatever we want to do. It also does not mean that we should fall into any form of inaction or passivity whatsoever. When we get in touch with what connects us to the super-intelligence of the natural order of everything, then we have immense power, force and super-intelligence in our own lives. The practical application of this power is expressed in the world as skillful means and wisdom. When we are truly familiar with open intelligence, we have the skillful means to be superbly helpful, and that is accompanied by the wisdom of knowing what to do and how to act in all situations.

Here is a very simple proposition: by the power of the single practice of relying on open intelligence for short moments, many times, anything we've ever thought about being or doing can come about. We will see a way of becoming more beneficial in all circumstances than we'd ever imagined possible. We will be able to discover the wisdom that is required to solve the tremendous problems facing our species.

We can't deny that we have all kinds of problems. They need to be solved, and they can only be truly solved with the wisdom solution. In this way we can come together as a grassroots global community gaining confidence in open intelligence to solve our individual problems and the problems of the world. Getting into rarified states of altered consciousness has not solved the problems of the world. Only open intelligence, which is beyond time, space and causality and which has no attachment to any convention can see solutions to problems that have not yet been solved. Formerly unsolvable problems—people not having clean water and nourishing food to eat on a daily basis, environmental degradation, endless wars and conflicts between peoples, nuclear missiles pointed everywhere—are solvable. However, the thinking that created these problems will not solve them. These problems will only be overcome by the power of open intelligence and the insights that cannot be found within conventional conceptual frameworks.

There is no one who doesn't want to be of benefit. Even someone like a gang member or a social deviant wants to be of benefit; it's just that their angle of vision is angled in a mistaken direction. Everyone has this urge to freedom and to be of benefit; however, unless someone shows us how to really bring that into full being within ourselves, we won't know how to do it. If we're not shown how, or do not find it for ourselves, we'll spend our entire lives dreaming small dreams and settling for a mere glimpse of our genius.

When we are interested only in our appearances and involved in a life of self-concern, then we are blind to the power of our own being. Trapped in our own personal identity we become tense and frightened and start looking for ways to advance ourselves, substantialize ourselves and prop ourselves up with our data. We might want to appear beneficial to others so that people will think well of us, but when we do this we grossly limit our true identity. Our true identity has no need to attract notoriety. When we rely on open intelligence, we acknowledge the sovereign fundamental reality that knows no pride. In open intelligence, all the beautiful dreams we dream become possible: people can have a good standard of living, and the world can become a place where human beings are of profound benefit to each other and to their habitat.

Don't ever settle for some kind of image of yourself that is based on needing to puff yourself up and then competing with other people and showing how great your abilities are in order to feel like you are somebody. That's a waste of a life. Even if you were to feel somewhat better some of the time by doing that, know that you can feel a lot better by simply gaining confidence in open intelligence! Beyond the personal identity is something that is incredibly immense and profound. I invite and encourage everyone to discover what that is by the power of relying on open intelligence.

It's Up to You, and It's Up to Me!
CHAPTER TWENTY-SIX

> *"By the power of maintaining open intelligence, a strong compassion will emerge within us that has the capability and determination to bring about direct change. We will find the solutions for both personal and global problems by going beyond data such as "us and them."*

"It's Up to You and It's Up to Me!" is the title of a kind of theme song we had in the Balanced View community in Rishikesh, India. Every day when I was giving talks there in the early months of 2007, we would have a songfest as part of our meetings, and one of our lovely participants wrote this song and sang it to us a number of times. The chorus goes: "It's up to you and it's up to me; together there's nothing we can't be! It's up to me, and it's up to you; together there's nothing we can't do!".

(Words and music by Shantam Zohar)

It truly is up to us to bring about the transformation we want to see in our world, and the demonstration of this will happen at the grassroots level. Where are the grassroots? They're right here in each one of us, and they're in Europe, Asia, Africa, Australia, South America, North America—everywhere that people are gaining confidence in open intelligence. The unifying nature of open intelligence is what unites all of us in a common bond, and it's up to us to bring about the global healing and unity that is possible.

When we are relying on open intelligence, we're enabled to find solutions to our own personal concerns as well as solutions to the problems facing the world. We must be clear, though, that the only way we can tap into that resource of wisdom is to become deeply acquainted with it. To the extent that we become familiar with the wisdom inherent in open intelligence, we will be less ruled by the obsessive self-focus that has compelled us to put our attention into our own personal circumstances. As a result we will see very profoundly that not only do *we* need to eat and be housed and clothed, *everyone* needs the same things. As we know, many people on Earth don't have these basic things. Instead of this being a fact that we gloss over or feel powerless to deal with, we need to fully acknowledge these facts and find the determination to do something about it. By the power of maintaining open intelligence, a strong compassion will emerge within us that has the capability and determination to bring about direct change. We will find the solutions for both personal and global problems by going beyond data such as "us and them."

The usual way of treating the mind is to chase down thoughts, emotions and sensations and then label them as positive, negative or neutral. We try to accumulate more of the positive ones and get rid of the negative ones. Instead of bringing real benefit, this way of relating to our mind only creates greater tension and unease within us and with others and can never provide long-lasting solutions for the problems we're facing.

No matter how advanced our science and technology may appear to be from the conventional point of view, their benefit remains limited at best if it's only being expressed within the boundaries of conventional thought, and not within the context of what will be of most benefit to all. In fact, unless science and technology are aligned with the wisdom of all-encompassing open intelligence, they will remain part of the problem. Only in growing confident in open intelligence as an alternative to ordinary thinking are we going to be able to truly solve our problems, whether they are our own individual difficulties or those of the world.

We have to let go of all the conventional reference points, allow ourselves to discover open intelligence and be guided by its inherent power of wisdom that is beyond ordinary thinking. This really is the only hope we have. The good news is that the powers of great benefit that come from open intelligence are tremendously potent and are fully capable of bringing about the changes required for the human race to not only survive but thrive. These are changes the conventional mind cannot even imagine.

The crisis facing humanity today is not just one of external problems such as poverty, pollution, terrorism and the threat of nuclear war; the root of this crisis is in the mind. The conflict and environmental degradation we see manifesting all around the world reflect the way we relate to our own thoughts and emotions. Chronic anger, violence, despair, depression and drug and alcohol addiction are pervasive in the modern world. We have great conflict within ourselves as individuals, and as a result we also have conflicts in our families, our communities and in the world as a whole.

Whatever goes on within individuals will also be played out on a global scale among nations. The constant battle waged in the mind through the attempt to correct and control our thoughts and emotions has never brought us inner peace. It is really foolhardy to keep doing the same things over and over again, when we can see the detrimental or half-baked results those approaches have brought. The best way to be freed from this destructive cycle is to become familiar with open intelligence by relaxing mind and body for short moments, repeated many times, until it becomes continuous; this is something each one of us can do. When we simply get familiar with our own open intelligence, we find solutions that are entirely beyond what we have devised until now. As more and more people around the world learn to enjoy stable open intelligence, we will be empowered to bring about transformations that are truly beneficial for the planet and its inhabitants.

Our natural disposition as human beings is mutual enrichment, and we come to know we are truly capable of that in the certainty of open intelligence. If we want to better ourselves as a human species we need to look to where the greatest power resides. Open intelligence is the source of powerful wisdom and is limitless by nature. When we rely upon stable open intelligence again and again, rather than upon ordinary thinking, it will become perfectly clear what needs to be done to provide lasting benefit to the world. And we will be empowered with the skill and determination to do what needs to be done.

The question sometimes comes up, "How can I just continue to rely on open intelligence when there is so much suffering in the world? If I just do that, isn't it like checking out and ignoring the big problems facing humankind?" The answer is, no; gaining confidence in open intelligence is the *best* solution to the problems facing humankind. When we maintain open intelligence, we begin to know ourselves as an integral part of the natural order, rather than as being something apart from it. By the power of open intelligence we increasingly settle into the ease of our natural being, and the result is that the tremendous power of timeless open intelligence can flow in us unobstructedly.

Nature is at ease with whatever is occurring, and this is how we are meant to be as well. Nature is at ease with all extremes. Whether the ocean is rough and tumultuous or still and calm, you could say that it is content with itself. It isn't trying to fiddle around with the big waves to make them smaller or trying to make the calm areas rise up into waves. It is simply at ease as its own nature, letting the waves be as they are.

This is how we are meant to relate to our thoughts and emotions. Rather than trying to control each wave of thought and emotion as it appears, we rely on open intelligence, seeing each wave as a perfect expression of that open intelligence. In this way we live in harmony and peace with whatever appears in our mind from moment to moment, identified only with the all-encompassing open intelligence that is our true nature.

We are meant to be completely relaxed. Look at the trees, flowers, birds, the Earth and all its aspects. They are all effortlessly in harmony with nature, no matter the conditions. The wind may be raging, but its essence is totally at rest. There isn't any resistance; everything is just the way it is, and because there's no resistance, the great power and ease of open intelligence is effortlessly present.

Through relying on open intelligence we can discover the same power. If we need to move forcefully and powerfully at a given time, the best way to do that is to allow the wisdom that emerges from open intelligence to both empower us to act and show us exactly how to act. As we gain confidence in open intelligence, our actions will be ever more clearly guided by nature's intelligence.

Without the decisive experience of our open intelligence, all of this will remain only an intellectual understanding. But when we experience the presence of open intelligence again and again, our vision will become very clear. When we repeatedly rely on open intelligence, we enter into and rely on its extraordinary wisdom that has the power to solve problems such as global warming, famine, lack of clean water and proper health care. Only through the power of open intelligence can lasting solutions for grave problems such as these be found.

By being at ease in open intelligence with everything that goes on within us, we discover wisdom. As we do so we experience firsthand the amazing benefit of wisdom. Please don't just accept what I'm saying; I'm inviting you to test these things for yourself, like a scientist who has a hypothesis and then tests it to see the result. Rely on open intelligence yourself and then see what comes about as a result.

Once our open intelligence is sufficiently well-established, there isn't constant distraction by data. It is then that the benefit of naturally occurring wisdom becomes very obvious. The first level of benefit comes to us as individuals as self-benefit; we attain equanimity of mind and unshakeable happiness and peace within ourselves, and that's not a small thing! Once we've benefited ourselves in that most essential way, there will be no stopping the inexorable flow of compassionate feeling and action that arises. This is the dignity, confidence and elegance of service inspired by profound wisdom and charged with the limitless energy of open intelligence. From open intelligence beyond learning and thinking, solutions arise that could never have been arrived at through ordinary thinking.

I want to make a very important point regarding coming to know our true identity as open intelligence. If we decide that we do want to discover our true identity, then we need to become *totally committed* to relying on open intelligence. In Robert Frost's poem "The Road Not Taken" he writes, "Two roads diverged in a wood, and I took the one less traveled by, and that has made all the difference." If we retain our belief that thoughts and emotions have the power to rule us, and we only rely on open intelligence part of the time, then that will be the road traveled all too often—the road of partial commitment and half measures, and it doesn't lead to real mental stability and wisdom.

But if we are truly committed to becoming confident in open intelligence for the benefit of all, then we will take the road less traveled. We'll choose the road of relying on stable open intelligence no matter what our thoughts, emotions or experiences may be. We'll say to ourselves, "I will never give up, no matter how long I live. I will rely on open intelligence until I have the vantage of its wise intelligence in all my activities. I will persevere no matter what happens, until open intelligence becomes completely spontaneous and I no longer need to try to maintain open intelligence. For the sake of everyone and myself, I will continue without fail. I will draw on the wisdom resources of stable open intelligence to support my decisions until it becomes obvious at all times." These are the two choices: a partial commitment, or a complete commitment that guarantees the desired result. The commitment must be one hundred percent, because only then can wisdom come fully alive.

The truth is that we can only exercise our commitment one moment at a time. Our decision to rely on open intelligence must be continually reaffirmed by the practice of relying on open intelligence, moment by moment. We can say, "I am committed forever," but in living that commitment, it must be continually reaffirmed by choosing to rely on open intelligence one thought at a time, one emotion at a time and one experience at a time whenever we remember to do so. In this simple way, brief moments of open intelligence gradually gain momentum and become continuous.

Q: How does relying on open intelligence need to be understood in terms of developing the leaders of the future?

A: In the same way that relying on open intelligence brings us great insights, open intelligence can also create leaders of great wisdom. Leaders need to be people who are able to manifest extraordinary mental stability, compassion, profound insight and skillful activities in all situations, and these attributes should be the primary criteria for any national leader. By the power of open intelligence, leaders at every level of human culture can share in this reservoir of attributes.

In open intelligence we have a balanced view. We are aware not only of what *we* are thinking and feeling, but also what other people are thinking and feeling. If we're all wrapped up in our own emotions, thoughts and desires, we won't have the openness and spaciousness to understand what other people are thinking and feeling or to see with clarity how our actions will affect others. Without that instinctive connection with the minds of everyone around the globe, it's very difficult for a leader to make decisions that truly benefit everyone.

If we take ourselves to be an individual who is an accumulation of thoughts, emotions, experiences, achievements and failures, then we'll spend our whole life trying to further that identity. We'll cling to certain data and reject other data and then compete with everyone around us by displaying our abilities in order to prove that our data are right. We will be living under the assumption, "My data are right and yours are wrong, and because my data are right I am somebody special, and because I'm special, my decisions are right, no matter what you say!" We may develop contrived listening skills in order to gain the favor of others in furthering our own agenda. True leadership can never come from that way of thinking and living. Only a continuation of these aggressive forms of relating will come from that way of thinking, and there is plenty of it on display throughout human culture.

However, when we rely on open intelligence we find within ourselves the wisdom that has no pride or aggression. Increasingly, there is a completely balanced view of everything that occurs. With that balanced view we have the spontaneous ability to act in a way that is beneficial to everyone. Not only that, we can laugh a lot more!

Q: You have mentioned a number of problems the world is facing. Can you speak about the problems economically wealthy countries like America have?

A: All countries have problems, even places like America where there are a lot of resources. America as a whole enjoys a level of economic wealth and advantage that is almost unimaginable for people in some parts of the world; yet, America is quite troubled in its own way. This country has all the material things, but in some cases very little wisdom about what we really are as human beings. There is so much distraction by the desire for material possessions—and the enjoyment of the personal pleasure and comfort derived from them—that there can be a tendency to become enraptured with this way of life rather than looking to see how resources can be distributed throughout humankind.

We who enjoy such incredible privilege are living an illusion if we think that this privilege could never be taken from us. I have so many friends around the world who have suffered from tremendous political upheavals and who have had to flee their own countries and seek refuge elsewhere, usually under very difficult circumstances. I really want to emphasize how quickly that can come about for any of us. We should never feel that we are safe from unexpected tumultuous events, because anything can happen. What is happening to people in conflict-torn countries can also happen to those of us who are presently living in great security and comfort.

The only way to be prepared for any event is to gain confidence in open intelligence and to find that within ourselves which is unaffected by any circumstance. In finding peace within ourselves we can open our hearts to helping others find peace, too.

The truth is that those who want to rely on open intelligence can do that anywhere. People living in the U.S. are as fully imbued with open intelligence as anyone else in the world, and although the U.S. has its problems, there is a wonderful openness to new ideas that has always made it a fertile ground for new approaches to living.

Q: If everything is a perfect expression of open intelligence, then where is the need to save the world or solve its problems?

A: Everything *is* a perfect expression of open intelligence, including the world and all the suffering in the world. Another way to say this is that everything is *equally* an expression of nature's intelligence. Whether solutions are found for all the problems our species is facing, or whether the world is saved or not, in the final analysis it is not going to affect the timeless intelligence at the basis of everything. However, when we have confidence in open intelligence, intense compassion naturally arises within us for all who suffer, along with a firm commitment to do whatever we can to bring genuine relief.

To say, "Everything is open intelligence, therefore the world does not exist, so I don't need to do anything to help the suffering," is an extreme view. Such extreme ways of thinking actually perpetuate the suffering in the world, making us blind to the pain around us and to the practical ways we can help others.

Open intelligence is the mainstay and support both of our individual well-being and our well-being as a species. When we gain familiarity with open intelligence, there is a tremendous amount of energy that is generated from letting go of all the fixed reference points of ordinary thinking. We find the energy of superb helpfulness and compassion. These are an inherent aspect of our own open intelligence, an actual feeling of warmth and goodwill within us. We can really know if we are relying on open intelligence, because kindness and compassion will naturally well up within us and begin flowing out towards everyone. Moreover, this will be obvious to us and to others.

Wisdom is the understanding that everything is fundamentally equal by nature. We are either lost in the world of data and cause and effect, or we recognize all appearances as wisdom appearances. Perfect wisdom and perfect understanding will prevail in every situation when we have found that equal vision. It becomes impossible to act in any way that is not beneficial. No matter what attributions of good and bad or right and wrong we've had before, they are all gone beyond in wisdom. This super-complete wisdom that is mutually enriching and interpenetrating is so much needed today. Through the natural ease of completely open intelligence, one knows what to do and how to act in a simple, beneficial way.

At this point in history it should be obvious that all of our philosophies about right and wrong, sin and virtue have not enabled us to solve either our individual problems or our problems as a species. In fact, if we consider the fact that almost all wars have been fought on the basis of such ideas, we might conclude that those ideas are some of humankind's greatest problems! It's only the wisdom that's beyond all science and philosophy that can bring lasting solutions to the huge problems the planet and its inhabitants are facing.

Q: *But surely all political action isn't futile. Haven't there been many people who brought about great change in the world through their actions?*

A: There's no denying that good things have come about from people's political efforts, but no matter how much good has come about in that way, infinitely *more* good can come about from the wisdom of open intelligence. Only when people get familiar with the pristine wisdom at the basis of all appearances will we truly be able to resolve the monumental problems we face in the modern age. From open intelligence we will have a much clearer and more balanced view than we could ever have from any extreme political position. There is something in true wisdom that goes far beyond all political or philosophical ideals, no matter how amazing those ideals may seem to be.

When I was a young woman, I was very much involved in political issues, and I saw all kinds of extremism on all sides of the political spectrum. I was firmly committed to many of the liberal ideas of the day, but I saw so much infighting, competition and fanaticism within the organizations with which I was involved that I very quickly became disillusioned with political activism. We were looking for world peace, love and the end of war, but what we actually ended up with was factionalism and watered down idealism due to all the fighting and disagreements we had. Most often the most powerful faction would assert its power; in other words, the group that could muscle its way through to victory via power-driven actions would win.

I could see that this kind of decision-making was inadequate for bringing about world peace. I thought to myself, "What's going on here? Most of these people, including me, are not peaceful within themselves! How can a group of such people bring about a peaceful world?" It didn't seem to matter which side we were on. Our lack of inner peace, whether it was due to anger, pride, fear, desire, depression or ignorance, would eventually lay ruin to even the most beautifully peaceful ideals. Protesting for peace without inner peace would never bring about world peace.

So what to do? I finally came to a point where I saw that all of the ideologies I'd come up with had led absolutely nowhere. They didn't show me how to solve my personal problems, they didn't show anyone how to work powerfully together in an organization, and they weren't really changing anything worldwide. Holding to those ideologies was just another way of getting lost in extremes.

Thankfully, I realized that all of us have to first come to terms with the struggle for peace *within ourselves*. That's where the primary struggle has to be resolved; only then can we succeed in creating organizations that are truly loving, peaceful and beneficial. If we don't come to terms with ourselves as individuals and make peace within ourselves, then there's no way we can make peace with one another or in the world.

Political extremism has only resulted in greater conflicts among people. Revolutions based on power struggles and hatred only create bloodshed and a new kind of bondage. Institutions or political movements that are based on extremism are places filled with pain and chaos. They just replicate what is going on inside us. We copy our inner suffering and paste it into an organization! Can such an organization bring peace to the world?

I am firmly convinced that humankind *does* have the capacity to form wisdom-filled organizations, but they can't be structured in the hierarchical and confrontational way in which many organizations are structured today. The ideal organization is one of participatory democracy, where leaders see their roles as ones of encouragement and inspiration that will bring out the strengths, gifts and talents of everyone in the organization. In this kind of organization there is a great deal of dignity, confidence and mutual support as people share with one another with the intention of reaching a common goal.

When people rely on open intelligence, they are empowered to create institutions and organizations that are truly happy, enjoyable and supportive places to be. To do that in an optimal fashion we must rely on open intelligence rather than ordinary thinking. Stable open intelligence brings about a new kind of thinking that is rich with effectiveness.

Whenever we are looking for peace anywhere else, we must first look to find it within ourselves. By the power of open intelligence, humankind can find the inner and outer peace that we've been looking for.

There is something about each one of us that is completely at peace, and if we become familiar with that equanimity, then so many of the things to which we have aspired become possible. When we know ourselves to be naturally resourceful, dignified and confident, then our families, communities, institutions and world can become that way too. This is truly something to aspire to and work towards.

It's up to us.

BALANCED VIEW RESOURCES

There are many resources available for anyone who is interested in knowing more about the Balanced View Training. The main source for this information is the Balanced View website at www.balancedview.org. Posted here are numerous public talks, videos and texts (including this book). While contributions are gratefully accepted, all media are available free of charge. Talks can be easily downloaded in MP3 format to a computer or MP3 player; they range in length from a few minutes to an hour or more and are of great assistance to anyone interested in gaining confidence in open intelligence.

Also listed on the websites is a schedule of Balanced View Trainings around the world. There are face-to-face trainings and public open meetings, as well as trainings and meetings offered via free teleconference bridge.

For many people the primary introduction to relying on open intelligence comes from listening to the free downloads described above. Further support for relying on open intelligence is offered through Balanced View's Four Mainstays and three series of written trainings: "Everyday Open Intelligence: The Twelve Empowerments," "The Power of Benefit" and "The Principles of Benefit."

An Introductory Training is offered in which participants receive direct instruction in the practice of relying on open intelligence for short moments, repeated many times, and that is the prerequisite for participation in the Twelve Empowerments. The Empowerments are the preliminary training of Balanced View, and through them participants are introduced to the fundamental nature of mind, open intelligence and data. They provide pivotal instructions that evoke a direct and decisive experience of open intelligence. An outline of the Twelve Empowerments Training is available on the website.

The Power of Benefit Series fully supports the fruition of the powers of great benefit: complete emotional and mental stability, profound insight, unstoppable compassion and skillful activity in every moment.

For those committed to sharing the vision of Balanced View—open intelligence for all—the Principles of Benefit are provided, along with direct guidance from a certified Balanced View trainer. These show us how to work together as an organization and as a global human family, providing structures that ensure peace, harmony and respect in all circumstances.

For more information concerning any of these trainings, please visit our website.

The Four Mainstays are the context for all Balanced View offerings. This support is available to participants through: 1) relying on open intelligence, 2) the training, 3) the trainer, and 4) the community. Each of the trainers in Balanced View is committed to providing all the necessary support to any person who is relying on open intelligence. Any request for support from a participant will be replied to within twenty-four hours.

For participants who wish to contribute to the Balanced View Training, donations are gratefully accepted. All are welcome to participate, regardless of ability to contribute.

Made in the USA
Las Vegas, NV
31 May 2025